JAMES BOND

JAMES BOND

*The
Authorized Biography
of 007*

A Fictional Biography
by

John Pearson

Grove Press, Inc./New York

First Black Cat Edition 1986
First Printing 1986
ISBN: 0-394-62140-9
Library of Congress Catalog Card No. 85-45544

Printed in the United States

GROVE PRESS, INC.,
196 West Houston Street
New York, N.Y. 10014

5 4 3 2 1

Contents

1

'This is Commander Bond'

I like to think that the plane was Urquhart's idea of a joke.
He was the only one of them to have a sense of humour (he
must have found it inconvenient at times in that grey morgue
of a building up by Regents Park where they all still work)
and since he booked my tickets when he made arrangements
for my trip he would have known about the plane. It left
Kennedy at 4 p.m. for Bermuda. What Urquhart failed to
tell me was that it was a honeymooners' special, crammed
with newly-weds on packaged honeymoons in the sun.

There is something curiously unsettling about mating
young Americans *en masse*. I had already had a two-hour
wait at Kennedy from London, this on an icy January
Saturday with the authentic New York sleet gusting against
the windows of the transit lounge. Now for a further three
hours I had to share this nuptial flight on mercifully false
pretences. The roses, the Californian champagne were not
for me.

'Welcome aboard – this is the sunshine special, folks.
For all of you just setting out together on life's greatest
adventure, the congratulations of your captain, crew and
PanAm, the world's most experienced airline.'

Polite laughter. Some cheery fellow clapped. And in my lonely gangway seat I started worrying about *my* adventure.

Where did old Urquhart's sense of humour stop?

Between me and the window sat a nice young couple, suitably absorbed in one another. She was in pink, he in dark grey. Neither of them spoke. Their silence was disturbing, almost as if in disapproval of my so-called mission.

Dinner was served – a four-course plastic airline meal, a triumph of space-age packaging – and, as I munched my Chicken Maryland, crunched on my lonely Krispee Krackers, my *angst* became acute. Strangely enough, until this moment I had not bothered over my arrival in Bermuda. Urquhart had said I would be taken care of. 'It's all laid on. Everything's arranged, and, from what I gather, they do one rather well.' In London, words like these had sounded reassuring. One nodded and said 'quite'. Now one began to wonder.

I had a drink, and then another and, as the big, warm aircraft thundered its way towards the tropics, tried going over in my mind the succession of events that had brought me there.

* * *

They had begun almost two years ago, after I published my 'official' life of Ian Fleming. It was an unusual book in the sheer spate of correspondence I received – from ballistic-minded Japanese, French teenage Bondphiles, crime-crazy Swedes and postgraduate Americans writing their theses on the modern thriller. I did my best to answer them. But there was just one letter which I had found it difficult to deal with. It was from Vienna from a woman signing herself Maria Künzler.

It was a long, slightly gushing letter written in purple ink and it described a prewar winter spent in the ski-resort of Kitzbühel with Ian Fleming. In my book I had dismissed this period of Fleming's life somewhat briefly. Fleming had been to Kitzbühel several times, first in the 1920s when he stayed there with some people called Forbes-Dennis. (Mrs Forbes-Dennis was, incidentally, the novelist, Phyllis Bottome.) Theoretically Fleming had been learning German, though in practice he had spent most of his time enjoying the mountains and the local girls. From the letter it seemed as if Miss Künzler had been one of them. Certainly her information about Fleming seemed authentic and she described certain friends from Kitzbühel I had interviewed for my book. This made a paragraph towards the end of her letter all the more baffling.

'So you can understand,' she wrote, 'the excitement we all felt when the good-looking young James Bond appeared at Kitzbühel. He had been in Ian's house at Eton, although of course he was much younger than Ian. Even in those days, James was engaged in some sort of undercover work, and Ian, who liked ragging people, used to make fun of him and tried getting information out of him. James would get very cross.'

When I read this I decided, not unnaturally, that Miss Künzler was slightly mad – or, if not mad, then in that happy state where she could muddle fact and fiction. I thanked her for her letter, and merely wrote that her anecdote about James Bond had caused me some surprise.

Here I should make it plain that when I wrote the *Life of Ian Fleming,* I never doubted for a moment that James Bond *was* Ian Fleming, a Mitty-figure Fleming had constructed from his daydreams and his childhood memories. I had known Fleming personally for several years – the very years in fact when he was writing the early James Bond books – and I had picked out countless resemblances between the James Bond of the books and the Ian Fleming I worked with on the *Sunday Times.* Fleming had even endowed his hero with certain of his own very personal trademarks – the clothes, the eating habits, even the appearance – so much so that whenever I pictured James Bond it was always Fleming's face (and not Sean Connery's) I saw.

True, there had been certain facts which failed to tally with the Bond-is-Fleming thesis. Fleming, for one, denied it

3

– strongly. In a way he had to, but it is a fact that the more methodically you read the Bond books, the more you start to notice details which refer to James Bond's life *outside* the books – details about his family, glimpses of his life at school and tantalizing references to his early secret-service career and love-life. Over the thirteen James Bond books the sheer weight of all these 'outside' references is surprising, especially as they seem to be remarkably consistent. It was this that originally gave rise to rumours that Fleming, whilst including something of himself in James Bond's character, had based his hero on a real-life agent he had encountered during his time with British Naval Intelligence in the war.

One theory was that the 'real' James Bond had been a captain of the Royal Marine Commandos whose deeds and personality inspired Fleming. Another held that Fleming had carefully studied the career of the British double-agent, James Morton, whose body was discovered in Shepheard's Hotel in Cairo in 1962. There were other rumours too. None of them seemed to hold much water, certainly not enough to make me change my mind about the Fleming–Bond relationship. Then the second letter came from the mysterious Miss Künzler in Vienna.

It arrived some three months after I had written to her, apologized for the delay and said that she had not been well. (From what I could work out, she would now have been in her mid-sixties.) It was a much shorter letter than the earlier one. The florid writing was a little shaky, but everything she wrote was to the point. She said that there was not much she could add to her earlier account of young James Bond. That Kitzbühel holiday had been in 1938, and she had never seen James Bond again, although she was naturally amused at the world-wide success of Ian's books about him. After the way that Ian had behaved it was funny, was it not? She added that Bond had written her several letters after the holiday. She might have them somewhere. When she could summon up the energy she would look for them and let me have them. Also she thought there were some photographs. In the meantime, surely there must be

4

people who had known James Bond at Eton. Why not contact them?

I replied immediately, begging her to send the letters. There was no reply.

I wrote several times – still without success. Finally I decided to take Miss Künzler's advice and check the Eton records for a boy called Bond. Fleming had entered Eton in the autumn term of 1921. Apart from saying that James Bond was younger than Ian Fleming, Miss Künzler had been vague about his age. (Supposing, of course, that an Etonian called Bond had really been at Kitzbühel in 1938.) I checked through the whole of the 1920s. There were several Bonds, but none of them called James and none of them in Fleming's old house. Clearly Miss Künzler was wrong, but out of curiosity I checked on through the early thirties. And here I did find something. There actually *was* a James Bond who was recorded having entered Slater's House in the autumn term of 1933. According to the Eton list he stayed just over two years; his name had disappeared from the spring list of 1936.

So much for the records, which neither proved nor disproved what Miss Künzler said. An old Etonian called James Bond certainly existed, but he seemed too young to have known Fleming. It was unlikely that anyone of this age could have been caught up in the secret service world by 1937.

I tried to find out more about this young James Bond, but drew a blank. A puzzled secretary in the school office said there appeared to be no file on him – nor had they any records of his family, nor of what happened to him. She suggested contacting the Old Etonian Society. I did, but again without success. All they could offer were the names of some of Bond's contemporaries who might have kept in touch with him.

I wrote to eighteen of them. Six replied, saying that they remembered him. The consensus seemed to be that this James Bond had been an indifferent scholar, but physically strong, dark-haired and rather wild. One of the letters said he was a moody boy. None of them mentioned that he had any particular friends, but no one had bullied him. There was no definite information about his home life or his relatives. The nearest to this was a passage which occurred in one of the letters:

> *I've an idea [my correspondent wrote] that there must have been some sort of trouble in the family. I have no details. It was a long time ago and boys are notoriously insensitive to such things. But I have a clear impression of him as a boy who had suffered some sort of loss. He was the type of brooding, self-possessed boy who stands apart from his fellows. I never did hear what became of him.*

Nor, it appeared, had anybody else.

This was distinctly tantalizing for, as close readers of the Bond books will recall, these few extremely inconclusive facts find an uncanny echo in the obituary of James Bond, supposedly penned by M. himself, which Fleming published at the end of *You Only Live Twice*. According to this source, James Bond's career at Eton had been 'brief and undistinguished'.

There was no reference in any of the letters to the reason M. gave for James Bond's departure – 'some alleged trouble with one of the boys' maids'. But there were two other interesting parallels. According to M. both of Bond's parents were killed in an Alpine climbing accident when he was eleven and the boy was subsequently described as being athletic but 'inclined to be solitary by nature'.

None of this proved that the mysterious James Bond who had entered Eton in 1933 was Fleming's hero. As any libel lawyer knows, coincidences of exactly this sort are a hazard every author faces. Just the same, it was all very strange.

My next step was clear. Bond's obituary goes on to say that, after Eton, the young reprobate was sent to his father's old school, Fettes. Accordingly I wrote to the school secretary asking if he could tell me anything about a boy called Bond who may have entered the school some time in 1936. But before I could receive a reply, another letter came which altered everything. Inside a large brown envelope bearing a Vienna postmark was a short official note from an Austrian lawyer. He had the sad task of informing me that his client, Fraulein Künzler of 27, Friedrichsplatz had died, not unexpectedly, in her sleep some three weeks earlier. He had the honour now of settling her small estate. Among her papers he had found a note saying that a certain photograph was to be sent to me. In accordance with the dead woman's wishes he had pleasure in enclosing it. Would I be so kind as to acknowledge?

The photograph proved to be a sepia enlargement of a snapshot showing a group of hikers against a background of high mountains. One of the hikers was a girl, plump, blonde, extremely pretty. On one side of her, unmistakable with his long, prematurely melancholy Scottish face, stood Ian Fleming. On the other was a burly, very handsome, dark-haired boy apparently in his late teens. The trio seemed extremely serious. I turned the photo over. On the back there was a note in purple ink.

This is the only picture I could find. There seem to be no letters, but this is James and Ian out in Kitzbühel in 1938. The girl with them is me, but somehow I don't think you'd recognize me now.

So much for poor Miss Künzler.

The photograph, of course, changed everything. If the young tough really was James Bond – and why should the defunct Miss Künzler lie? – something extremely odd had happened. The whole idea of Fleming and the James Bond saga needed to be revised. Who was this James Bond Fleming had evidently known? What had happened to him since 1938? How far had Ian Fleming used him as a model for his books? The reality of Bond opened up a range of fascinating speculation.

I had not heard from Fettes, and there was still precious little evidence – a photograph, an entry in the Eton Register, a handful of coincidences – enough to pose the mystery rather than solve it. But there were certain clear lines now which I could pursue and did – but not for long. I had barely started contacting several of Fleming's friends from the Kitzbühel days when I was rung up by a man called Hopkins.

Once a policeman, always a policeman – there was no mistaking Mr Hopkins's voice. He understood from certain sources that I was making certain inquiries. He would like very much to see me. Perhaps we could have lunch together? Somewhat incongruously he suggested next day at the National Liberal Club in Whitehall Place.

Mr Hopkins was an unusual Liberal: a big, bald man with outsize eyebrows, he was waiting for me by the bust of Gladstone in the foyer. Something about him seemed to make old Gladstone look a little shifty. I felt the same. We had a table by the window in the big brown dining-room. Brown was the dominating colour – brown Windsor soup, brown walls and furniture. Mr Hopkins, as I noticed now, was wearing a somewhat hairy, dark brown suit. When the soup came he started talking, his sentences interspersed with noisy spoonfuls of brown Windsor soup.

'This is all off the record, as you'll understand. I'm from the Ministry of Defence. We know about your current inquiries. It is my duty to inform you they must stop.'

'Why?'

'Because they are not in the national interest.'

'Who says they're not?'

'You must take it from me they're not.'

'Why should I?'

'Because if you don't, we'll have the Official Secrets Act down on you just so fast that you won't know what's hit you.'

So much for Mr Hopkins. After brown Windsor we had cottage pie, apparently the staple food of Liberals – nutritious doubtless, but no great stimulus to conversation. I tried getting Mr Hopkins to reveal at least something of his sources. He had been at the game too long for this. When we parted he said, 'Remember what I said. We wouldn't like any unpleasantness.'

'Tell that to Mr Gladstone,' I replied.

It was all most unsatisfactory. If there were really any reason for keeping quiet about James Bond, I felt I had a right to know. I certainly deserved an explanation and from someone with a little more finesse that Mr Hopkins. A few days later I received it. This was where Urquhart comes upon the scene. Another invitation out to lunch – this time to Kettners. I said I wouldn't come unless he promised no more threats at lunchtime. The voice at the other end of the telephone sounded pained. 'Threats? No, really – how unfortunate. Simply an intelligent discussion. There are some slightly sensitive areas. The time has come to talk . . .'

'Exactly.'

Urquhart was very, very thin and managed to combine baldness with quite startlingly thick black hair along his wrists and hands. As with the statues of Giacometti he seemed to have been squeezed down to the stick-thin shadow of his soul. Happily his expense account, unlike his colleague's, stretched to a bottle of respectable chianti.

From the beginning I attempted a bold front, and had produced the photograph of Bond and Fleming before we had finished our *lasagne*.

'Well?' I said.

'Oh, very interesting. What a good-looking chap he was in those days. Still is, of course. That's half his trouble.'

'You mean he's alive? James Bond's alive?'

'Of course. My dear chap. Why else d'you think we're here?'

'But all this nonsense from your Mr Hopkins – the Official Secrets Act. He almost threatened me with gaol.'

'Alas, poor Hopkins. He's had a dreadful lot of trouble with this case, a dreadful lot. He has a hernia too. And an anaemic wife. Some men are born to suffer.'

Urquhart smiled, exposing over-large false teeth.

'No, Bond's an interesting fellow. He's had a dreadful press of course and then the films – he's not at all like that in real life. You'd like him. Perhaps you ought to meet him. He enjoyed your book, you know – your Life of Ian. Made him laugh, although, between the two of us, his sense of humour's not his strongest point. No, we were all extremely grateful for your book. Hopkins was certain that you'd smelled a rat, but I told him not to worry.'

'But where is Bond and what's he doing?'

Urquhart giggled.

'Steady. We mustn't rush our fences. What do you think of this chianti? *Brolio*, not *Broglio* as Ian would insist on spelling it. But then he wasn't really very good on wines. All that balls he used to write about champagne when the dear old chap couldn't tell Bollinger from bath water.'

For the remainder of the lunch we chatted about Fleming. Urquhart had worked with him during the war, and, like everyone who knew him, was fascinated by the contradictions of the man. Urquhart used them to avoid further discussion of James Bond. Indeed, as we were leaving, he simply said, 'We'll be in touch – you have my word for that. But I'd be grateful if you'd stop your investigations into James Bond. They'd cause a lot of trouble if they reached the papers – the very thought of it would do for Hopkins's hernia.'

Somewhat lamely I agreed, and walked away from Kettners thinking that, between them, Hopkins and Urquhart had managed a deft piece of hushing up. Provided I kept quiet I expected to hear nothing more from them. But I was wrong. A few weeks later Urquhart rang again, asking me to see him in his office.

It was the first time I had entered the Headquarters building up by Regents Park which formed the basis for Fleming's 'Universal Export' block. I was expecting something altogether grander, although presumably all secret services adopt a certain camouflaging seediness. This was a place of Kafkaesque oppressiveness – grey corridors, grey offices, grey people. There were a pair of ancient milk-bottles outside Urquhart's door. Urquhart himself seemed full of bounce. He offered me a mentholated cigarette, then lit one for himself and choked alarmingly. The room began to smell of smouldering disinfectant, and it was hard to tell where Urquhart ended and the smoke began.

'This business of James Bond,' he said. 'You must forgive my seeming so mysterious the other day. I really don't enjoy that sort of thing. But I've been contacting the powers that be, and we've a little proposition that might interest you.'

He paused, tapping a false tooth with a cheap blue biro.

'I'll be quite honest with you. For some time now we've been increasingly concerned about the Bond affair. You are by no means the first outsider to have stumbled on it. Just recently we've had some nasty scares. There have been several journalists. They have not all been quite so, shall we say, cooperative as you. It's been sheer murder for poor Hopkins. The trouble is that when the story breaks – and of course it will, these things always come out in the end – it will be damn bad for the Service. Seem like another gaffe, another Philby business, only worse. Can't you just see those headlines?'

Urquhart rolled his eyes towards the ceiling.

'From our point of view it would make far more sense to have the whole thing told responsibly.'

'Meaning suitably censored.'

'No, no, no, no. Don't bring these obscene words in unnecessarily. This is a story we're all proud of. I might almost say that it is one of the most startling and original coups in our sort of work. Without exploring it completely it would be hard to understand just how remarkable it is.'

I had not suspected quite such eloquence in Urquhart. I asked him to be more explicit.

'Certainly. Forgive me. I thought you were with me. I am suggesting that you write the full life story of James Bond. If you agree, I'll see that you have full cooperation from the department. You can see his colleagues. And, of course, I'll make arrangements for you to meet Bond in person.'

*   *   *

As I learnt later, there was more to Urquhart's plans than he let on. He was a complex man, and the years he had spent in undercover work made him as secretive as any of his colleagues. What he failed to tell me was the truth about James Bond. I had to piece the facts together from chance remarks I heard during the next few weeks. It appeared that Bond himself was facing something of a crisis. Everyone was very guarded over the details of his trouble. No ailing film-star could have had more reverent discretion from his studio than Bond from his colleagues at Headquarters. But it seemed clear that he had been suffering from some complicated ailment during the previous year which had kept him entirely from active service. The symptoms made it sound like the sort of mental and physical collapse that overworked executives succumb to in their middle years. Certainly the previous September Bond had spent over a month in King Edward VII Hospital for Officers at Beaumont Street under an assumed name (no one would tell me what it was). He seems to have been treated for a form of acute hepatitis and was now convalescent. But, as so often happens with this uncomfortable disease, he still had to take things very easy. This was apparently something of a problem. The doctors had insisted that if Bond were to avoid a fresh relapse he simply had to have total physical and mental rest from active service and the London winter. James Bond apparently thought otherwise.

He was insisting forcefully that he was cured and was already clamouring to return to active service. People appeared to sympathize with his anxieties, but the Director of Medical Services had called in Sir James Molony – the neurologist and an old friend and ally of James Bond in the past – to back him up. After seeing Bond, Sir James had raised quite a furore in the Directorate. For once they really had to use a little sympathy and imagination for one of their own people. Something concrete had to be done for Bond, something to take his mind off his troubles, and keep him occupied and happy while he recuperated. According to Sir James, Bond had been complaining that 'with liver trouble it's not the disease that kills you: it's the bloody boredom.'

Surprisingly, it was M., rarely the most understanding of mortals where human weakness is concerned, who had come up with at least a partial solution.

One of the few men M. respected in the whole secret-service world was Sir William Stephenson, the so-called 'Quiet Canadian' who had been the outstandingly successful head of British Intelligence in New York through the war. For several years now this lively millionaire had been living in semi-retirement on the top floor of a luxury hotel in Bermuda. Both Bond and Ian Fleming knew him well. Why not, suggested M., have Bond sent out to stay with him? They would enjoy each other's company and Bond could swim, shoot and sail to his heart's content. Sir James approved the idea of Bermuda. The climate was ideal but, as he said, the last thing Bond required was a vacation. He'd had too much vacation as it was. His mind needed to be occupied as well.

It was here that Head of Records (a distinguished Oxford don and former agent who acts as the historian of the different branches of the Secret Service) put up the idea of getting Bond to write his memoirs. For him it was a perfect opportunity to get the authentic version of the career of the most famous British operator of the century. But it was M. who pointed out that Bond was the last man to expect to write his story. It had always been hard enough to get the simplest report from him after an assignment. It seems that at this point Urquhart had brought up my name as a solution to the problem. Why not send me out to Bermuda once Bond had settled in? Together we could work on his biography. Bond would have something definite to do. Head of Records would get his information. And he and Hopkins would at last be well rid of the nightmare of an unauthorized account of the whole extraordinary James Bond affair reaching the newspapers.

'You mean,' growled M., 'that you'd let this writer fellow publish the whole thing?'

'If he doesn't,' Urquhart apparently replied, 'someone else is bound to before long. Besides, that whole business between you and Fleming and 007 is going to rank as one of the classic pieces of deception in our sort of work. The opposition know the truth by now. It's time a little credit was given publicly where it is due.'

According to Urquhart, M. was susceptible to flattery. Most old men are. Somewhat reluctantly he finally agreed to back my mission.

Back in London, all this had seemed quite logical and clear. If Urquhart told me Bond was alive and well and living on some distant island, I believed him. Now, with the first lights of Bermuda gleaming below us in the darkness, I wasn't quite so sure. The air-brakes grumbled down, the undercarriage thudded into place; Hamilton lay straight ahead.

The night air was warm and scented. Stepping down from the aircraft was like the beginning of a dream. There were palm trees beside the airport building, hibiscus and azaleas in bloom. For the first time I began envying the honeymooners. I trailed behind them, feeling conspicuous and lonely. Urquhart and London seemed a long way off. Urquhart had told me I would be met at the airport. I hadn't thought to ask him how. Stupidly I hadn't even an address.

In immigration I produced my passport. The official looked at me suspiciously, then signalled to somebody behind him. A good-looking coloured girl came across to me, smiled, said she hoped I'd had a lovely trip and would I come this way? Outside the airport concourse a large negro chauffeur was just finishing putting my luggage aboard a large gold-coloured Cadillac. He saluted lazily, opened the rear door for me, then drove us effortlessly along a road beside the sea. I tried making conversation, without much success. I asked where we were going.

'You'll see,' he said. 'We'll soon be there.'

We purred across a causeway. There was a glimpse of palm trees, lights that glittered from the sea. Then we drove through high gates, along a gravelled drive, and there before us, floodlit and gleaming like that party scene from *High Society*, stood the hotel – old-style colonial, pink walls, white

14

louvered shutters, pillars by the door. The pool was lit up too. People were swimming, others sitting on the terrace. A doorman in top-hat and wasp-coloured waistcoat took my distinctly meagre luggage to the lift.

Urquhart had said, 'they do one rather well.' They did. Bath already run, drinks waiting on the table, a discreet manservant to ask if I had eaten or would like something from the restaurant. I told him 'no', but poured myself a good slug of Glen Grant on ice. I felt I needed it.

'Sir William asked me, sir, to kindly welcome you and tell you to treat this place as your own home. When you are ready, sir, say in half an hour, please ring for me and I will take you to Sir William.'

I bathed luxuriously, changed into the lightweight suit purchased three days before from Aquascutum on Urquhart's expense account and, after more Glen Grant, I rang the bell. The manservant appeared at once, led me along a corridor, and then unlocked a door which led into a private lift. Before starting it the man picked up a telephone inside the lift.

'Augustus here, sir. Bringing your guest up now.'

I heard a faint reply from the telephone. The lift ascended, slowly.

At the top there was a slight delay, as the doors evidently opened by remote control from the other side. When they did I walked straight into an enormous room, most of it in shadow.

On three sides long, plate-glass windows looked out on the dark night sea. Along the fourth side there were chairs, a radio transmitter, two green-shaded lamps. By their slightly eerie light I could make out only one man at first – elderly, grey-haired with a determined, weather-beaten face.

'I'm Stephenson', he said. 'London have been telling me about you. Glad you could come. This is Commander Bond.'

2
Boyhood of a Spy

So this was Bond, this figure in the shadows. Until this moment I had taken it for granted that I knew him, as one does with any familiar character in what one thought was fiction. I had been picturing him as some sort of superman. The reality was different. There was something guarded and withdrawn about him. I felt that I was seeing an intriguing, unfamiliar face half-hidden by an image I could not forget.

It was a strong face, certainly – the eyes pale-grey and very cold, the mouth wide and hard; he didn't smile. In some ways I was reminded of Fleming's own description of the man. The famous scar ran down the left cheek like a fault in the terrain between the jaw-line and the corner of the eye. The dark hair, grey-streaked now, still fell in the authentic comma over the forehead. But there was something the descriptions of James Bond had not prepared me for – the air of tension which surrounded him. He had the look of someone who had suffered and who was wary of the pain's return. Even Sir William seemed to be treating him with care as he introduced us. We shook hands.

'The authentic warm, dry handshake,' I said, but Bond didn't laugh. Levity was clearly out of place. There was an awkward silence, then Bond lit a cigarette, inhaling deeply.

'I'm not sure,' he said, 'that I'm going to be much help to you. This seems a half-arsed sort of project.'

'Why?'

'Because there's not a great deal I can tell you. Quite frankly, I'd like to hang on to the few shreds of private life that Ian left me.'

Sir William tactfully remarked that he was sure that his private life was the last thing I was interested in; before I could object, he had brought the subject round to Fleming. Bond softened up a little then. I asked him how well he had known him.

'Extremely well – if it was ever possible to know him.'

'And you didn't object when he started writing about you in the books?'

'Did I, Bill?'

The old man chuckled, as if the whole question of the books were something of a private joke between them.

'That's something,' said Sir William, 'that's going to take a little explanation.'

'And has M. given his authority for me to tell the whole grisly story?'

'Apparently.'

'Incredible,' said Bond. 'Well, if *he* says so, I've no objections. Quite the reverse in fact. I'll be relieved to have the truth recorded over that little episode. Rather too many people still seem to think that I agreed to Ian's efforts out of vanity. If they only knew the trouble those damned books have caused me.'

'Come now,' said Sir William. 'They were a master-stroke at the time. And they undoubtedly did save your life. It isn't fair to start complaining because they got a little out of hand.'

Bond sniffed and looked annoyed.

'What are your plans?' I asked.

'You mean, what is my future?' Bond shrugged his shoulders. 'Good question. Only wish I knew the answer. Officially I'm now too old for active service, but I don't know. How old's too old? Abel was fifty-five when he came up for trial – three years older than I am now. I suppose it all depends.'

'On what?'

'Chiefly upon the little man in Harley Street, Sir James Molony. You remember him. Ian writes about him somewhere. Official head-shrinker to the Secret Service – and a great man in his way. My future's in his hands. He's due here shortly. If he decides I'm fit for duty, I'm back to London like a flash.'

He dropped his voice, and stared out at the dark ocean. The lighthouse on Lighthouse Hill flashed and subsided.

'It's not a question primarily of age,' he said. 'The little that you lose in stamina you make up in cunning. What really matters is something deeper; whether your courage lasts.' He turned impatiently and faced me.

'As for this present business, I'd like to get it over and done with quickly. What can I tell him, Bill?'

'Virtually the lot. He has total security clearance.'

'Headquarters will be checking what he writes?'

'Naturally.'

'That makes it easier. When shall we start?'

'Tomorrow morning if it suits you.'

'And where do you want me to begin?'

'At the beginning.'

* * *

Bond was a punctual man. (As he told me later, punctuality was one of the prosaic qualities essential for an undercover agent, although in his case it also seemed to match his character.) Next morning, at 9.30 precisely, my telephone rang.

'If you're ready we might as well begin this ghastly chore.' The telephone served to exaggerate the curiously lethargic drawl to the Commander's voice. I had been finishing my breakfast and hoping for a second piece of toast. Bond however made it plain that he was anxious to begin.

'Where would you like to work?' I asked. I was curious to

see where he was living, but he said quickly,

'Oh, I'll come down to you. More peaceful in your place.'

Two minutes later there was an authoritative rap on the door. James Bond entered.

Somehow he looked completely different from the night before – no sign now of tension or of that wariness he had shown then. He was fit, bright-eyed, positively breezy. He was wearing *espadrilles*, old denim trousers and a much faded dark blue T-shirt which showed off the width of shoulder and the solidity of chest. There was no hint of a paunch or thickening hips. But he seemed curiously unreal this morning in a way he hadn't previously; almost as if he felt it necessary to act a role I was expecting. (Another thing I was to learn about him was the extent to which he really was an actor *manqué*.)

He talked about his early-morning swim. Swimming, he said, was the one sport he still enjoyed.

'And golf?' I asked.

Golf, he replied, was much too serious a matter to be called a sport. He added that he really hadn't played much recently. As he was talking, he loped around the room, looking for somewhere that suited him to sit. Finally he settled on a bamboo chair on the balcony from where he had a fine view across the harbour. He breathed deeply, stretched himself, and stared at the horizon.

'Now,' he drawled, 'what can I tell you?'

'Something that Fleming never mentioned is where you were born.'

Bond swung round immediately.

'Why ask me that?'

'You said begin at the beginning.'

Bond smiled, somewhat ruefully, and paused before replying.

'I suppose you have to know. The truth is that I'm a native of the Ruhr. I was born in a town called Wattenscheid – that's near Essen – on Armistice Day, 11 November 1920. I have not, I hasten to add, a drop of German blood in my veins – as far as one can ever be certain of such things. As Fleming says somewhere, my father was a Highland Scot, my mother Swiss.'

'So how come the Ruhr?'

'My father, Andrew Bond, was, as Fleming rightly says, an engineer who worked for Metro-Vickers. In 1920, though, he was attached to the Allied Military Government with the rank of brigadier. He was responsible for helping to dismantle the empire of our old friends Alfred Krupp and Sons – unfortunately he was not allowed to perform this most valuable task as well as he might have. He had this house at Wattenscheid – I don't remember it of course, but I did see it just after this last war – big, ugly, rambling place. My mother always said she hated it. Apparently she had to have me there because of a rail strike. She was all set to have me back in England, but it was suddenly impossible to leave. By the time the strike was settled I had arrived. The damage, as they say, was done.'

'But was it damage? Has it ever caused you any trouble?'

'Being officially a native Kraut? Oh certainly. Government departments can be very wary of such things on your records. At one time it looked like dishing my chances for the Royal Navy. Also, I think it's always made me very touchy about our friends, the Germans. Shall we say I don't care for them. Fairly illogical reaction. Probably all stems from this accident of birth. But I still don't like them.'

Once Bond had settled the question of his birth, he seemed to relax. He suggested that we order coffee, which he drank strong and black – always a good sign with him as readers of Fleming's books will remember. For the rest of that morning we went over the basic facts about the Bonds. Fleming, who used to get very bored with families, had been predictably brisk over James Bond's ancestry. Apart from some hypothetical dialogue in *On Her Majesty's Secret Service* suggesting that James Bond might be descended from the Bonds who gave their name to Bond Street – dismissed by Bond himself as 'sheerest eyewash' – all that he disclosed were the bare facts of his hero's parentage. The father, Andrew Bond, had come from Glencoe in Argyll whilst the mother, Monique, was a Delacroix from the Swiss canton of Vaud.

I was surprised to see that James Bond was evidently proud of his Scottishness, talking nostalgically about the stone house in the Highlands which was still the centre of the family. He said the only roots he felt were there. 'I always feel myself emotionally a Scot. I don't feel too comfortable in England. When I die I've asked that my ashes be scattered in Glencoe.'

He talked a lot about the early Bonds, tough, warlike people who followed the MacDonalds and had lived in Glencoe for generations. Three Bonds, all brothers, were slaughtered in Glencoe during the massacre of 1692. Later Bonds preserved their sturdy independence; during the eighteenth century they had prospered, whilst by the nineteenth they had produced a missionary, several distinguished doctors, and an advocate. But, as with many Highland families, the Bonds clung to their identity as Scots. They had avoided being softened up like Lowlanders. They still regarded Glencoe as their home. The men remained big-boned and wild. One of them, James Bond's great-grandfather and his namesake, won a V.C. with the Highland Infantry before Sebastopol. His sword still hangs in the house in Glencoe. Other male Bonds were less impressive. One of them, Great-Uncle Huw, drank himself determinedly to death in his mid-thirties. Great-Uncle Ian was sent down from university for shooting his law books one night with a ·45 revolver. The present head of the family, Bond's Uncle Gregor Bond is a dour, drunken old gentleman of eighty-two.

According to James Bond, the men in his family all tend to be melancholics. Through this side of the family he evidently inherited his shut-in, brooding quality. There is a lot of granite in James Bond. He also got the family determination and toughness mixed with a solid dose of Calvinism. The Bonds, as true Scotsmen, believed in guilt, great care with money and the need for every man to prove himself.

Bond's father, Andrew, was a true Bond. Extremely gifted, he appears as something of a paragon during his boyhood – prize scholar and captain of games at Fettes, he went on to Aberdeen to study engineering with considerable success. In his early twenties when the war began, he joined the Royal Engineers, survived the Somme, and was seconded to Ian Hay's staff at Gallipoli. Here he lost an arm but gained a D.S.O. and also a lifelong admiration for the Turks. When the war ended, he was an acting brigadier and joined the Allied Military Government to supervise the dismantling of the Ruhr, a task which must have suited this puritanical young engineer.

But the real passion in his life was mountains. Climbing suited his strenuous nature, and late in 1918 the handsome young ex-brigadier spent his first peacetime leave climbing the mountains he had dreamed of – in the Swiss Alps. He was trying to forget the horror of the war, but he did more than that. He found a wife.

Whatever else they were, the Bonds were great romantics, and Andrew's marriage was in character. Just as Garibaldi saw the woman that he married for the first time through a telescope, so Andrew Bond caught his first glimpse of his future wife half-way up a mountain. She was suspended at the tail-end of a rope of mountaineers ascending the spectacular peak, the Aiguilles Rouges, above Geneva. Climbing conditions were appalling. From below, Andrew Bond admired the tenacity of the climbers. When, later, he went to congratulate them, only to find that the final climber was young, female and extremely pretty, his fate was sealed. So was hers. Nothing deterred him – neither the fact that she was barely nineteen, nor that her family opposed the match, nor that she was already officially engaged to a Zürich banker three times her age. The same spirit that had inspired old James Bond against the Russians at Sebastopol urged on his grandson for the girl he loved.

The Delacroixs were rich and obstinate and somewhat staid. Their reaction to their daughter's one-armed suitor was predictable. Had Andrew Bond possessed a modicum of tact he might still have won them round. Tact was, alas, one of his several deficiencies. After a stormy interview with the man he wished to make his father-in-law, he delivered a brief ultimatum, had it rejected, and stormed out of the big white house, slamming the ornate front doors behind him. Two days later, he and Monique eloped.

The elopement was to cause years of bitterness which helped sour much of James Bond's childhood. Monique was instantly disowned and cut off without the proverbial Swiss franc. Andrew, in return, would never let the name Delacroix be spoken in his presence. From now on he did his climbing in the Pyrenees. The prompt birth of a son and heir, James's elder brother Henry, nine months to the day after the wedding, made little difference. The Bonds and Delacroixs were not on speaking terms.

This was a pity, especially for Monique. Pretty, high-spirited and frivolous, she clearly found the early days of marriage far from easy. Apart from the baby and their mutual love of mountains, she and her formidable husband had little in common, and, as she was soon pregnant again, mountain-climbing hardly seemed advisable. The elopement had been the great adventure of her life. Once it was done she started missing Switzerland, the nice big house in Vaud and the warm, reassuring flow of funds from Papa Delacroix. She would have probably done better with her sexagenarian from Zürich.

As always in such cases, one wonders how two human beings can have been so painfully mistaken over one another. How could Andrew Bond possibly have been the sort of husband she required? He was profoundly serious and solitary, a dedicated engineer and something of a puritan. Worse still, he had no money. His old employers, Metro-Vickers, were prepared to have him back. There was a job for him in Birmingham. Monique, for the first, but not the last time, kicked. Andrew gave in; to keep his young wife happy, he accepted his secondment to the Allied High Command in Germany. James Bond was born the autumn after they arrived.

It should have been an idyllic childhood for two small boys. Their parents doted on them and they had everything – love, comfort, playthings and security. In this defeated country, they were like spoiled young princes. The house at Wattenscheid had its own grounds and was filled with servants, nannies, dogs and horses. Summers were spent along the Baltic coast or down the Rhine, Christmases at Glencoe where all the Bonds would gather and stay for Hogmanay like the old-fashioned tribal clan they were.

This was where James Bond saw his paternal grandfather, old Archie Bond for the first time. He was terrified of him; and the old man spoke such broad Scots that the child, who already spoke better German than English, could understand little that he said. There were the wicked uncles too, his father's brothers – whisky-sodden Gregor and wealthy Ian who was such a miser. But the one relative they both adored was their father's only sister, their Aunt Charmian – sweet, sad Charmian, bride of three weeks, whose husband had died at Passchendaele. She lived in Kent, grew dahlias and believed in God.

James adored his mother; indeed, the more that she despaired of him, the more he loved her. Even today James Bond still keeps her miniature beside him, and regards her as a female paragon. When he describes her he uses words like 'fresh', 'gay', 'irresistible'. Neither her *affaires*, her dottiness, her wild extravagance can dim her memory.

Unhappy marriages often produce devoted children; the Bonds were no exception. The family was held together by its tensions. James loved his father but could not speak to him of anything that mattered, worshipped his mother, but could not forgive her for rejecting him. In years to come a lot of women were to pay the price of this rejection.

Even as a child, James was finding that life had certain compensations. One was his strength; after the age of eight he found that he could always beat his brother in a stand-up fight – and did so frequently. Another was eating; he became known as a greedy child and, for a period, was extremely fat. (As Fleming noted, even in manhood James

Bond remains addicted to double portions of whatever he enjoys.) Fighting and eating and long rambles with his dog – these were the consolations of the young James Bond.

Another feature of his boyhood was the continual movement that went on – the Bonds were wanderers. After Monique's refusal to settle back in Birmingham, Andrew accepted a succession of overseas assignments from Metro-Vickers when his attachment with the Military Government ended. From Germany they moved to Egypt, where Andrew worked as consultant for three years on the Nile dam project above Aswan. By now James was five, and, just as in Germany, he proved himself adaptable in his choice of playmates. Soon he had his private gang of small boys from the neighbourhood, most of them Egyptian. James seemed to find no difficulty communicating with them, or with asserting his leadership. He had always been big for his age. The Bond brothers had an elderly French governess. James could elude her, and for days on end would roam the city with his gang of guttersnipes. Sometimes they played along the river, scampering along the waterfront and living on their wits. At other times they flitted round the market-place, picking up money where they could and playing their games with other gangs.

With Andrew away for days on end, and Monique occupied with a new admirer, nobody appeared to mind what happened to the boy. He must have picked up more than a smattering of Arabic (much, to his regret, entirely forgotten) and with his dark complexion seems to have become almost an Arab boy himself. One of his strangest memories of this period is of waiting with his followers one evening outside a big hotel in Cairo, watching the cars arrive. Suddenly a black and yellow Rolls drew up. Out stepped his mother followed by a fat man with a monocle. James recognized him as an Armenian contractor who had visited the house on business with his father. The man seemed so gross that he couldn't imagine what his mother was doing in his company. James called out to her, but the smart Mrs Bond failed to recognize the street Arab as her son. Next day, when he asked his mother what she was doing at the hotel, she became furious, insisted she had been at home, and ordered James to his room for insolence.

This was, as Bond says wryly, his first real lesson in the female heart.

Finally, there seems to have been some sort of family crisis – the boys were getting used to them by now – and, on the grounds that Cairo heat was bad for his wife's health, Andrew Bond was once again transferred – this time to France. For Andrew, the worse his marriage, the better his career, and by now he was becoming one of the Metro-Vickers' key men in the power stations they were building through the world. Once more he took a big house for his family – this time along the Loire, not far from Chinon – and once more the same old pattern seemed to reassert itself, with all the erratic ups and downs of an unhappy family. Theoretically they were quite rich, but there was never money to go round. Monique was wilder than ever. Servants would come and go.

France suited James. He picked up the language, loved the food and made a lot of unexpected friends – the boatmen on the river, the village drunk, the gendarme and the madame who kept the café in the village. He also fell in love for the first time – with the butcher's daughter, a sloe-eyed, well-developed girl of twelve, who deceived him for an older boy who had a bicycle.

*   *   *

James Bond remained in France a year – then his world changed again. In 1931 the Metro-Vickers combine won an unprecedented contract from the Soviet Government to construct a chain of power stations around Moscow as part of Stalin's policy for the electrification of Russia. Inevitably, Andrew Bond was despatched with the advance party of British engineers. Three months later he sent for his family to join him.

The Metro-Vickers representative in Paris had booked the

Bonds a first-class sleeper to themselves, and Bond can still remember the small details of the journey – the rare excitement of eating a meal with his mother in the restaurant car, the white gloves of the waiters, the mineral water and the reading lamp beside his bed. As the train thundered east towards the Polish frontier, he can remember dropping off to sleep to what Fleming called 'the lullaby creak of the woodwork in the little room', then waking drowsily to hear the porters calling out the names of German stations in the night. This was Europe, the grey Prussian plain as dawn was breaking, Warsaw by breakfast-time. That evening he watched as the train slowed down and passed the red-and-white striped posts marking the Russian frontier.

James saw his first Russian policeman then – a large silent man in dark blue uniform and red-starred cap who checked their papers. Grey-tuniced porters helped the family aboard the Moscow Express, a magnificent relic from pre-Revolution days. Once more the Bonds had their own compartment – this time with rose-pink shaded lamp and Victorian brass fittings. In the restaurant car, as foreign visitors with roubles, they ate even better than the night before – it was here, incidentally, that Bond formed a life-long love of caviare. All this made the arrival next day at Moscow something of a shock.

The British families had been herded together in Perlovska, a small place twenty miles from Moscow. By Russian standards the little wooden house the Bonds were given was the height of luxury – for Monique it was unspeakable. There were no shops, no night-life and no entertainment. With winter coming, life was bleak. There was famine in the land.

Ten-year-old James Bond was getting an impression of Soviet Russia that has never really changed. Deep down he still believes this is a land of starving peasants, cowed citizens and an all-powerful secret police. These conclusions must have seemed dramatically confirmed by the events he witnessed in the early months of 1932.

Historians are still arguing the causes of the so-called

Metro-Vickers trial of that year, when several of the leading British engineers on the power-station project were put on trial in Moscow, charged with sabotage.

For the Bond family, huddled in their freezing house in Perlovska, it was all hideously real. Andrew Bond's friend, the minister Tardovsky, had already been arrested. Rumours were everywhere. Then the six British engineers – the Bonds knew them personally – were carried off to the fearful Lubianka prison, by the secret police. It seemed a miracle that Andrew was not among them.

Throughout the desperate weeks of the trial that followed, James Bond was to become one of the few westerners to have lived through a Russian purge at first hand. (Those who condemn him for his anti-Communism should remember this.) He has not forgotten the scared families, the hopelessness of waiting, the cold dread of the next move of the police.

Andrew was something of a hero, always on the move between the Kremlin, the British Embassy and the Lubianka, briefing the lawyers and helping to keep the prisoners' spirits up. Monique was less resilient. As James Bond says, it was easier for his father – he had something to do. Monique could only wait. Under the tension and privation of the camp, her health suffered and her nerves got worse. She could not sleep, complained of headaches, and begged her husband to get them out of Russia. Sternly he told her that they would not leave until the trials were over.

During this period, James Bond had an uncanny glimpse into the future. Several of the accused engineers had been released on bail, and were waiting in the compound of Perlovska for the trial to start. James, along with most of the English nationals, was with them. Suddenly a car drew up, a big, official-looking limousine. Out stepped a tall, impeccably-dressed young Englishman, looking for all the world as if about to enter some St James's club. Sounding distinctly bored, he introduced himself. He was a Reuter's correspondent, sent out from London for the trial. His name was Ian Fleming.

The two things about him that stuck in James Bond's memory were his suit – an outrageous check, the like of which had not been seen before in Moscow, let alone Perlovska – and his unruffled ease of manner. Despite himself, James Bond was most impressed, and there and then changed his mind about being an engineer when he grew up. All these things considered, it seemed a better bet to be a journalist.

Although he had to stay on at Perlovska throughout the trial, James heard all about it from his father. It was from him that he learned of the impassioned speech of Andrei Vishinsky, the vitriolic Russian prosecutor. When the verdicts were announced they amounted to a triumph for Andrew Bond. All but two of the engineers were acquitted. Andrew was congratulated by his company and marked out for promotion. Still more important for the Bonds, their ordeal was over. The Metro-Vickers mission was withdrawn from Russia. The family was coming home at last.

With Andrew appointed to head office, he took a house in Wimbledon, 6 North View, an echoing Victorian monstrosity facing the Common. Here the Bonds settled for the summer. They must have appeared an odd, outlandish family. Andrew was thirty-eight, but looked much older, his big-nosed, craggy face now lined and battered by the last few years. The two boys also must have borne the marks of their ordeal. They, too, looked older than their years and both of them seemed strangely out of place among the well-to-do children of their neighbours. They were oddly dressed. James Bond ascribes his subsequent sartorial conformism to childhood anxieties on this score. He still remembers other children laughing at his *lederhosen*. He says he also felt distinctly foreign here in Wimbledon. He was not used to hearing English spoken – he and his mother generally conversed in French. As a result, he felt himself painfully unwanted. Although back in England, he was as much of an outsider as ever.

But the member of the family who fared worst was undoubtedly Monique. During the long months in Russia she had hung on, because she had to. The boys depended on her. Now that all this was over, she fell to pieces. Her zest for life deserted her. A photograph taken that July gives an idea of what was happening. The face is still beautiful but white and drawn, the thin hair turned prematurely grey, and there is a hunted look about the eyes.

James's brother, Henry, was the only one who seemed unscathed by life. The two boys were entered for the summer term at Kings College School. This was something of a stop-gap, since Andrew, possibly as a gesture against the wealth of the Delacroixs, had entered the boys for Eton when they were born. But the school was convenient, barely five minutes' walk across the common. Henry settled in and soon became a favourite pupil. James was difficult and withdrew in on himself. Then came the disaster that shaped his life.

*   *   *

It started with his mother's nervous breakdown towards the end of that July. She had been acting strangely for some time, complaining that the Russians were pursuing her and that she had seen several of the Soviet secret police from Perlovska watching the house from the Common. Then one night she went berserk and tried to stab Natasha, the Bonds' devoted Russian maid. Fortunately, Andrew Bond was at home. The doctor came and Moñique was sent off to a sanatorium at Sunningdale. She soon seemed to recover, but the specialist advised a change. At his instigation, Andrew Bond decided that the time had come to forget the past, make peace with the Delacroixs and take his wife home. It must have been a difficult decision for a man of his proud nature.

James Bond remembers how his father saw him and his brother off from King's Cross for their summer holiday in Glencoe. It was an emotional occasion. Andrew Bond assured them that he was taking their mother off to Switzerland and that when she came back she would be cured and happy. He promised that the days of wandering were over. The family would settle down and they would love each other. It was an unusual speech for so reticent a man.

The boys had been at Glencoe nearly three weeks when they came back from a day on the moors to find the house in uproar. Aunt Charmian had suddenly arrived from London. James Bond remembers that his grandfather was in tears. The sight was so unusual that it took some while for him to understand what his aunt was saying. The boys were to get their things together. They were to be calm and sensible. From now on they would both be living with her at her house in Kent. There had been a frightful accident . . . climbing in Switzerland . . . their parents had been killed.

It was Henry who broke down and wept. James Bond surprised everyone by his self-possession. He says that in a strange way he was prepared for what had happened. When his father saw him off from King's Cross three weeks before, he knew that he would not be seeing him again. Now he remembered his father's words, 'You must look after yourself, laddie. If you don't there's no one else that will.'

The death of James Bond's parents remains a mystery to this day, although their son was gradually to piece together something of what happened. It seems that Monique had returned to her parents as planned. After an emotional reconciliation – her father was particularly shocked at her condition – she had stayed on for several weeks at her childhood home in the Vaud. Then Andrew came to fetch her; by all accounts there was a bitter argument between the husband and the family. All the accumulated resentments and recriminations were brought up. Andrew was shouting that Monique's place was back with him and her children. Her parents were insisting, just as forcefully, that she should stay with them, blaming Andrew for the state that she was in. As so often in such rows, the one person both sides were forgetting was the one that they were fighting over. During the uproar Monique fled the house.

It was some time before her absence was discovered, still longer before anybody found that she had taken a car and driven off towards Geneva. Andrew chased after her. He traced the car nearly as far as Chamónix. There he found it left outside a café. The café owner said that he had seen the woman who was in it heading for the mountain. Andrew Bond knew then where to find Monique; the great mountain towering above the valley was the crag of the Aiguilles Rouges.

It was past midday and Monique had more than two hours' start on him. But he remembered the climb up the sheer face of the mountain where he had first caught sight of her so many years before. Monique was making her escape at last.

She must have climbed with desperation. The route she took was one which is normally for well-equipped mountaineers, fully prepared and roped together. Despite this, she had almost gained the shoulder of the mountain when her husband reached her. She was crouched on a ledge too narrow for the mountain goats.

By now there were people watching from the valley. Through their binoculars they could see the pink dress she was wearing outlined against the red mass of the rock. They could see her husband edging close towards her, and, for a while, it seemed as if the chase continued. It was nearly dusk by now.

The watchers in the valley saw the two figures on the mountain close together. Evidently Andrew was trying to persuade her to come down. Finally she did; the pink speck started to move back towards him, edging along the sheer face of the rock.

Whether he tried to clutch her, whether she threw herself or slipped no one will ever know. James Bond believes she could not face leaving her husband or returning to him. At any rate, they were together when they fell and what was left of them was buried in the village cemetery below the mountain.

*　　*　　*

One thing the situation did was bring out the best in Aunt

Charmian. She was efficient, practical and calm – the only one who was. It was quite clear that no one in Glencoe could possibly take charge of the two boys and she was adamant against the Delacroixs doing so. She was the one who went to Switzerland, and saw that her brother was buried with the woman he had so disastrously loved. She also managed to convince the old man Delacroix that she was the best person to look after the two boys.

Pett Bottom is not far from Canterbury. This is a splendid part of Kent, some ten miles inland from the sea, a landscape of long valleys, undulating hills, and fertile orchards.

The name Pett Bottom – which inevitably appealed to Ian Fleming – is ancient, 'Pett' being Anglo-Saxon for a wood. Aunt Charmian's small house was still at the bottom of the wood, a few hundred yards from a small country inn, The Duck.

There is something wholly admirable about Aunt Charmian. In the two Bond boys she had found something her life had lacked – a purpose – and this slightly dumpy, gentle woman dedicated herself to them with all the single-mindedness of her family.

Early that autumn, Henry went off to Eton as arranged. There was inevitably strong pressure on Aunt Charmian to send James to a suitable preparatory school, 'to knock some sense and some behaviour into his young head', as Gregor Bond put it. She resisted – furiously. As she wrote to both sets of grandparents, 'If James is sent away again, after all he's been through, we'll have a problem on our hands for the rest of our lives.' Instead she said that she would keep him with her at Pett Bottom, and promised that she would coach him for the Eton examination. Finally everyone agreed. Aunt Charmian was a persuasive woman.

Certainly it was thanks entirely to her that James Bond passed the Eton entrance examination and went to join his brother Henry there in the autumn term of 1933.

*   *   *

Like Hobbes of Malmesbury's description of life in the state of nature, James Bond's career at Eton might be summed up as 'nasty, brutish and short'. Certainly it is not a period of life on which he looks back with pride or much regret, and it was evident from the day he went there that this was not the school for him. Despite all this, the strange thing is that Eton put its trademark on him. Indeed, in some ways, he seems a very typical Etonian.

From the beginning he found himself a rebel. It was a mistake to put him in his brother's house. Henry was predictably successful and had adapted well to school society; James was once more in his elder brother's shadow. As a result, he soon reacted against everything his brother seemed to represent. He refused to work. He saw the cliques of older boys as snobbery, the school traditions as tedious charade. He kicked against the fagging system and objected to the uniform. His contemporaries who wrote that he was 'moody and self-contained' seem to have had a point. He says now that once again he felt himself a complete outsider in this closed, upper-class society, and that for most of his time at Eton he was very lonely.

James Bond is probably exaggerating. It is hard to see him being victimized by anyone. At fourteen he was enormous for his age – already nearly six feet tall, good-looking and distinctly self-possessed. Older boys appear to have treated him with caution. Before long he enjoyed a certain status and he had a few, carefully picked friends, all of them outside his house. They were all members of what he called 'the unregenerate element' in the school, and most of them had a reputation, like James, for being 'flash'.

Bond's favourite crony was a boy called Brinton, nicknamed 'Burglar'. He was a year older, embarrassingly handsome, with the cool, *mondaine* sophistication of the cosmopolitan rich. He and James got on together. During the holidays, James visited his house in Shropshire, and later was invited to his father's place in Paris. Here, with his looks and his command of French, Bond impressed Burglar's father. It was this rich old rake who discovered the boy's natural talent for cards and love of gambling. He backed the two boys when they played bridge for money with his rich Parisian friends. The canasta craze was starting – James Bond cleaned up at that.

Burglar *père* introduced Bond to his earliest Morlands Specials, and also gave him his first taste of the life of the very rich – something which, in his way, James Bond has been seeking and rejecting ever since. He liked the Brintons' sense of style – the luxurious flat, the drinks, the dress, the servants, and the cars – particularly he liked the cars. Burglar's father was not only rich, he was indulgent, to a fault. As a final treat he lent the boys his big *café-au-lait* Hispano Suiza and a chauffeur, sending them down to Monte Carlo for a week's holiday in style. In theory the chauffeur drove; in fact the two boys took turns behind the wheel and Bond got his first experience of what has remained an unabated pleasure – driving a powerful fast car across the Continent. He also had his first glimpse of a casino. Burglar's father joined them in Monte Carlo. James Bond won 500 francs at roulette.

After all this, Eton seemed doubly boring. In his second year, James Bond did less work than in his first. He also started to antagonize his house master who saw him as a pernicious influence. Soon it was clear that Bond's days at Eton were becoming numbered. Despite this, he is still irritated by what he considers the poor taste of Ian Fleming's so-called joke about the reason why he was finally asked to leave, the coy reference to 'some alleged trouble with one of the boys' maids'. Bond says that Fleming knew quite well that the girl was *not* a housemaid, but Burglar's illegitimate half-sister, a very beautiful half-French girl of seventeen he was in love with. She had been staying with her father at the Dorchester. James Bond, aged fifteen, borrowed £5 and a motor cycle from Burglar, rode up to London, and took the girl out to dinner before riding back to college. It was his brother Henry who reported him. It was exactly the incident the house master had been waiting for.

3.

Les Sensations Fortes

Bond had been talking all the morning. I was surprised. After the ritual show of reluctance of the night before, I had expected to have trouble getting him to talk – quite the contrary. Indeed he showed all the symptoms of someone who had lacked an audience too long – now that he had one, nothing would stop him. He was clear-cut and businesslike, precise on facts and quite uninhibited about himself. After my unfavourable first impressions, I found myself starting to like him.

It was nearly one o'clock when he finally broke off and suggested we should have a drink down on the terrace. He had his favourite place near the pool, shaded by the succulent green leaves of several banana palms. As we arrived, couples were coming up from the beach for lunch; I was amused at the automatic way his grey eyes followed the plump bottoms of the girls. None of them seemed to take much notice, but I did wonder how they would have reacted had they known the identity of the lean iron-grey-haired man eyeing them so professionally.

The sight of female flesh clearly relaxed James Bond. He smiled to himself, leaned back in the steamer chair where he was sitting and, from his T-shirt pocket, produced a familiar object – the famous gun-metal cigarette-case. He flicked it open, offered it to me.

'The first today,' he said. 'I hope you weren't expecting Morlands Specials. Officially I've given up, but one can't be too strict about these things. These are the latest de-nicotined Virginian. I'd better warn you that they taste revolting.'

'Fleming would have a shock,' I said.

'After he had me smoking seventy a day? He exaggerated that, you know – as with a lot of other things as well. He was a strange fellow. With the cigarettes I'm sure it was an excuse for his own heavy smoking – he liked to think that there was someone who smoked even more than he did. In fact I never have been more than a two-pack-a-day man, and then only in times of tension.'

'And drink?'

'Oh, he got that about right. What did he say I drank – half a bottle of spirits daily? No one can call that excessive. Even Sir James Molony says it would be wrong to cut out alcohol entirely. Perhaps with his authority behind us, we should have something now to quench the thirst.'

'Shaken not stirred?'

Bond laughed. 'Precisely.'

By the telepathy that marks the finest waiters in the very best hotels, Augustus was waiting for our order just as James Bond finished speaking. I was intrigued to see how Bond treated him. In fact he gave the order just as Fleming had described in the precise, clipped voice of the man who knows exactly what he wants and is used to getting it – the vodka iced, the French vermouth specified by name, the single slice of lemon peel. I felt there was a touch of parody in the performance – Bond acting out the part of Bond – but he seemed unaware of this and coolly nodded to Augustus when the drinks arrived. Fleming had been right. This was a man who, as he said, took an almost old-maidish pleasure in attention to the minutiae of life.

As he drank, I had a chance to observe him carefully. He was, if anything, taller and slightly thinner than I had expected; the arms below the short sleeves sinewy rather than muscular. His denim trousers were unpressed, his hair was worn a little on the long side. What would one have thought of him from first impressions? A colonial administrator here on convalescent leave? An aging playboy between marriages? Only the face might make one wonder – that bronzed Scottish face whose hardness seemed so out of place among these lush surroundings.

'You takin' lunch today, Commander?' asked Augustus.

The commander nodded.

'Customary table?'

Bond grunted his assent. I checked an urge to smile.

'You must excuse me,' said James Bond. 'I am a creature of routine. A dangerous thing in my profession, but I feel here it does no harm.'

The customary table proved to be the best in the hotel – set well back from the pool and shaded by a great hibiscus, busy with humming birds. Clearly the birds delighted Bond, taking up most of his attention so that it was harder to get him to continue with the story of his life. Once more he did the ordering – 'I always have the lobster done with coconut and lime juice, and avocado salad; then perhaps some guavas and blue mountain coffee. Suit you? The usual, twice, Augustus.' When the food came, he ate with relish.

I asked him about getting thrown out of Eton. How did Aunt Charmian react?

'Oh, she was wonderful, although I know that she was bitterly upset. You see, the dear old thing had this firm idea that I was infected with what she used to call "the curse of the Bonds", and that her task in life was to save me from it. When I got into Eton she thought that I would be a gentleman at last. Now that I was leaving under a cloud she really thought that I was going to the dogs.'

'Wasn't she angry?'

'No. That was the marvellous thing about her. She never blamed me. She blamed herself. Made me feel dreadful. There was quite a rumpus in the family about me. My mother's people seemed to think that I should go to Switzerland and live with them. The family in Glencoe seemed in favour of sending me to prison. As a compromise I was finally packed off to my father's old school, Fettes. I rather liked it after Eton, stayed there until sixteen, then got fed up with it. Decided it was time to move on. Got to Geneva University. And that was where the trouble really started.'

*   *   *

Bond explained that the strange decision to study at Geneva came through the Delacroixs. Ever since the Eton episode old man Delacroix had kept pressing for him to spend some time in Switzerland. Finally James Bond suggested the idea of studying at the university as something of a compromise. The Delacroixs would pay but he would naturally have rooms close to the university; for by now James Bond was keen on having his independence. Above all, he wanted the chance to live his own life free from the crush of communal living in a boarding school.

Surprisingly, he liked Geneva. One says "surprisingly" because the prim, staid city is hardly the background one associates with Bond. And yet as soon as he arrived he felt at home here. Part of the explanation may be that he was half Swiss, and part that he was suddenly experiencing freedom here for the first time in his life. But there was something else about Geneva that appealed to him, and he agreed with Ian Fleming on the subject. For both of them it had, what Fleming called, a 'Simenon-like quality – the quality that makes a thriller-writer want to take a tin-opener and find out what goes on behind the façade, behind the great families who keep the banner of Calvin flying behind the lace curtains in their fortresses in the Rue des Granges, the secrets behind the bronze grilles of the great Swiss banking corporations, the hidden turmoil behind the beautiful bland face of the country'.

This then was Switzerland for Bond, and he was fascinated by it. He had two rooms with a respectable Swiss lady over a sweet-shop off the Quai Gustave Ador. In theory, the good lady was supposed to keep a strict eye on him both for the university and the family. In fact, James Bond soon used the charm on her that worked infallibly with elderly ladies of all nationalities; within a month he had Frau Nisberg round his little finger. For the first time in his life he found himself free to do exactly as he wanted.

He worked – a little; enough at any rate to satisfy the university. He attended lectures in psychology and law and read quite widely. Otherwise, he amused himself. Right from the start, he showed himself quite self-sufficient. He was completely selfish. Apart from girls, he had no need for other people in his life, and was extraordinarily single-minded in the way he went after what he wanted. That first winter in Geneva he fell in love with winter sports.

As with his golf, James Bond was not a stylish skier. He was too wild to become a star. But he had total dedication, outstanding stamina, and he loved taking risks. Near Chamonix there is a famous ski-run, the so-called Aiguilli de Midi, which in its day was the supreme test of all the top-flight internationals. One of the young instructors with the university ski-club constantly referred to it. He was a conceited and unpleasant young man who liked to show off to the novices. These included Bond, who was officially still in the beginners' class. Bond resented him. He, in turn, took every opportunity to make a fool of Bond. After one final training session during which the instructor behaved more obnoxiously than usual, Bond decided he had had enough. The instructor had been making fun of James Bond's style, or lack of it, and saying that he should try it out on the Aiguilli de Midi – then he would see how long he lasted.

'Fine,' said James Bond, 'we'll try.'

The instructor said this was impossible. Chamonix was two hours' drive from Geneva, and he was only joking. James Bond replied that he never joked. Early next morning the two of them set off. By the time they had reached the top of the ski lift, the instructor was begging Bond to come to his senses. He apologized for seeming to make fun of him. He would make any restitution that he pleased. But he must realize that if he attempted the Aiguilli he would quite certainly be killed. Bond made no reply, except to ask him if he wanted to go first or second. The instructor, thinking that Bond would need help, said he would follow him.

'Please yourself,' said Bond as he checked his skis.

The beginning of the Aiguilli is spectacular. There is a straight drop of more than a mile between the narrow shoulders of the mountain; from there the ski-run passes between rocks and clumps of pine then plunges down into the valley. The hazard comes from the sheer speed of the descent – after that first drop the skiers are hurtling on at speeds approaching sixty miles an hour. To keep control at such a speed is a supreme test of nerve and skill.

Bond put on his goggles and, without looking back, thrust himself off. To this day he is not sure how he survived. Some instinct from generations of mountaineers must have helped preserve him – also his strength and his beginner's luck. For the hair-raising first mile of the descent he thought that he had gone. He had no control – nothing except the will to stay alive. But then he realized that he was winning. His mind was very clear. The closeness of death was sharpening his reactions; for the first time he was enjoying the one drug to which he would always be addicted – danger.

The remainder of the run was an experience of pure exhilaration which he has never forgotten. At the bottom of the slope he didn't wait for the instructor, and never spoke to him again – nor did he ever go back to the beginners' class.

But this piece of bravado was important for James Bond. Once he had tasted such excitement he needed more. From that moment on, life became a pursuit of such extremes. It was around this time that he met a Russian student called Gregoriev – a drunken, violent youth with a black beard. He was an anarchist, and Bond enjoyed hearing him rail against society, morality and all the forces of their so-called civilization. Something deep down in Bond agreed with him and they often drank together late into the night. It was during one of these drunken sessions that Gregoriev introduced James Bond to Russian roulette. He produced a rusty ·32 Smith and Weston, put in a single bullet, spun the chamber, put it against his forehead and pulled the trigger.

Bond asked him why he did it. Gregoriev's reply was to provide James Bond with something of a motto in the months ahead.

'*Ah*,' said Gregoriev, '*mais j'adore les sensations fortes.*'

As a gambler, Bond could appreciate the logic of Gregoriev but he loved life too much to follow him. When the Russian offered him the gun he refused it. He had other ways by now of finding *les sensations fortes*.

One was through skiing. Now that he had conquered the Aiguilli, nothing could hold him back, and he soon gained a reputation as the wildest skier in the university. When he was writing of the events described in *On Her Majesty's Secret Service*, Fleming was impressed to discover that Bond had been down the Cresta run in a bobsleigh about this time. Bond also mountaineered under the most hazardous conditions. It was all a way of proving himself and of enjoying *les sensations fortes*. For Bond insists that he took these risks out of sheer joy of life, and was indignant when a psychiatrist suggested that he was suffering from an acute death wish. Fleming understood him here. In *Dr. No* he writes of Bond's 'usual blind faith that he would win the duel'. Bond says that this faith has never quite deserted him.

There were other motives though behind Bond's mountaineering which Fleming failed to understand. Bond climbed because his father had. At times he bitterly regretted that Andrew Bond was dead. In *From Russia With Love*, Fleming described him flying above the Alps and, looking down, imagining himself again 'a young man in his teens, with the leading end of the rope round his waist, bracing himself against the top of a rock chimney on the Aiguilles Rouges'. What Fleming didn't know was the emotional battle there had been behind the climb. As he looked down from his aircraft, Bond was not having the nostalgic memories that Fleming seemed to think. He was remembering a very private battle long ago as he had forced himself to follow a certain route up the mountainside in an attempt to lay the ghosts of his dead parents.

During his first months at Geneva, Bond had been developing his appetite for life. He was voracious. The same greed which had made him a glutton as a small boy was now directed outwards, and he was hungry for experience. One of his girl-friends was to compare him with the character of Nora in Ibsen's *The Doll's House* – always waiting for something *wunderbar* to happen. But that first Easter in Geneva, it must have seemed as if this 'something *wunderbar*' had finally arrived.

It was the beginning of April. Term was over, but James Bond was in no hurry to leave Geneva. He enjoyed the rackety routine of life with old Frau Nisberg; he enjoyed the silence of his room with its views across the lake; he enjoyed Frau Nisberg's cooking. He had told Aunt Charmian that he would be back with her for Easter, but the thought of England secretly depressed him – that grey weather, that appalling food and all those boring dreary people. Even the thought of dear Aunt Charmian failed to reconcile him to England. He would recognize the anxiety behind her smile. She would be worrying what he was up to. And brother Henry would be there. He would much rather not see brother Henry. So James Bond decided to stay in Geneva just a few days longer.

The day after he made this decision, he was awakened by the noise of a car hooting in the street outside. This was unusual in that sleepy side-street and Bond, who had been late to bed, tried ignoring it. The noise continued. Finally Bond, bleary-eyed, looked through the window. There in the street below stood the gleaming form of a *café-au-lait* Hispano-Suiza. In the driver's seat, thumb firmly on the horn, sat his friend 'Burglar'. Bond forgot his tiredness. He forgot Easter in England. Within half an hour he was dressed, packed, breakfasted and sitting beside Burglar bound for Paris.

Although Bond had had little contact with the Brintons since leaving Eton, he was as fascinated as ever by the rich. From that previous trip to Paris, he had picked up the idea of money as a source of freedom, glamour and excitement –

in short, for those *sensations fortes* for which he craved. Now he was having a fresh chance to sample them, for Burglar wanted him to spend Easter with him. Without a second's hesitation Bond agreed.

It was a memorable day with the great car sweeping towards Paris through the early spring. They stopped at Mâcon where they lunched off *Poulards comme chez soi* at the Auberge Bressane. Burglar insisted on champagne. When they drove on to Paris, he promised Bond that they would have a night to remember. Bond, slightly drunk, agreed. And so occurred that evening which Fleming has described as 'one of the most memorable of his life'.

As a keen reader of the old Continental *Daily Mail*, Bond remembered the advertisements for Harry's Bar. This seemed the acme of sophistication and it was there that they began. They drank more champagne. They dined in style at Fouquets (on Brinton *père's* account). Inevitably, they wondered where they could find a woman.

'Nothing but the best,' said Bond.

'Naturally,' said Burglar.

At this time the most notorious, if not quite the most fashionable, brothel in Paris, was the Elysée on the Place Vendôme. Le Chabanaif was wilder, Le Fourcy enjoyed a reputation still for the blowsy splendours of *la belle époque*. The Elysée was different. The superb eighteenth-century house was run like a London club, complete with doorman in full livery, smoking-room with hide armchairs and library smelling of cigar smoke where it was strictly forbidden to talk. The one unusual feature of the place was the presence of a lot of pretty girls with nothing on.

Although distinctly drunk by now, Bond seems to have treated the whole situation with the self-assurance one would hope for – Burglar likewise. The Brinton name secured them entry. According to Fleming, Bond was still a virgin. Bond, in the interests of strict accuracy, insists that technically this was not quite true. But he agrees that this was the first time that he enjoyed the real pleasure that would loom so large in all his subsequent adventures.

'Until then I hadn't really known what it was there for.'

The girl's name was Alys. She was from Martinique – short, slightly plump, demure and adept in the arts of love. She giggled at him (thus revealing dimples and small perfect teeth), praised his looks, admired his virility, and, in a 500-franc room on the second floor, gave him the courage to accomplish creditably what, by its nature, was still unfamiliar. As an afterthought she stole his pocket book. It contained 1,000 francs, a passport and photographs of his parents. Bond noticed his loss just as he was leaving..

It was stupid of the girl, for the Elysée was respectable. So were its clients. None of them went there for the pleasure of losing pocket books. None of them wanted trouble. So when James Bond, aggressive, outraged and fractionally drunk by now, knocked out the liveried doorman and began shouting for the manager, the manager arrived. Her name was Marthe de Brandt.

Although forgotten now, Marthe de Brandt was famous in her day. The daughter of a judge and a famous courtesan, she was something more than the successful harlot she became. She was beautiful, abandoned and ambitious. She was also undoubtedly intelligent and well-educated. By twenty she was rich, by twenty-five, notorious. Thanks to the generosity of de Combray, the armaments king, she attained sufficient capital to open her own establishment. Thanks to her own attractions, she made the place something exceptional in the pleasure-life of Paris. It was her idea to call it the Elysée after the presidential palace. It was also her idea to base the décor on a London club. Within a few months of opening, it had become an unofficial centre for the political élite of France.

Like many of her kind, Marthe de Brandt was something of a spy. It was not hard for her to gather information from her guests and it was mere common sense to sell it to the highest bidder. At the time that James Bond met her she was already in her late twenties and a little past her prime – small, very blonde, with a determined mouth and periwinkle eyes. She was very rich. As far as one can be precise about such things, she worked mainly for the Eastern powers.

It is hard to know what such a woman can have seen in young James Bond. Hardly sex – she must have had enough of that. Nor love – the idea seemed absurd. At the time the general explanation was that she wanted someone to corrupt. If by corruption in this context one means teaching a younger person every known form of copulation, then Marthe de Brandt corrupted him. But there was more to the relationship than this. Both of them must have found something they needed in each other. For James Bond she may have been the amorous equivalent of the Aiguilli run. For her the precocious English boy was probably the son she wanted.

The strange thing is that she fell for him at once. Even young Brinton was surprised at the apologetic way this famous woman treated him, reprimanding the unfortunate doorman, summoning the girl, and, after slapping her face, dismissing her on the spot. Then Marthe de Brandt promised Bond that he would have his property returned the morning after, when she had finished her enquiries.

Bond spent the night at the Brinton flat on the Boulevarde Haussmann. When he awoke a messenger had already brought him an envelope. Inside was his pocket-book. It contained two crisp ten-thousand franc notes – also a letter from Marthe de Brandt inviting him to supper.

The remainder of that Easter holiday is something Bond won't talk about. His friends, the Brintons, saw little of him. Nor did Aunt Charmian. Marthe had a small flat in the tiny Place Furstenburg off the Rue Jacob. For the next few months this became his home.

He obsessed her as no man had done before. She obsessed him as no woman would again. His studies suffered – so did her business. Neither of them seemed to notice. The *amour fou* between Marthe de Brandt and her young Englishman became the talk of Paris.

It was a Chéri-like *affaire*. She indulged and spoiled him. He appeared to be her creature. During that Paris springtime they went everywhere together – to see the horses run at Longchamp (where he was bored), to watch the twenty-four-hour race at Le Mans (where he wanted to drive) and to the latest show at Le Boeuf sur le Toit (where, for the first time in her life, she felt jealous). They drank a lot, fought a lot and loved a lot. She had his suits made by a famous tailor in the Rue de Rivoli, arranged him boxing lessons with Charpentier. When they felt bored, they drove down to Antibes where she had a wistaria-covered villa hidden among the pines. She bought him the famous Bentley with the Villiers supercharger. (Fleming got the details of the purchase slightly wrong – also, of course, the date, one of a number of inaccuracies which have caused Bond subsequent embarrassment.)

Despite their difference of age, they seemed to have appeared a well-matched couple; she was so small and fair and doll-like, he so tall and mature for his age. For these few months they led a charmed existence, almost oblivious of others. Aunt Charmian wrote anxious letters until old Gregor Bond told her he would get over it. Burglar's father tried to warn him of a woman like de Brandt. One night, as they were dining in the crowded Restaurant des Beaux Arts, they heard a drunk American call out, 'Here is the lovely Marthe and her English poodle.' It was a well-known brawler called Sailor Hendrix. Bond hit him very hard between the eyes, then pushed his head into his onion soup.

Another time he thought that she had been unfaithful with a former lover, a distinguished figure on the Paris Bourse. The following night she invited the man to their apartment and made him watch as she and Bond made love.

In fact there was only one man in the whole of Paris who could come between them. James Bond met him early that summer. His name was Maddox. He was a curious, dry, bespectacled man of totally indeterminate age, tough as a prewar army boot, and very rich. Bond met him through the Brintons. He appeared a typical wealthy foreigner, a collector of paintings and of pretty women, gourmet and wit and friend of many politicians. Officially, he was military attaché at the British Embassy. Unofficially, he ran the British Secret Service inside France. As an old lover of Marthe de Brandt, he had observed Bond's success with interest. A methodical man, he had checked on him as matter of routine. Then he decided he should get to know him better. But Maddox was a cold fish. Having met James Bond he did what he often did with people he thought might prove useful – he pigeon-holed him carefully away, but kept his tabs on him.

Maddox was always proud of his ability to use unlikely people for his work. A good judge of character, he used to claim that he had rarely been let down. He used to talk about his 'cellar' of potential agents. 'Let them mature,' he'd say, 'wait until they're ready to be drunk.' For James Bond this moment came quicker than Maddox had expected.

At the beginning of 1937 the British Secret Service faced a sudden crisis. For the past year the energies of the British government had been directed to cementing ties with France and with out-manoeuvring the extreme right wing which was pro-German, anti-British and which later formed the main support for Pierre Laval and Vichy France. The British had been having considerable success. As the German menace grew, there had been discreet cooperation between the French and British High Commands, who were unofficially exchanging plans and information. This was all very secret, but in January reports reached London that this information was known in Berlin. Rumours were picked up in Paris and soon published in the right-wing press. Official French government denials followed.

Two days later came the bombshell. A Berlin newspaper published photographs of French High Command documents together with comments by the British General Staff. They were repudiated by the French, but in Paris the right wing was in full cry. The President was said to be distressed, and behind the scenes the whole policy of military cooperation between France and Britain now seemed threatened. Maddox had frantic messages from London. However the leak of documents had happened, it must be found and blocked. Immediately. Maddox had several suspects. One of the major ones was Marthe de Brandt. Von Schutz, the German military attaché, was an habitué of the Elysée. Marthe had done business with him in the past. Maddox was informed that she was the source this time. She needed money for her fancy boy. He half suspected her already. Even so, normally he would have checked more thoroughly. There was no time with London clamouring for action. That same evening Maddox had dinner with James Bond.

Maddox wrote later that he found him quite insufferable – arrogant, ill-educated and drinking far too much. (How much simple jealousy was motivating Maddox is anybody's guess.) But Maddox found no difficulty breaking down the arrogance. He probably enjoyed doing it. He seems to have played upon Bond's anxiety for a purpose in his life. He claimed to have known his father. He got him talking and then asked him if this life was really what he wanted – acting the kept man to a notorious tart.

Normally Bond would have hit him as he once hit Sailor Hendrix, but Maddox had handled situations of this sort before. Besides, he wasn't drunk. Bond was. Maddox asked him why he stayed with a woman who was flagrantly unfaithful to him. Bond asked him what he meant. And, in reply, Maddox produced photographs of Marthe de Brandt with a variety of men. They were not the sort of pictures that one enjoys seeing of the woman one loves. Bond was too shocked to realize that they had all been taken at least two years earlier.

Maddox knew then that the time had come to mention patriotism to James Bond. It was not difficult. One of the main performers in the photographs was recognizably von Schutz. As Bond could see, Marthe de Brandt was not only betraying him – she was betraying France and Britain to the Hun.

Maddox outlined the damage caused already by the leakage of the documents to Berlin. Once war came, as come it would, this woman's action could cost fifty thousand British lives, more still if she were permitted to continue.

Bond was silent.

'What do I have to do?' asked Bond.

'I am afraid she has to die,' said Maddox. 'The only question that remains is how to do it. I don't want you involved or hurt, but I must know that I can count on your discretion – if not exactly your cooperation.'

'How soon must this happen?'

'As soon as possible.'

There was a long silence then. Maddox puffed softly at a large cigar. Finally James Bond said, 'I'll do it – personally. I don't want anyone else to touch her.'

'I hardly thought you would,' said Maddox.

The next day was a Saturday. The day after was to be Marthe de Brandt's thirtieth birthday. She dreaded being thirty. To make her happy, Bond had arranged a long weekend with her and some old friends at a small hotel beside the Seine where they had often enjoyed each other in the past. The place was called Les Andeleys. It has a famous castle built by Richard the Lionheart and Monet painted here along the river.

Bond felt curiously cold and self-possessed, and, from the moment that he woke, he treated Marthe de Brandt with exceptional affection. He had spent all his money on a ring for her – an amethyst and diamond which she loved – and put red roses on her breakfast tray. They made love, and Marthe de Brandt seemed happy at the idea of their weekend in the country. All the way down in the Bentley she chattered gaily. Bond thought that she had never been more beautiful.

Just after midday they reached the long road from Les Thilliers. The Seine was on their left, its waters shining through the leafless poplars. The road was empty. On the far hill stood the ruin of the Norman fort. The Bentley sang at something over eighty.

'Darling,' said Marthe de Brandt, 'I do hate being thirty. It's so old. I can't bear being old.'

'You never will be,' said James Bond. He jammed his foot down to the floor-boards as the bend approached. The great car lifted, kicked like a jumping horse against the verge, then somersaulted slowly into the lilac-tinted river.

4

Luminous Reader

When Bond had finished telling me his story he fell silent. At first I thought that he was deeply moved: then I realized that he was simply watching the two humming-birds that were still flickering like small blue lights against the coral flowers of the hibiscus. By now the sun was at its height and they were the only things that moved. The empty pool was bright-blue plastic, sea and terrace had become some over-coloured photo on a travel brochure. Bond sipped his coffee. His grey eyes still followed the two birds intently. It was impossible to tell what he was thinking.

'Strange business,' he said finally. 'Still, it taught me a lesson I've remembered ever since. Never let a woman rule you – total disaster if you do.'

'A pretty drastic lesson.'

'Yes,' he said, smiling faintly. 'Yes, it was.'

'What happened?'

'To the car? Oh, it was salvaged. Cost quite a bit, but it was finally all right.'

'And you?'

'I was salvaged too. Went through the windscreen. That's what did this.' He touched the long scar down his cheek. 'Fleming was always trying to find out how I got it. Now

51

you know. I was quite knocked around in other ways – several bones broken, mild concussion, but one floats, you know. One floats. I was picked up by one of those big Seine barges.'

'And the woman?'

'Oh, she had had it. Very swift death. She was still in the car when they pulled it out. Her neck was broken. The ironic thing about it all was that Maddox told me later it was a mistake. It hadn't been her at all. The real spy had been some wretched fellow in the British Embassy. They caught him a few days later.'

'Weren't you horrified?'

'Of course. But there was no use blaming Maddox. It was terrible for him, and he had done his duty. Besides, I owed an awful lot to him. He cleared up the mess, settled the French police, somehow avoided having me involved in the inquiry. God knows how he did it. These things are very difficult in France. It was through Maddox that I got my real start within the Service.'

I tried getting Bond to continue with the next stage of his story, but he seemed reluctant. He had been talking for a long time. Clearly he needed his siesta, but, before he went, he promised to see me that evening over dinner. Then he would continue with his début with the British Secret Service, the famous affair Fleming mentions of the Roumanians at Monte Carlo.

Before going down to dinner, I rang his room. There was no answer. Nor was there any sign of Bond that evening. I asked Augustus if he had seen the Commander.

'No, sir. The Commander ain't dining in tonight.'

'You sure?'

'Quite sure, sir. He left the hotel with his lady. Somehow I don't think the Commander will be back tonight.'

Nor was he back the morning after. I spent the morning lying in the sun and swimming. There seemed no need to worry about Bond. It would have been strange had he not had a woman with him, but I wondered who she was. I also wondered how long she was keeping him.

My second question was soon answered. Punctual as ever, Bond appeared for lunch, dressed as the day before – same T-shirt, same old *espadrilles*, same uncreased denim trousers. There was, alas, no sign of any lady. Nor did he offer an excuse or explanation for the night before.

Otherwise the routine followed the previous day's, even down to the lobster done with coconut and the guavas. Bond was in lively spirits, chatting quite confidently about his return to active service. He seemed to think that this could happen any moment. Clearly there was something in the wind but when I asked him about possible assignments he clammed up fast. I felt I had committed something of a solecism and, to change the subject, asked about Maddox.

'Funny character – part of the old guard of the Secret Service. Straight out of Ashenden; in fact he knew Maugham and used to claim that he had based one of his characters on him. He taught me a lot and certainly he influenced me at the time. The after-shave and the cigars and all the people that he knew – I was terribly impressed. He was quite unlike your modern operator; he wouldn't last ten minutes under our present set-up. But he had something. He was a hard man, and he had an instinct for the telling gesture. He was good to me in the beginning.'

After Bond was rescued from the Seine, Maddox had taken care of everything. Bond's name was kept out of the papers and Bond himself installed in a discreet nursing home in the woods near Fontainebleau. The doctors said that he would need several weeks before he was on his feet again but were confident that with his youth and his physique there was no real danger. The only thing they overlooked was the gash on his face. When Maddox saw the scar left by the stitches he was furious.

'Don't worry,' said the surgeon. 'He has kept his looks and the women will find it irresistible.' But Maddox wasn't thinking about women. He knew the danger of a trademark in the career he had in mind for Bond. He called in LaPointe, the Swiss plastic surgeon who later worked with McIndoe. LaPointe did his best, but, as he said, he had, as usual, been consulted when the damage was already done.

During these weeks in the nursing home Maddox was a frequent visitor. He and Bond talked a lot and Maddox was able to sum him up and learn a great deal more about him. He also made inquiries on his own among a lot of contacts back in London. After some hesitation, Headquarters had given him a provisional go-ahead.

The evening James Bond left the nursing home, Maddox took him out to dinner – at the fashionable Orée de la Forêt. The food was somehow typical of Maddox – *fonds d'artichauts au foie gras, tournedos aux morilles*, a bottle of Dom Perignon – and over the brandy and cigars, Maddox outlined his proposition. He did it with great charm and skill. James Bond has never forgotten the small, frog-like man with the bald head and bright black eyes who gave him his first introduction to the life he was to follow. It was a Faust-like situation with Maddox playing Mephistopheles. Bond had little chance against the future that fate had in store for him.

Maddox began by breaking the news of Marthe de Brandt's innocence. Bond was deeply shocked. Maddox did nothing to lessen the boy's sense of guilt. Instead, he cleverly exploited it. Such things, he said, did happen. Bond should forget the whole affair.

Bitterly Bond asked how he could possibly forget? He had killed the woman he loved, for something she had never done. How could he go on living with such a load of guilt?

Maddox was sympathetic then. If Bond really felt like that, there was something he *could* do – something dangerous, something which could save countless lives. Here was a chance for Bond to expiate his hideous mistake.

'War is coming. It is a matter now of months not years; and there are certain ways in which you can help your country. You possess qualities which we can use. At times the life will seem glamorous and exciting, but I must warn you that your chances of ever seeing a comfortable old age are slim.'

There was no real decision to be made. James Bond

agreed to work for the British Secret Service as Maddox knew he would.

At this period Maddox was still dealing with the mess left by the stolen documents affair. Officially the incident was closed. Behind the scenes it was regarded as a considerable loss of face for the British; in the undercover world of secret agents such things matter.

The Germans were exultant – the French mistrustful. Somehow the British needed to regain their credibility – with their own agents, with their allies, and, most of all, with the enemy.

Maddox was an aggressive man. In time of crisis his instinct was to attack. The early part of 1938 saw him mounting several swift operations aimed at restoring the prestige and confidence of his network. As a small part of this, James Bond was to perform his first assignment or as he calls it now, 'my apprentice piece'.

It was an unlikely business for the British Secret Service to become involved in. Maddox would normally have steered well clear of it. But these were not normal times, and when Maddox heard of the chaos being caused at Monte Carlo by the Roumanians, he smelled his opportunity.

In the long history of the great casino there have been just a few notoriously successful players – Taylor, the professional gambler from Wyoming who had his *succès fou* back in the high days of the 1890s, Fernande, the little Belgian and the extraordinary Charles Wells, the original 'man who broke the bank of Monte Carlo'. (In fact he did this six times before his luck ran out.) Such men were considered good for the casino. They were showmen who encouraged other gamblers, raised the stakes and brought Monte Carlo valuable publicity. The Roumanians were different. From their appearance at the beginning of the previous season, they had spelt bad news for the casino.

They were a syndicate of four, headed by a man called Vlacek. No one had heard of them before, but in the season which had just ended they had played steadily and won remorselessly. Nobody knew quite how they did it.

Naturally there had been endless speculation over the systems they were using, but as the four Roumanians lived in seclusion in a walled villa down the road at Juan les Pins, they kept their secrets to themselves. The casino had automatically investigated them – supervised their play, checked their credentials, attempted every known test against cheating – without result. The Roumanians, whatever else they were, were clean. And night after night, like dark automata, they had continued their inexorable game. Against all known odds they had continued steadily to win. Nobody seemed to know how much, but, according to Maddox's informant inside the casino, they had milked the tables of something over £12 million during the last season.

For the casino all this was far more serious than most outsiders realized. In the first place, most of this money ultimately came from the bank – the casino paid. And in the second, these invulnerable Roumanians had begun to scare off the big-time gamblers. The entry every night of this inscrutable quartet into the grande salle, had a depressing influence on play.

For the management it was an anxious situation and Maddox had decided to make the most of it. This golden corner of the South of France had long been a centre of intrigue. Like most of his profession, Maddox was often there; as something of a gambler himself he knew how the casino always attracted that 'floating world' of spies and diplomats and women of the world who were his clientele. Anything that he could do to help the management would inevitably pay off – Maddox knew how useful it could be to have the powerful Société des Bains de Mer who ran the casino in his debt. And it would do no harm if word got round that the casino had been saved by the British Secret Service.

During those weeks when Maddox had been visiting James Bond in the nursing home at Fontainebleau, they had often played bridge together in the evening. For Bond it passed the time; for Maddox it gave just the chance he wanted to assess Bond's character and capabilities. For as a

56

one-time international bridge player – he had represented Britain in the Biarritz Tournament of 1929 – Maddox believed the card-table was the perfect place to reveal an opponent's strength and weakness. In Bond he recognized something quite unusual. Despite his youth, Bond was that rarity – a natural player whose instinct was to win. Even Maddox often had his work cut out to beat him; more to the point, he could recognize in James Bond's play that combination of daring and stamina, memory and rigid self-control that makes great gamblers and secret agents.

All this made Bond the natural choice for the assignment taking shape in Maddox's extraordinary imagination. It also meant that James Bond's basic secret-service training was, to say the least, unorthodox.

He was brought back to London with strict instructions to stay incognito. Maddox arranged for him to stay in the now defunct Carlton Hotel on the corner of Haymarket under the pseudonym of Haynes. Maddox was staying in the hotel as well. From time to time he would appear and then haul Bond before a bewildering succession of medical experts, language and firearms experts and men behind large desks in Whitehall. Throughout these encounters Bond always had the uncomfortable feeling that they knew far more about him than they said. Nobody told him anything specific – even Maddox had become curiously reticent – but Bond gathered that he was on probation for the Secret Service. He had been chosen for an unusual assignment. His training would begin within a day or two.

Maddox explained all this over dinner in the grill room. He also said that he would be saying goodbye to Bond for a month or two. Now that he had started him on his career he must return to Paris where he had work to do. But quite soon now, Bond would be meeting his instructor.

Bond was becoming slightly bored with the whole air of mystery.

'Why the delay?' he asked.

'Because it's taking just a little while to get him out of prison,' Maddox replied.

'Prison?'

'Yes, Wormwood Scrubs. A splendid fellow called Esposito – Steffi Esposito. American, I'm afraid. And, as you'd imagine with a name like that, he's a professional card-sharp. Scotland Yard tell me he's the best in Britain.'

'He must be if he's in Wormwood Scrubs.'

'That's not the point,' said Maddox. 'He's going to teach you everything he knows. Work hard. You've a lot to learn.'

Bond tried to find out more, but Maddox's wrinkled monkey-face was now impassive. All that he would tell Bond was to take his work seriously.

'They're letting this Esposito off a nine-month rap in your honour.'

*   *   *

James Bond met his teacher three days later in an over-furnished flat off Baker Street. He was expecting someone seedy from the underworld (Bond's experience of criminals was limited). Instead, he found himself greeted by an impeccably dressed, plump, grey-haired man with sad eyes and a pompous manner. Something about him made Bond think immediately of the chaplain at Eton.

'I am informed, sir, that I must teach you all I know.' Esposito sounded much put out by this. His voice had traces of New York and Budapest. 'I tried to tell the fools that it would be impossible, and probably not in anybody's interests, but the police have never understood my sort of work. Your Mr Maddox seemed a cut above the rest of them. He and I agreed upon a basic course for you on the manipulation of the pack. May I see your hands?' He felt Bond's fingers, tested the suppleness of the joints, and sighed impatiently.

'You will have to work. You, my friend, possess the hands of a karate expert. Instead you need the touch of a virtuoso with the violin. Perhaps we should begin with the bread-and-butter business of our art. We call it the Riffle Stack, a straightforward matter of shuffling the cards to produce a desired pattern for the dealer. When – and I use the word 'when' advisedly – when we have mastered that we can move on to more artistic things, until we can deal our aces, kings and any card at will. The aim, dear Mr Bond, is to make those fifty-two cards in the pack our devoted servants.'

Esposito, for all his talk, was an iron teacher; for the next week, ten hours a day, he kept Bond practising the Riffle Stack. Bond used to dream of cards at night, but after ten days of this gruelling work, Esposito let drop his first hint of encouragement.

'You are learning, Mr Bond. Slowly, but you are learning. The fingers are becoming suppler. Within a year of two you might even make a living from the cards.'

But this was not the purpose of the course, and now that Bond was beginning to achieve the basic skills of the card-sharp, Esposito started to introduce him to the main tricks on the repertoire – how aces could be slightly waxed so that the pack broke at them, how cards could be marked on the back with faint razor cuts, and how the whole pack could be minutely trimmed to leave just the faintest belly on a few key cards.

Finally Bond graduated to the gadgetry of the profession – 'Shiners', small mirrors fixed into rings or jewellery, devices that would feed cards from underneath the sleeve, electric gadgets that could signal an opponent's hand.

Bond worked for two whole months in that flat off Baker Street. Apart from Esposito he met no one and heard not a word from Maddox. Despite this he had an uncomfortable feeling of being watched; on the third day of each month £100 would be deposited into his bank account. Then at the end of August, Esposito relaxed. He announced that they would soon be leaving London.

'Time for a little field-work, my friend.'

Bond packed his passport, dinner jacket, half a dozen shirts, and the next day he and Esposito caught the morning train to France. Esposito was in his element. 'I feel that I can *breathe* at last,' he said, inhaling the mackerel-scented air of the main quay at Dieppe. He wore co-respondent shoes and a violently checked suit that made Bond think of someone on a racecourse. There was a jauntiness about him now that Bond had never seen before. They had lunch together in the Hotel Windsor. Esposito did the ordering in florid French. For a while he reminisced about his past adventures and about certain 'colleagues' he had known – tales of extraordinary coups and instant fortunes gained and then squandered over the green baize of the French casinos.

'If I had kept a tenth of what I've won, I'd be a millionaire. But what is money, my dear friend? Simply a game of chance. It's the game that matters.'

Esposito looked mournfully across the esplanade. The sea was blue, the beaches thronged with regiments of bourgeois families. Bond thought the time had come to ask him when the field-work began. Esposito revived.

'Tonight, my friend, we make our début. We shall see how good a teacher Steffi Esposito has been.'

'You mean . . . ?' said Bond.

'I mean that we shall try our luck – and also just a little skill. It is your Mr Maddox's idea. He feels that, after your training, you should have a trial run. He wants you to know just what it feels like to manipulate the cards.'

'You mean I have to cheat?' said Bond.

'Cheat?' replied Esposito, looking pained. 'Please do not use that word. I am an artist and I have tried to teach you just a little of my art. Cheating does not come into it.'

Rather than start an argument, Bond asked him where he planned his trial run.

'Not in Dieppe. I am known here and it could be embarrassing. There is a place along the coast – quite near Le Touquet. A good hotel, a small casino. It will suit us nicely. It is called Royale-les-Eaux.'

*　　*　　*

Bond liked the little town immediately. It had a certain style about it, an air of well-fed tolerance. It was not pretentious, but seemed the sort of place where comfortable French families had come for generations for their holidays. There were fat plane trees in the square, an ornate town-hall, several tempting-looking restaurants. There was also a casino, almost a Monte Carlo in miniature. Bond's heart sank when he saw it. Silently he cursed Esposito.

Esposito was in his element. They booked in at the Splendide. They dined together (although for once Bond wasn't feeling hungry). And then they strolled to the casino. Bond could not help but be impressed now by Esposito. As he followed him into the *salle des jeux* he was reminded of a great musician walking towards the podium. The room was crowded, and for a while Esposito and Bond surveyed the table. The play was high. Royale-les-Eaux was currently attracting an exclusive clientele and suddenly Bond felt an excitement he had never known before. He had known the thrill of gambling for high stakes with the Brintons. This was different. He was experiencing the forbidden pleasure of the card-sharp ready to pit his skill against the table.

After that evening Bond could understand the thrill of beating the system. He and Esposito were playing baccarat. The stakes were high – a group of businessmen from Paris were pushing up the odds and for a while Esposito played along with them. So did Bond. They played cautiously and unobtrusively. After half an hour Esposito was down and Bond about even.

Bond kept his eyes upon Esposito. When card-sharps work in pairs, one is invariably the leader; during those weeks in Baker Street, Bond had learned to follow Esposito minutely. There were certain signs by which Esposito could signal advance details of his play. Suddenly the way he held his cards told Bond that he was about to force the pace.

The bank was held by a balloon-like man with tiny eyes. Bond could detect the avarice with which he fondled the barricade of chips before him. Esposito's signals told Bond that the bank was standing on a five. This was a risky thing to do, but would still leave the odds slightly in the fat man's favour.

There was a murmur of excitement as Esposito put ten red

chips – 100,000 francs – on to the table. It was by far the largest bet of the evening and Bond could appreciate the practised way he did it. There was no hesitation and Esposito's bland face was quite impassive. At the same time he signalled Bond to follow. Bond held a nine and eight of clubs – a reasonable, but by no means a decisive, hand. If Esposito were right about the banker's hand, Bond would unquestionably win. But was he right? How could he possibly be sure?

Bond is essentially a cautious gambler and normally would not have dreamt of taking such a risk. And yet Esposito was quite emphatic. Bond hesitated. Everyone was watching him, and at that moment his nerve failed. 100,000 francs was over £800 – all that he possessed. Warily he placed five white chips – 5,000 francs – down on the table.

All eyes were on the fat man then as he turned his cards. A nine of clubs, a six of hearts. In baccarat it is the last figure of the count that signifies. It was a five, exactly as Esposito had said.

There was that faint murmur from the players – part envy, part excitement – as the croupier pushed Esposito's ten red plaques across the table. Bond felt a twinge of regret as his white ones followed. The play continued, but his opportunity was over. Esposito made no more signals, nor did he gamble heavily again. Half an hour later he rose, tipped the croupier, nodded towards the banker, and departed. Five minutes later James Bond followed him. Bond found him in the bar. Esposito was laughing.

'Well, my friend, and how does it feel to win illicitly?'

Bond replied sharply that he disapproved of it. Esposito still laughed.

'Quite, quite, your attitude does you great credit. It was most necessary though. Your Mr Maddox was insistent. What was it he said – something about needing to have poached to be a game-keeper? I don't understand these English phrases.'

Early next morning, Bond and Esposito left for Paris. Here they made contact with Maddox. That same evening,

Maddox and James Bond dined together at the Brasserie Lipp. Maddox was looking tired. The hollows of the eyes were darker, the thin hair slightly greyer than when Bond saw him last. But he seemed in the best of spirits. He ordered steins of Pilsener, and whilst they drank, he outlined Bond's assignment. The Roumanians had just arrived in Monte Carlo with the beginning of the new season, and already they were winning. Maddox had seen de Lesseps, the casino manager. The poor man was desperate. He had appealed for help to their old friends and rivals, the French Deuxième Bureau. One of their smartest operators, a young man called Mathis, was already working in the casino, so far without success. The Roumanians appeared more confident than ever. The casino was fighting for its life.

Bond was to catch the Blue Train to the Côte d'Azur. An apartment was reserved for him in the Hôtel de Paris. He could draw on virtually unlimited funds. But he was on his own. There must be no scandal and no violence – nor must the management of the casino become implicated in anything he did. For cover he would play the part of the spoiled son of a South African millionaire. His pseudonym was Pieter Zwart. After his training with Esposito he was to challenge the Roumanians. He must either beat them or discover the secret of their operation.

'But if there is no secret?' Bond asked anxiously.

'Then you must make up one. I want those four Roumanians back in Bucharest within a fortnight.'

* * *

At Monte Carlo, Bond was in his element. The character of the wild young Pieter Zwart appealed to him. He hired himself a car – an electric-blue Bugatti. He had silk shirts and pink champagne sent up to his room. Above all, he was thrilled to be back in France and in such circumstances. He never gave the memory of Marthe de Brandt more than a passing thought.

His first evening he dressed carefully, dined well, then

strolled for a while along the Grande Corniche. The evening was beautiful. Down in the harbour there were moored the yachts of the very rich. The lights of Cap Ferrat winked from the headland. Back in the rococo palace of the casino, the chandeliers were lit, the halls were filling, and the early gamblers placing their first bets. It was all totally unreal, but something about its unreality appealed to Bond. He was developing a marked distaste for the realities of life. He was nearly seventeen, but looked a handsome twenty-five. Behind the cold mask of his face, he felt even older. When Marthe de Brandt died, something had died in him. All that he wanted now was action and the sort of life that Maddox offered.

He was glad too that he was on his own. Already this was how he liked to work and he was grateful to Maddox for understanding this. Esposito had stayed behind in Paris, but it was understood that if Bond needed him he would come at once.

Bond took his place in the *grande salle* early, anxious to secure a good seat and to have a chance of seeing who was there. The great room was crowded and Bond played the usual game of trying to pick the genuinely wealthy from the would-be rich. Esposito had told him there was something in the eyes. Bond believed him, but was still not certain what it was. He wondered what his own eyes gave away.

He did his best to play the part of the extravagant young gambler, buying some half million francs worth of chips from the *caisse* and wagering them wildly. He was successful here. By midnight, when the Roumanians were expected, he had already squandered over £500 at baccarat, and was beginning to attract attention. This was what he wanted.

Almost on the stroke of midnight the Roumanians appeared. Bond watched them carefully. All were short, swarthy men wearing tight-fitting dark suits like uniforms. They were unsmiling and formidable, entering the room like a troupe of well-trained acrobats. They stood out from the other players by the certainty and calm which made them curiously forbidding. Now that he had seen them, Bond could understand the anxieties of the casino. These men would take a lot of stopping.

Bond looked across at Vlacek. The only way that one could pick him out was by his enormous head. It was completely bald and tanned the colour of brown paper. His features were inscrutable for, like his three colleagues, he wore large dark glasses.

As soon as he appeared, a place was cleared for him as if for royalty. He was exactly opposite James Bond. Although it was impossible to penetrate the dark pools of the lenses, Bond felt his eyes on him. It was an uncomfortable sensation and he recalled Esposito's advice, 'Always watch their eyes and always smile.' Bond smiled. Several shoes were played. Vlacek was a computer in a dinner jacket. The huge naked head showed no expression, and with each hand unerringly he won. Vlacek was a machine for winning.

Finally Bond challenged him, and as he did he watched for any of the countless give-aways Esposito had taught him to observe. There were none. The stubby fingers with their backing of obscene black hair handled the cards mechanically. There was no sign of pleasure as he gathered in his winnings from James Bond. By 2.30 it was over. The 500,000 francs had crossed the green baize of the table. Bond was cleaned out.

Bond did his best to bear his losses as he imagined any well brought-up millionaire's son would. He shrugged, grinned, tipped the croupier and nodded towards Vlacek, who made no sign of having noticed him. But as he got up from the table a girl brushed his arm. She was tall, beautiful and very blonde. Bond apologized to her. She smiled; he noticed she was very young.

'Sorry you had such bad luck tonight,' she said.

Bond thanked her.

'You'll have to try again tomorrow. Your luck is bound to turn.'

'Do you guarantee it?' said Bond.

'Certainly,' she said, and smiled again, a very special smile which Bond remembered.

'Will you be here?' he asked.

'I'm always here,' she said.

Bond would have offered her a drink for she appealed to him. He had not had a woman now since Marthe de Brandt. Until tonight the idea would have shocked him but in his present mood it seemed permissible. He was not James Bond now – he was Pieter Zwart, a rich South African, and he had just lost 500,000 francs. Something told him it would not be difficult to get the girl to bed.

But Bond had other things to do. De Lesseps, the casino manager had asked to see him, and there was much to be discussed. De Lesseps had his office on the second floor. Bond took no chances. He left the casino, waited half an hour, then doubled back and used the side staircase.

De Lesseps was a bird-like man who seemed to flutter as he talked. He was profoundly pessimistic. He explained to Bond that he had hoped that the Roumanians had won enough the previous season to be satisfied. Instead, now they were back and were winning more than ever. The casino had tried everything. There seemed no hope, no hope at all.

Bond asked whether they had checked the croupiers.

'We have even checked the lavatory attendants. I hardly trust myself. I have my own security men on every table, and yet still they win.'

He sat down weakly behind the largest buhl desk Bond had ever seen, and, for a moment, seemed on the point of tears. Bond felt embarrassed and a little helpless. Neither were emotions he enjoyed. He was relieved when someone knocked at the door.

Bond recognized the broad-shouldered man who entered as one of the uniformed attendants from the *grande salle*. He looked intelligent, with a lively Gallic face. De Lesseps introduced him as Mathis from the official French Deuxième Bureau. Ever since Maddox had mentioned that their French opposite number was working on the case, he had been looking out for him.

Mathis was perfectly polite but Bond felt an air of condescension in the Frenchman's attitude. Like De Lesseps,

Mathis seemed to have checked everything and hinted that the affair was now so serious that 'other means' might have to be employed against the Roumanians. Bond knew enough about the French to understand what these 'other means' might be. Just as Bond was leaving, Mathis asked him how he had got to know Vlacek's mistress. Bond asked him what he meant.

'That tall blonde girl you talked to when you left the table. She's always there with him. Surely you knew?'

Bond was surprised – and put out by the Frenchman's knowingness. He remarked that Vlacek had appeared totally sexless. De Lesseps laughed.

'Sexless? A Roumanian? Our inquiries show that all four of them avoid tobacco and alcohol, but consume women in large quantities. They seem to think that sex helps clear the brain.'

'Perhaps it does,' said Bond.

Although it was nearly four by the big yellow clock on the casino before Bond got to bed, he was up early. The sun was shining, there was a splendid day ahead, and he had plans for using it. Now that he had finally met Mathis he was on his mettle. He liked the spur of competition – there would be a very private pleasure in showing that Frenchman how to settle an assignment.

First he ordered breakfast. This was his favourite meal of the day. During his time with Marthe de Brandt he had discovered how a successful breakfast sets the pattern for the day. In her French bourgeoise way, she had taught him to pay attention to such minor details of life, and he gave precise instructions to the room-service waiter – double fresh-squeezed orange juice, strong black double-roast coffee, whole-wheat toast and two boiled eggs. Clearly the habits that so fascinated Fleming were formed early, for Bond even gave the time the eggs were to boil – three minutes, twenty seconds. As Fleming noted, Bond really did believe there was such a thing as a perfect boiled egg.

While he was waiting he booked a call to Paris. He had just finished eating when Esposito was on the line. Bond thought that he was sounding slightly hurt at being left behind in Paris, but once he began describing the Roumanians he brightened up. For several minutes Bond outlined the details of their play. Esposito asked certain questions.

'The croupier's involved,' he said.

'That's what I thought,' said Bond. 'But how's it being done?'

'A very old trick,' said Esposito. Bond detected just a touch of smugness in his voice as he continued. 'Only an expert would know – de Lesseps should have spotted it at once. I don't know what he thinks he's there for.'

'What should he have spotted?'

'The dark glasses. They give the game away at once. It's years since I've heard of it actually being used, but Matignon does mention it in his monumental *Treatise on Cards*. It's called the Luminous Reader. You'll find it in the index.'

*   *   *

During the next few days, James Bond played the part of spendthrift Pieter Zwart with gusto, driving the blue Bugatti wildly, eating splendidly, gambling recklessly. He made a point of losing three or four thousand pounds a night, yet always having a quick smile for everyone in the casino – including Mathis, who was convinced by now that he was mad. He also made a point of always chatting to Vlacek's mistress. Although so beautiful, she struck him as a shade pathetic. She was English and her name was Pamela. He recognized the type and wondered how she had become involved with the Roumanian. Did she love him? He would find out, but first he had to speak to Maddox. He was soon dealt with. There was a predictable explosion when Bond rang to say that he had got through £15,000 in four days, but Bond could cope with this side of Maddox. He knew how he admired extravagance, and confidently promised him that by the weekend the Roumanians would all be back in Bucharest. In return Maddox gave him three more days' unlimited credit.

The girl was even easier. She was scared of being seen with him during the day, but otherwise appeared delighted to be driven in a Bugatti by a young millionaire. Bond took her to Menton, where he gave her lunch at a discreet restaurant owned by an Italian. Later, in the pine woods, he discovered that she did not love Vlacek. When they were dressed again she told Bond how she had got into his clutches – gambling debts at the casino; Vlacek had paid but still held her receipts; she had had no alternative. There were hints of the Roumanian's gross depravity. Bond listened sympathetically. They made love again, had drinks together at the Eden Roc, and Bond assured her that he would settle her debts with the casino – on one condition.

* * *

The next day was a Friday. He had two days left. Reluctantly, he decided that to keep his promise now to Maddox he needed Mathis's help. At first the Frenchman was distinctly sceptical of Bond and treated him with much the same courteous disdain that he had shown before. He also made it plain that his own plans for dealing with the Roumanians 'in the only way that's left' were well advanced.

'Rather than that,' said Bond, 'let us at least try out a little hunch of mine.'

Mathis asked what this would involve.

'Simply to find the finest optician in the South of France.'

Mathis was efficient. He thought that this ridiculously rich young Englishman was mad – but in the end he got him what he wanted. Alphonse Duverger was from Cannes. A shrunken, stick-like man with a blue beret he was the senior oculist from the main opticians in the city. Fortunately the firm also had a branch in Juan les Pins. It was there that Bond and Mathis met him early that afternoon. Bond explained what was at stake and what he needed. It would mean a long night's wait and then a period of frantic work. Alphonse Duverger asked certain questions. When Bond had answered them he smiled, exposing over-white false teeth and promised he would do his best.

That Friday night, Bond followed what had now become his regular routine, entering the *grande salle* before midnight, watching the Roumanians arrive, then losing several thousand pounds to them. He purposely avoided looking at the girl, but Vlacek for once appeared almost genial. As well as Bond there were several rich Americans, all of whom gambled heavily and lost. Vlacek was managing to smile. When Bond withdrew he said to him, 'Please don't lose heart, Mr Zwart, your luck is bound to change.'

'Let's hope,' said James Bond.

Mathis was standing just behind his chair. Bond thought he saw him wink.

It was to be a night of waiting. It was gone four when the casino had begun to empty and the Roumanians had won enough. Bond was sitting in a hired Peugeot opposite the main entrance when they came out. Mathis had joined him, and they saw the Roumanians troop out, solemn as four constipated undertakers. The girl was with them. A big limousine purred up with darkened windows. They got in and drove away.

There was no hurry. It would take the Roumanians twenty minutes to reach their villa. According to the girl, Vlacek was a leisurely lover. It would be an hour at least before he was asleep. So Bond and Mathis made sure that the Roumanians were well ahead before they set off for the villa. They drove slowly, then took up position near the small tradesman's door at the rear. Several lights were on. One by one they were extinguished. At ten past five the back door opened. Keeping to the shadows Bond walked across. The girl was waiting. Neither of them spoke as she handed something to him and then closed the door.

Then the rush started. It took the Peugeot three minutes flat to reach the opticians in the Rue Marechal Leclerc. The lights were on and, still in his blue beret, Alphonse Duverger was waiting. Bond handed him a pair of heavy dark spectacles.

'The lenses must be indistinguishable,' he said.

The blue beret nodded.

Before six was striking, Bond and Mathis were back safely at the villa. As they arrived, the back door opened and Bond was able to give the girl back Vlacek's spectacles. For her sake he hoped Duverger knew his job.

During September, Saturdays at the casino were a gala night. In an attempt to bolster up the casino's failing fortunes, de Lesseps had been trying to attract the wealthiest visitors to the Riviera. There had been a ball up at the castle, and, as Bond arrived at the casino, the square outside was jammed with a small fortune in expensive motor-cars. The casino had been floodlit, fireworks were lighting up the bay. There was an air of carnival and celebration. Bond wondered grimly whether it would be for him or the Roumanians.

The casino was crowded, with the rich elbowing the would-be-rich for places at roulette; in the *grande salle* the croupiers were performing miracles of speed as they kept the cards and the counters on the move. There was excitement in the air, that unique excitement of high gambling in a great casino where fortunes and human lives are desperately at risk. The heavy money seemed to be originating from a group of South Americans – sallow men with diamond-covered wives. Bond wondered how they would react to the Roumanians when midnight came.

But the Roumanians were late. For the first time since Bond had been there, there was no sign of them at 12.15. Had the girl been seen? Had Vlacek's suspicions been aroused by some difference in his spectacles? Suddenly Bond realized that if he had failed, it was the end of his career. Maddox would somehow manage to explain away the money he had spent to Whitehall. But there could be no explanation for himself. In his business failure was the only sin against the Holy Ghost.

Then suddenly the Roumanians had come. The usual rigmarole began. Vlacek took his customary place. There was a hush. The dealing started. Bond watched him carefully. Vlacek picked up his cards and, for the first time,

Bond saw him falter. Instead of that mechanical inhuman play, Vlacek was pausing. And, for the first time since Bond had watched him, Vlacek lost.

There was a buzz of interest. People were watching now. The croupier, a white-faced, elegant young man gathered the cards, replaced them in the shoe, then dealt again. As Vlacek held his cards this time his hand was shaking, but he kept his self-control and bet high as he always did. Bond noticed two small beads of oily sweat starting to trickle down his cheek. He turned up his cards – a seven. The banker had a 'natural'. It was the third hand that seemed to crack Vlacek. He was sweating freely now and placed an even higher stake on his cards. Again he lost. Then something unexpected happened. The Roumanian clutched at his dark glasses and pulled them off. For the first time Bond saw his eyes. They were staring straight at him and they were full of fear. Vlacek tried to rise, but Mathis was behind him.

'Sit, monsieur,' he said, 'the game goes on.'

Then Bond produced his own dark glasses. Duverger had made them up for him with Vlacek's original lenses. Bond put them on. The cards were shuffled from the shoe and Bond could finally see the trick which had come so near to ruining the casino. On the back of every card were clear luminous signs – dots for numbers, crosses for kings, circles for queens, and so on. This was the famous 'Luminous Reader' – with these extraordinary dark glasses, Bond could tell everybody's hand, even the banker's. He could see now how the Roumanians had always won.

For the next half-hour James Bond played – the game of a lifetime. Mathis kept Vlacek at the table and James Bond destroyed him. He had some £50,000 in chips before him. Bond took it all, and only then did Mathis let Vlacek rise.

The final act took place that night on the second floor of the casino in de Lesseps's office. All four Roumanians were there. So was James Bond along with Mathis and de Lesseps and a group of top-security officials from the casino. As a policeman, Mathis had been in favour of making the whole case public, but de Lesseps had argued him out of this. This was Monaco – not France. The publicity of a big trial would be unwelcome, and the outcome could be uncertain.

Instead the Roumanians had agreed to refund most of their winnings, and had signed an undertaking never to enter a casino again. Mathis could ensure that they never entered France either.

So they agreed, and Bond saw them walk down the grand staircase and across the foyer for the last time. It was a moment not without its pathos. The big limousine was waiting.

Bond went to send Esposito a cable – 'Luminous reader triumphant.' And as he came back from the desk to have a drink with Mathis, a tall, blonde girl brushed against his arm. The drink had to wait.

5

Eve of War Games

Bond seemed to have enjoyed telling the story of the luminous reader. There was no mistaking the nostalgia with which he talked about those far-off days.

'So,' he concluded, 'I like to think that I'm the man who *saved* the Bank of Monte Carlo.'

'But was it really useful to the British Secret Service? Did it work the way that Maddox planned?'

Bond laughed good-humouredly.

'Well, yes and no. The undercover world was very different then. There was a lot of make-believe and some extraordinary characters. When I look back it seems a sort of game – but I did take it all extremely seriously. We all did. Maddox especially. He enjoyed planning an affair like that and got a great kick from its success. The night after the Roumanians left, he arrived in Monte Carlo. Of course he was in his element. De Lesseps gave us dinner – and what a dinner. Mathis was there, and most of the directors of the Société des Bains de Mer. I took Vlacek's girl. Maddox had some actress with him. It was an incredible affair. And in a way old Maddox was quite right.

'The defeat of the Roumanians really was a great boost to the morale of the whole Service. It happened at a time when we needed a success. It certainly did win us friends inside the casino – after this, nothing was too much trouble for them where we were concerned – and it did a lot for our good name with the French Deuxième Bureau. Over the years, Mathis has been a good friend, you know. I'm not so sure though that it was good for me to start off with a success like this. In some ways I think that I've been paying the price for it ever since.'

It was unlike Bond to indulge in this sort of introspection. Self-doubt was not a failing that he suffered from. On the other hand, I longed to know how self-aware he really was – how consciously he analysed himself.

'What price?' I asked.

Bond glanced up quickly, and then shrugged his shoulders.

'I'm not sure myself. I suppose that you could say the price of never being quite like ordinary people.'

'You'd like to be?'

'Of course. I realize it now, but it's too late. I'm what I am. I know myself quite well enough to know I'll never change. I need this life – I'm hooked on it. Why else d'you think that I'm so anxious for that damned call back to London? But sometimes I'd give anything not to have to worry. And in a way, you know, I blame it all on Maddox that I do.'

'Why Maddox in particular? Surely your whole life had been setting you apart from other people? You were a born outsider from the start?'

'Touché,' said Bond. 'Of course I was. I was a very mixed-up adolescent. Whatever happened, life could not have been that easy for me, given my background and what happened. The point was, Maddox saw all this. He understood. In his own quiet way he was a very wicked bastard. He indulged me, gave me exactly what I wanted, and made me what I am. It's only now I realize how much he was enjoying it.'

Bond grinned, revealing strong, faintly discoloured teeth. We had stayed too long at the table. The last of the coffee had gone cold, the waiters had already laid the other tables for the evening meal.

'Time we moved,' he said. 'I tell you what. Why don't we

have a tour of the island? There's a car here, belonging to a friend. While we're driving I can try and tell you just what happened. Then perhaps you'll understand.'

The car turned out to be a white Rolls Royce Corniche. It had been parked in a lock-up garage under the hotel. As Bond drove it out I saw that the whole rear offside wing was buckled and an expensive gash ran the whole length of the body.

On the front seat there was a woman's pink towelling beach coat, also a pair of gilt-and-diamanté framed sunglasses.

'Shove them in the back,' said Bond.

He drove with a relaxed control which somehow matched the car, but seemed to have a faint contempt for it.

'Pity the way the Rolls Royce has become like any other car – just one more status symbol now for rich Americans.'

'You don't like it?'

'Everything about it's soft, ridiculously luxurious. This isn't what a car should be. The last real car that Rolls produced was the 1953 Silver Wraith. One of those with Mulliner coach-work, and you have something.'

It was somehow typical of Bond to be complaining about luxury whilst still enjoying it.

I asked him about his favourite cars. The old Bentley was the best. The essense of a car is that it should be part of you, an expression of your character. He explained that for him a motor-car was as personal a possession as his wrist-watch or the clothes he wore. It needed to be absolutely perfect.

We had taken Black Hole Lane – the ocean was bright blue, the island very gentle, like an Isle of Wight gone tropical. There was a pleasing quality about it, something not completely real. The same with Bond – the island suited him. He insisted on stopping at the old fort of St Catherines, and for a while talked knowledgeably about the pirates and the privateers. Bond looked out to sea, and spoke of the ruin of the fauna, and the island.

'I can remember the same thing with Europe. It's hard you know, not to feel nostalgic for that bad old world. For one thing it had such variety. And, for another, one could still enjoy oneself – if one had money and a little freedom. I had both.'

He returned to the aftermath of the casino job and how perhaps it had been bad for him.

'There I was, still only seventeen, with suddenly the run of Europe. I'm not complaining. It was a great time – a splendid period to be alive. Perhaps it's only now that I am having to pay the price for all of it.'

After the casino business, Bond was officially enrolled by the Secret Service. He was attached to Station P, controlled from Paris, and used as an operator in the field. But certain things – his youth, his strength and great good looks, his obvious success with women – all placed him in a certain category. As he says, 'I had a somewhat gilded image.' Some of his colleagues called him 'Casino Bond' – others, more sourly, 'our young gigolo'. He inevitably attracted envy, but this never worried him. He was a loner. Maddox was the only man he trusted. He was responsible directly to him. He was kept very busy.

For cover, Maddox insisted that he made a show of picking up his studies at the University of Geneva. This he did at the beginning of 1938. Life there was undemanding for a rich young student, and Frau Nisberg was delighted to have him back. He seemed thinner and much older than she remembered him – also quieter. The easy-going, wild young boy had turned into a man. There were no more late-night drinking sessions with the other students, no more skiing escapades to prove himself. He was more reserved, more noticeably Swiss.

He also seemed much more sophisticated, dressing so elegantly now, smoking his foreign cigarettes that made the whole house smell like a bordello. He had his great grey battleship of a motor-car which Herr Nisberg garaged for him behind the shop. He used to drive off in it for days, sometimes for weeks on end. Frau Nisberg was certain that the young Herr Bond had got himself a rich, demanding woman. Frau Nisberg knew the signs. She would hear his telephone ringing in the night and in the morning his room was always empty. He would never leave a note or any hint when he was coming back. She used to tidy up a bit while he was away – he was even more untidy than she remembered – and when he reappeared he was often in a dreadful state – unshaven, hollow-eyed for lack of sleep. 'Women,' Frau Nisberg thought, 'keeping the young Herr Bond away from his studies.'

But young Herr Bond was learning – things which would have turned Frau Nisberg's iron-grey Swiss hair snow-white had she suspected them. On one occasion Herr Nisberg did notice three neat holes in the offside door of the Bentley and wondered. On another, young Herr Bond had been confined to bed after an absence of some weeks. There had been bloodstains on his clothes and instead of old Herr Doktor Neuberg there had been some funny foreign doctor she had never seen before. As she told Herr Bond, he must really be more careful.

But Bond *was* careful; it was how he survived. One of the highest words of praise in Maddox's vocabulary was 'professional', meaning a man who knew his job. Bond liked to think that he was rapidly becoming a true professional.

For several months after the Roumanian job, he had been employed on what was known as 'bread-and-butter work' – the essential, down-to-earth, prosaic work of the European secret agent, working for Maddox as a carrier or as a contact man. This involved long, often hazardous trips across Europe. There were certain routes he got to know – passing through Strasbourg into Germany, or through the Simplon into Italy or taking the unsuspected paths between the customs' posts to enter Spain across the Pyrenees. He would use different covers, sometimes an English student travelling to learn the language for the Foreign Office examination. His favourite cover was to be the self he hankered after – a rich young Englishman on holiday, driving the Bentley, preferably with some glamorous young thing beside him.

It was a vital training, for, as Maddox told him, it taught him Europe – not the Europe of the tourist, but the undercover Europe of the spies, conspirators and double agents. He learned how to cope with the police – when to bribe and when to bluff and when to bluster. He discovered how to employ disguise (the unobvious detail was the secret here – change just the few key features people recognize). And he found out the hard way how to guard himself, rapidly developing a sixth sense for the face, the gesture that proclaimed danger.

He had a natural instinct for this sort of life. His skill with languages and experience with foreigners gave him an advantage from the start. But there was more to it than that. The agent's life was often an extension of that strange childhood he had lived when he had played his undercover games with Arab guttersnipes or young French hooligans. It was the same world he had glimpsed in his escapades in Russia. He was still juggling with reality as he had done in his days at Eton, half in society and half against it. He was the privileged outsider, carefully planning his adventures, and avoiding all emotional entanglements. Above all, he was enjoying *les sensations fortes* which were the private purpose of his being.

It was in Berlin that James Bond first killed a man. It was a bizarre affair. Bond says that 'it gave me the creeps for quite a while.' He is fortunate that this was all it did.

The assignment was a routine affair which Bond had already carried out before. During these early months of 1938, British Intelligence was fostering connections with a small resistance group in Germany – a dedicated band of anti-Nazis with plans for the assassination of various top Nazi leaders. It was an offshoot of this group which brought about the so-called Stauffenberg plot against the Fuehrer in 1944. But even in 1938 the conspirators were busy. British money was helping finance them and in return top-secret information was being sent to Britain. Much of this two-way traffic was controlled from Station P, and inevitably Bond's fluent German fitted him to play the part of courier. He used to travel to Berlin and always stayed at the Hotel Adlon. This was a hotel Bond disliked intensely. It was the epitome of a Germany he had hated almost as long as he remembered – heavy and stuffy and authoritarian. And in those days it was cram-full of party members and their fat supporters. It was Maddox's idea that Bond should stay there, on the grounds that he was less likely to attract attention under the very noses of the Nazis. Bond was not sure that he agreed. He had had one uncomfortable moment there already when the Gestapo carried out a sudden check on the whole hotel because Goering was guest of honour at a banquet. Bond escaped having his luggage searched by sheer effrontery and arrogance. He could be very German when he had to and calmly informed the Gestapo sergeant that he would be searched *only* with the official order of his friend, Reichsführer Himmler. The sergeant blustered. Bond coldly ordered him to get him the Reichsführer on the telephone, banking on the fact that no mere sergeant would risk bothering the head of the Gestapo at a time like this.

Bond was lucky. Had the sergeant carried out his search and found the false bottom in Bond's suitcase, there would have been some awkward questions to be answered.

Bond's way of making contact was a well-tried one and all but foolproof. On his way out for dinner he would leave the key with the concierge at the Adlon, tipping him well, and explaining that a young lady would probably be calling for him. In prewar Berlin, this was an accepted way of meeting one's mistress, and there was never any trouble. What could be more in character than for a good-looking rich young foreigner like the Herr Bond to wish to have a woman for the night? When he returned from dinner he would find his contact waiting for him in his bed.

For fear of hidden microphones, they would not talk of anything important. Instead they would act out their roles of foreigner and call-girl. There would be champagne, a lot of laughter, and, as he paid the girl, they would exchange whatever documents they had. They would then make love.

On each of Bond's visits to the Adlon, there had always been the same girl – a tall, slim, aristocratic-looking blonde. He never learned her name but says that she was the most accomplished mistress that he has ever had. Danger heightened passion. The calm knowledge that they could well be making love for the last time in their lives gave poignancy to their embraces. Each time the girl appeared more beautiful – and desperate. When they had finished making love the girl would sleep a while. Then at three or four o'clock she would wake, dress and, without disturbing him, she would depart. He almost loved her then, for this was his ideal situation with a woman – passion and anonymity and no entanglements. The thought of seeing her again almost made Berlin enticing.

It was in May of 1938 that Bond made his fourth and final trip to the Adlon. He had come via Munich – all the way he was thinking of the girl. Against all the rules he had brought a present for her – a mammoth bottle of Guerlain's *L'Heure Bleu*. Its nostalgic fragrance seemed to suit her. He left it in his room, and, as usual, tipped the concierge and went out for dinner. He returned earlier than usual, eager to see the girl.

To this day, Bond is not sure what put him on his guard. It was probably a subtle difference in the smell inside the room as he opened the door. Only the rose-silk covered bedside lamp was on; the girl was lying with her back to him, apparently asleep, her honey-coloured hair spilling across the pillow. Bond called to her. She stirred, but she still seemed half asleep, and made no reply. The light was dim, her face was hidden in the shadows. Bond undressed, and as he slipped in beside her, she rolled towards him. Then suddenly, she lashed out, and for the first time, Bond saw her face. In one nightmare moment he realized the truth. This was not his mistress – but a man.

It was a gruesome fight, for the Nazis were evidently taking no chances. The man they had put to wait for Bond was a trained killer. But once he was over his surprise, Bond found he had the advantage as he hurled himself against him.

There was a blonde wig. This came off as Bond grabbed at it, revealing a close-cropped scalp beneath. The face was cruel – and looked depraved with its layer of thick, woman's make-up. But as they fought, Bond could feel steel-hard muscles under the silk of the expensive night-dress. For a while they grappled silently. Bond reached the throat and began to press. The man groaned softly. Bond eased his grip, and at that moment the man heaved himself sideways and threw Bond across the bed. Bond smashed against the dressing table and the man was on him. He had the advantage now and knew how to use it. Bond felt a staggering blow to his throat and as he heaved with the pain, the man had got a scissors grip around his neck. Bond reached out with his one free arm – an instinctive movement of survival. His consciousness was going and he wanted anything to strike his enemy. His hand found something on the dressing-table. He grabbed at it, then brought it up with all his force against the man's unprotected throat. Something smashed then and the man screamed. Bond was aware of wetness on his arm and the sweet scent of carnations. The man relaxed his grip. Bond struck again. The scream choked to a gurgle. As Bond staggered forward he could see the weapon he was holding – the jagged top of his bottle of *L'Heure Bleu*. The blood and scent were mingled on the floor.

As Fleming says of Bond, he is always at his keenest in a crisis, and at this moment he found his brain was curiously clear. The man was dead. He looked grotesque, with his distorted face and shaven head and pale pink night-dress. There was no sound from outside. Bond had a gun and was prepared to use it, but it wasn't necessary. When they set the trap, the Germans had been careful to do nothing that might raise his suspicions. They were still keeping clear.

Somehow he hoisted the dead man back into the bed, replaced the wig, and tidied up the room. Swiftly he changed his own clothes, packed and made his exit via the window and the fire escape. By next evening Bond was back in Switzerland.

Not all of Bond's assignments were as violent as this. The majority were quite straightforward and went off without a hitch. And just occasionally Bond would make a mistake –

like the time he was in Istanbul.

The Istanbul affair began as a routine assignment – so routine that Bond now admits that he did not take quite the care with preparations that he might have. It came a few weeks after the Adlon business, and he was frankly looking forward to the trip as a holiday to help forget that hideous affair.

There had been some trouble with the Turkish network. Normally the few British agents around Istanbul were run and paid from Station N in Cyprus, but a courier had been arrested by the Turks, and as something of an emergency measure it was arranged for funds to be transmitted through Station P. Maddox gave Bond the task of taking them. Fortunately Bond still enjoyed long rail journeys. Packing a lightweight suit and an early novel by Eric Ambler he travelled overnight from Paris on the Simplon-Orient. Sewn into the lining of his jacket was a bearer draft for £20,000 on the Etibank of Turkey.

Bond loved the train. He remembered the trip he took to Russia with his mother aboard the Moscow Express and savoured every moment of the journey. He enjoyed the food, the service and the constant change of scenery as the train roared and clanked its way through Eastern Europe. This was true Ambler territory; Bond was excited at the thought of what might happen. Nothing did. There were no breakdowns, no disasters, no mysterious strangers. Even the customs men gave Bond no more than the most perfunctory of nods before chalking his suitcase and bidding him goodnight. Barely an hour late the train steamed in to the grey Sirkeci Station. Bond alighted and took a taxi – a battered Chrysler, one of the very few in Instanbul. It was nearly dark and Istanbul, that sleazy relic of Byzantium, appeared the most romantic city in the world. The moon was rising over the great mosque of Suleiman, the Bosphorus was shimmering with light.

Maddox had suggested Bond should stay at the old Pera Palas hotel, scene of so many real-life thrillers in the grand days of the Turkish Empire. And there, amid the chandeliers and potted palms, Bond the romantic felt that he had finally discovered his true spiritual abode. He had a palatial apartment, all mirrors and gilt furniture, a balcony that faced the Golden Horn. That night, tired as he was, he could not sleep. Instead he wandered through the city until nearly dawn.

He had arrived on Wednesday night, and had to meet his contact Thursday afternoon. His instructions were quite clear. The man he had to meet was Turkish. His name was Azom. Maddox had several photographs of a beetle-browed, crop-haired individual with eyes like currants and a fine moustache. He had shown them to Bond. 'That's your man. He'll be aboard the Bosphorus Ferry at 3.30, Thursday afternoon. You won't have much difficulty picking out a character like that.' And Bond had nodded. He was told to put the bearer draft into an old black briefcase. Azom would have a similar briefcase. Bond would exchange them and his mission would be over.

The ferries across the Bosphorus are frequent, shuttling all day between Europe and Asia and linking the two halves of Istanbul. So Bond had to take great care in choosing one that left just before 3.30. Punctual as usual, he was early, but after some waiting boarded a ferry that left at 3.28 precisely. Under his arm he had the battered briefcase with £20,000 inside.

At first Bond thought he would never find Azom. Although it was nearly May, the Black Sea wind was cold and clouds were blanketing the Golden Horn. The boat seemed almost empty. Then Bond realized that most of the passengers were inside. There was a tea lounge and a place for passengers to sit. Azom was there.

He was exactly like the photographs – the same short hair and powerful moustache. Bond put his age at forty-five or so. He looked a shrewd, tough character. Bond decided that he was glad that he and Azom both worked on the same side. Azom was drinking tea – sweet tea with lemon, Russian-style. Bond loathes tea, but, for once, decided he should take a glass. Tea in one hand, briefcase in the other, he sat down beside Azom. Azom smiled. Bond nodded and suddenly regretted that he spoke no Turkish. Instead he sipped his tea. It was disgusting.

Bond found no difficulty switching the two briefcases. Azom's was identical with his, and at the far shore Bond picked it up, bowed to the smiling Turk and joined the jostling disembarking crowd. He then caught the next ferry back.

Bond had to hurry. He had a sleeper reservation in his name aboard the Simplon-Orient Express to Paris. It left at five. He just had time to pay his bill at the hotel, grab his luggage and reach the station with two minutes in hand. He felt quite satisfied with himself; it wasn't often that an assignment went so painlessly, and he felt better for the trip. He smoked a Turkish cigarette and ordered a glass of raki from the attendant – a poisonous form of alcohol, but he was feeling at peace with Turkey and enjoyed it. He read more Ambler, dined, and was just turning in, when something made him think of Azom's briefcase. By now the train was rattling through the Bulgarian night at sixty miles an hour. The briefcase was sitting on the luggage rack; Bond took it down and opened it.

Inside there was a sandwich, a Turkish paperback, some bills and an identity card. Bond examined it. The photograph was certainly exactly like the pictures of Azom he had seen in Paris; but, as he now realized, Azom possessed a very typical Turkish face. The card was made out in the name of Yusuf Rhazid. Azom must have missed the ferry. Bond had swapped cases with a total stranger.

For the remainder of the journey, Bond wondered what on earth to do. Should he go back to Istanbul and try finding Azom and Herr Yusuf Rhazid? It was too late for that. Should he tell Maddox? What could Maddox do? After a sleepless night, he decided to await events: events, for once, were on his side. In Paris, Maddox was in the best of spirits and praised him for a successful mission. Early next morning, Bond drove the Bentley back to Geneva. During the drive he was mentally preparing his explanations for when the inevitable complaints arrived from Turkey. They never did. Station N reassumed control of the Turkish network. Maddox was thanked for his assistance, and Bond decided to let sleeping Turks lie. Just the same he often wondered what did become of the £20,000 he had given to the stranger with the moustache aboard the Bosphorus Ferry. Eighteen years later he found out.

Bond was in Istanbul again for the events described by Fleming in *From Russia With Love*. He had a friend called Nazim Kalkavan, a generous host and a great good liver who was anxious to take him out for what he called 'a genuine *diner à la Turque*'. There was one place in Istanbul they had to visit. It was near the Sokullu Mehmet Paşa mosque. The owner was an old friend and according to Kalkavan he served the only really worthwhile food in Istanbul. Bond enjoyed Kalkavan's enthusiasm. He was a genuine gourmet and knew his city.

The restaurant was by the water, a beautiful old Turkish-style house, and Kalkavan was at his most effusive. As they entered he insisted on introducing Bond to the proprietor.

'James Bond – meet Yusuf Rhazid. He is a great friend and he owns the one good restaurant in Istanbul.'

The face had hardly changed. There was the same cropped hair, the same magnificent moustache that Bond had last seen eighteen years before on the Bosphorus Ferry. For a moment the sharp currant eyes caught Bond's – then, unmistakably, Herr Rhazid winked.

'Nazim Pasha,' he said quietly, 'Mr Bond and I have met – a long time ago – but we were never introduced. I have a lot to thank him for and now I must thank you for bringing him. Tonight you will be my guests. And Mr Bond, I hope that you will come again whenever you are in Istanbul.'

The dinner was one of the most memorable of Bond's entire career – he describes it as a 'banquet'. It began with caviare and vodka – Turkish government monopoly vodka – and heavy-grained grey caviare which, as Kalkavan explained, had come from Samsun on the Black Sea. This was followed by a Turkish speciality – Lufer fish, which exists only in the Bosphorus. The main dish consisted of small chickens, roasted whole and stuffed with *Pilav* (rice cooked with pine-nuts, raisins and diced chicken livers). And afterwards there were Turkish dishes with names that amused Bond so much that he can still remember them. One was called 'Vizir's finger', and the other 'lady's navel'.

Rhazid refused to produce a bill. This annoyed Kalkavan who tried to insist on paying, but as Bond said to him, 'I think the British government has already settled it.'

*   *   *

Throughout the long splendid European summer of 1938, Bond was busy. Apart from a snatched few days in Kent visiting Aunt Charmian, he had no real holiday.

He found his few days at Pett Bottom disturbing. The house was quite unchanged – so was his aunt. She was still growing dahlias, apparently untouched by time. But Bond felt he had aged a hundred years since last he slept in the little room beneath the eaves. His aunt was as gentle and uncritical as ever. She asked no questions but he knew her well enough to tell what she was thinking. Who was this hard young man? Were all those fears she had for him becoming true? He would have liked to reassure her but she was too intelligent for that. He left her, promising to come back quickly, but both knew that he wouldn't.

And yet the past still followed him. Within a few days he was sent to Russia; it was like a return to those hateful months at Perlovska during the Russian Terror. It was a routine trip – by rail through Negoreloye to make contact with a man in Moscow. There was no real danger this time. Bond was officially a King's Messenger, travelling on a diplomatic passport and covered by the British Embassy. But when he passed the final station on the Polish frontier he felt that strange oppression he had known in Russia as a boy. It never lifted for the whole time he was there, and, for the first time since childhood, Bond was afraid.

There was no difficulty making contact with the man he wanted. He was a scientist – a bio-chemist with an international reputation living with his wife and children in a two-roomed flat in the Leninskye Gory quarter near the university. London had heard through academic channels that he was frustrated with his work in Moscow and anxious to take up research in Cambridge. Cambridge was keen to have him. Bond had to tell him so and see what could be done.

Leninskye Gory was the new Moscow of the Russian Revolution – monstrous and unrelieved and grey with its cliff-like blocks of workers' flats. Fedyeov, the scientist, lived on the eighth floor of one of these. He was a small man with a three-day growth of stubble and bright scared eyes. Bond recognized the air of hopelessness within the flat. Fedyeov had given up. Bond was reminded of a bird with a broken wing he had once tried to nurse – Fedyeov had the same uncomplaining stillness. The man's eyes seemed to know exactly what was coming.

Bond was touched by his courtesy. His wife, a motherly plump woman, brought tea. Bond drank it dutifully and gave him his message. There was something quite pathetic about how the man received it. Tears filled his eyes, he stammered out his thanks, but said that it was quite impossible – the government would never let him leave. In that case, Bond replied, there might be other ways to get him safely to the West. Bond had never seen such terror as appeared on Fedyeov's face. He begged Bond to say no more. He was being watched – nothing was possible. He thanked him, but good-day.

Bond had not expected much success – even so he was disappointed. He spent a somewhat melancholy evening with an official from the Embassy, and since he was due to leave next day, went to bed early. He was staying in the annexe to the Embassy. This suited him. He didn't care for diplomats, but the embassy had two advantages – he was saved trouble with the Russian state police and he was guaranteed a decent breakfast. While he was eating it the Head of

Chancery came in. He was a plump, tweedy man in his middle thirties, who chatted for a while about life in Moscow.

'Nasty business about that scientist of theirs,' he said.

'What scientist?' said Bond.

'Haven't you heard? A man called Fedyeov – terribly distinguished. News came through from Pravda early this morning. Supposed to have thrown himself out of an eighth-floor window – typical of these bloody Russians. They're all mad, the lot of them.'

Bond was no longer very hungry.

'When did it happen?'

'Early last night.'

'D'you think it was really suicide?' Bond asked.

The diplomat shrugged his shoulders. "You never know in this God-awful country. It seems a dreadful bloody waste whatever happened.'

It was a haunted journey back. Bond tried to tell himself that Fedyeov was virtually a dead man when he saw him, but he could not stop thinking that were it not for James Bond, he would still be alive. At the same time Bond was troubled by his mother's memory. Suddenly it seemed as if everybody round him now was doomed – a melancholy, cold and grey as the Russian plains around him, gripped his soul.

He hoped that with his return to Paris all would be well. It wasn't. Something was hideously wrong. He couldn't sleep and when he did there was a recurrence of those nightmares which had troubled him after his parents' death. He drank. He went on sleeping pills. Neither did much good. And, as always in the past, Bond had no way of telling anybody what was wrong. Luckily Maddox noticed.

Maddox was sympathetic. Bond had been working much too hard. He needed fresh air, exercise, a holiday. He suggested Kitzbühel. And so began that curious series of coincidences through which Bond renewed his brief acquaintance with Ian Fleming. Without that trip to Kitzbühel, there would have been no James Bond books; nor for that matter, would I have heard that Bond existed. For, of course, it was at Kitzbühel that James Bond met Maria Künzler.

In 1938, Kitzbühel was still a sleepy little Tyrolean market town beneath the jagged mass of the great Kitzbüheler Horn. For years now it had been a favourite haunt of Fleming's who had been coming here since the 1920s. He was there late that autumn when Bond arrived at the Hirzingerhof Hotel. It was inevitable that they should meet in that closed circle of rich winter visitors. Most of them in those days were Austrian. Englishmen – and particularly good-looking Englishmen – were a rarity. It was also inevitable that they should clash. Fleming was something of a prima donna with a considerable following of adoring maidens. Bond, despite the difference in their age, was competition. They were both tough, both Scottish, both powerful characters. But whereas Bond was somewhat dour, Fleming was an inveterate deflater of other people's egos. He was a mocking, highly cynical Old Etonian. James Bond, another Old Etonian, was quite capable of taking care of himself against such opposition. In their different ways, both of them seem to have enjoyed it.

Certainly for Bond the presence of Fleming was a godsend. As he admits he 'stopped me brooding'. He also introduced him to a lot of girls – Miss Künzler among them. According to James Bond she was 'a cheerily amoral little thing, a sort of doll who slept with everyone'. He was upset to hear about her death.

Somehow Fleming knew of Bond's connection with the Secret Service. Bond confirms that he pulled his leg about it. 'It was wrong of him of course, but I imagine I must have been a little pompous about it all. Ian couldn't stand pomposity.'

Fleming apart, the most important person Bond met at Kitzbühel was a man called Oberhauser. Fleming, who knew him, wrote of his tragic death in *Octopussy*, and quotes Bond's words to his murderer, the pathetic Major Smythe – 'Oberhauser was a friend of mine. He taught me to ski before the war, when I was in my teens. He was a wonderful man. He was something of a father to me at a time when I happened to need one.'

As Bond says, the idea of Oberhauser teaching him to ski is a typical piece of Fleming exaggeration. As Fleming knew quite well, Bond could already ski – in his own rough and ready but effective way. But it was Oberhauser, an Olympic medallist and by far the soundest ski instructor in the town, who taught James Bond a little of the style he lacked. Also, as Fleming says, this Tyrolean succeeded in doing what no one else had done for Bond. He got through to him, persuaded him to talk and acted as a sort of father with advice. Bond believes he all but saved his life.

Oberhauser was a realist. Like Bond, he had often found himself face to face with death as he climbed the mountains. He had lost comrades, friends and those he loved; and yet his zest for life was undefeated. Bond talked to him of Fedyeov, of Marthe de Brandt and finally about his parents. The Austrian was sympathetic, but, as he said to Bond, 'so what?' Did he intend to live his life out with a load of guilt? Would he continually blame himself whenever things went wrong? If he went on like this, the past would finally destroy him.

What did he suggest, asked Bond, and Oberhauser pointed to the mountains.

'Climb them,' he said, 'and don't look back.'

During those weeks in Kitzbühel, Bond took his advice, and once again he felt the joy and the renewal of a whole day's climbing. By the time he returned to Paris, the mountains and Oberhauser's words had done their work. Bond had evolved a conscious plan for living. His aim was now to live entirely for the moment and to enjoy the pleasures of his calling to the uttermost. There would be no more remorse and no regret. He would turn himself into what Fleming called 'a lethal instrument'.

With Maddox's consent he left Geneva, and took a flat in Paris. It was a strange life he was making for himself. Three times a week he used to shoot on the revolver range of the Garde Mobile on the Boulevarde Lans. He swam in the Olympic pool at Vincennes. Kiebermann, the European judo champion, taught him unarmed combat at the Montparnasse Gymnasium. And twice a week he played expensive bridge with Maddox at the fashionable Club Fevrier. He rarely lost. His sexual needs were satisfied by several wealthy married women. It was an iron-clad routine.

Behind it all, Bond was attempting to destroy the softness and weaknesses that were in him. Usually it worked, but he was always conscious of his private enemies. Fleming described him getting sentimental when he heard *La Vie en Rose,* and there were similar occasions that Fleming never heard of. Sometimes, however hard he tried, his memory and his imagination tortured him. And always in the night there was the hideous fear of cracking. He describes himself as 'old before my time'. He was cynical and bored, and always in the background lurked something worse than any enemy – world weariness.

But nobody knew anything of this. Outwardly Bond was a young man to be envied – rich, handsome and invulnerable, living a life which would apparently go on for ever. It continued through 1939 like this – then in August, as the German armies massed on the Polish frontiers, he took his favourite married woman off on what he knew would be their final holiday. Cramming the Bentley with champagne, he drove her south. They ended at the Eden Roc at Antibes. Jean Cocteau had just left – the hotel was nearly empty. They had a memorable two weeks. The girl was beautiful, the weather perfect. Bond felt his youth was almost over. When the month ended, she had to join her husband and her children. Bond returned to Paris where he found a movement order from Headquarters to return to London. The big building overlooking Regents Park was claiming him.

6

Bond's War

'The war changed everything,' said Bond, 'but it's a complicated story and it will take a lot of telling. Right now I feel like a siesta. Perhaps we'll start again this evening after dinner.'

He had an abrupt way of dismissing one, almost as if suddenly upset at the thought of how much he had revealed. With an impatient gesture he pushed back the coffee and went loping off in the direction of the hotel. He had an odd walk, forceful yet relaxed. People made way for him. Whether he really would be taking a siesta, I had no idea.

That afternoon I took a motor-scooter – the standard means of tourist transport on the island – and rode off to the beach. It was a perfect day – the sun exactly the right temperature, the sea the ideal shade of blue. Lazy Atlantic breakers were arriving, as if by previous arrangement, on the meticulous gold sand. It was all most agreeable, but there was something wrong. Was this perfection just a little empty? Didn't this immaculate toy island act as a sort of limbo-land, a background against which one inevitably waited for something, anything, to happen. Already I could feel impatient, and, as for Bond, could all too easily understand his restlessness and longing to be back at work.

And yet the island suited him – the heavy sun-tans and the

golden girls, the long cool drinks, striped awnings, and hibiscus-scented evenings – in its own tiny way, Bermuda was authentic Bond-land.

At dinner I looked out for Bond – he wasn't there. But afterwards I saw him in the bar. There was a woman with him. Was this the mysterious companion of the last few days? I felt that Bond would want to keep his woman strictly to himself, but he must have seen me and immediately called me over. He was unusually affable, almost as if relieved to have me there. The woman was, I felt, less welcoming.

'This,' he said, 'is Mrs Schultz. Fleming described her in his book on Dr No, but she was still Miss Ryder in those days – Honeychile Ryder.'

He seemed amused by this. She was quite clearly irritated. She seemed a hard, bad-tempered, very beautiful, rich woman. Certainly she could hardly have been more different from that appealing child of nature Fleming had described living in the ruins of a great house in Jamaica. The golden adolescent with the broken nose had metamorphosed into a tough and all too typical socialite American in her early thirties. As Fleming had predicted, the nose had been remodelled – quite triumphantly; and Honeychile, like Miss Jean Brodie, was in her prime. Bond looked, I thought, a little hunted.

Rather as if making conversation, he told her about the plans for his biography. She thawed immediately – as some women do at the promise of publicity.

'But James, you never *told* me. You mean your *real* biography? Isn't that just what I always *said* that they should do? I mean those books of Ian's were *ridiculous*. I never will be able to forgive him for the way he described me in that *dreadful* book of his. But, darling, I'm so happy for you. Truly, I think that it's the greatest thing that possibly could happen.'

Bond grunted then and asked what I was drinking. He and the Mrs Schultz were taking bourbon on the rocks. I chose the same. Bond, as usual, made it doubles, then steered the conversation firmly away from literature.

'Honey,' he explained to me, 'is cruising. In her yacht. It's her own floating vodka-palace – all eighty feet of it. Twin diesels, state-room designed by David Hicks, a crew of twelve. Somehow she heard that I was here and paid a social call.'

She pouted. This did not improve her looks. She had, I noticed now, a thin upper lip.

'Don't think that you're the only reason why I'm here. When Mr Schultz passed on I was a nervous wreck. Mr Schultz worshipped me, and I felt I owed it to him to pull myself together. He would never have wanted me to sit there getting miserable. You know Mr Schultz's last words to me?'

Bond shook his head, resignedly.

' "Honey," he said, "be happy." So to respect his wishes I brought the *Honeychile* – he named her after me – down on a sunshine cruise. I feel that it's what he'd've wanted.'

'Indeed,' said Bond.

She prattled on about herself. Bond seemed in full retreat and I thought that she was set to stay all evening. But she refused another drink, explaining that she had to be back on board by nine and that her chauffeur was already waiting. We walked out of the hotel with her. A Rolls Corniche drew up as she appeared, and, as it purred away, I recognized its scratched bodywork and badly smashed rear wing.

Bond grinned, a little sheepishly, and said,

'Be sure, as dear Aunt Charmian would say, your sins will find you out. I always knew that girl would travel far – but not so far as this.'

'But didn't she marry some clean-cut young New York doctor after Dr No?'

'She did – and left him four years later to become Mrs Schultz – of Schultz Machine Tools Inc. He, I might add, was in his seventies. And now, unless I'm much mistaken, she's after husband number three. I recognize the look.'

He drained his glass and settled himself comfortably back into his chair. Without the woman he seemed more himself. Somewhere a band was playing a calypso. The bar was filling up. The big windows to the terrace had been drawn back and from the beach below came the faint murmur of the sea.

'I was telling you about the war,' he said.

I would have preferred to have known more about the spectacular Mrs Schultz, but Bond was obviously relieved to change the subject.

'I didn't realize at first quite what the war would mean. For years I had been thinking it would be my great moment. Instead, when I came back to London, I found that nobody was remotely interested in me. Maddox was stuck in France. Headquarters had just been moved into its present offices by Regents Park – sheer bloody chaos everywhere. When I reported there, the place seemed full of Oxford dons and refugee Hungarians. All of my records had gone astray and some moron would insist on calling me James Band. When I told him the name was Bond and that I'd been working for the Service for the last three years, he told me not to lose my temper, and gave me the "don't-ring-us-we'll-ring-you" routine. To cap it all, the Carlton Hotel was full.'

'Where did you go?'

'Where d'you think? Back to Aunt Charmian of course. But even she was busy winning the war – civil defence, evacuees, the Women's Services. Aunt Charmian was in the thick of it. It was the old girl's finest hour. I stayed with her for something like a month. I'm sure that she believed I was some sort of draft dodger, but she was too polite to say so. She would go on about my brother Henry though. He was in the War Office *and* he had a uniform. Two or three times a week I'd call Headquarters, but they had somehow found out I was born in Germany. At one stage I'm sure they wanted to intern me.'

Bond laughed and signalled to Augustus for some more to drink.

'It really was one of the most depressing periods of my life. I was just nineteen, and I felt useless and unwanted. It also dawned on me that my whole way of life was over. Nothing would ever be such fun again – and, to be quite honest, it never really has.'

By a strange coincidence the man who rescued Bond from the stagnation of the 'phoney war' was Ian Fleming. He was already working in intelligence – as personal assistant to Admiral Godfrey, Director of Naval Intelligence at the Admiralty – and he was on the look-out for suitable recruits to the Admiral's empire. He must have heard about the strange young man that he had met at Kitzbühel, checked on his records, and decided, as he often did, that this was the sort of man Naval Intelligence required. Thanks to his backing, Bond was commissioned as lieutenant in the Royal Navy with immediate secondment to the D.N.I. Bond's war had finally begun – and also the bizarre relationship with Ian Fleming.

M. has authoritatively described the two of them as 'personal friends'. If he is right, it was a most uneasy friendship, for they were very different characters.

Fleming was a dreamer, an intellectual *manqué*, the perfect desk-man at the D.N.I. Bond was essentially a man of action; he had inherited from his father the clear-cut mind of a good Scottish engineer. He was a realist, and his experience of life had taught him to keep his imagination in check and not to be too sensitive with people.

Fleming was witty, sociable and worldly. Bond was plain-spoken, wary of others and something of an outsider. And yet they seemed to complement each other. Each came to play a vital part in the other's life – so much so that today it is difficult to think of them apart; even in 1939 there are clear signs that this strange interdependence was beginning.

During this period Fleming must have seen that Bond had been living the life that he had dreamed of, the life which just conceivably *he* might have followed had he continued his original career with Reuter's instead of leaving it in 1936 and entering a City stockbrokers. And, similarly, Bond was acknowledging the power figure which he saw in Fleming. This was the person that *he* envied; and, as with Fleming, this was a self that he could never be – the settled, rich, impeccable insider, an influential cautious man who spoke to press lords by their Christian names, hobnobbed with admirals, and played bridge with members of the Cabinet.

During these first months in Naval Intelligence Bond was impatient for action. Finally, with one of Fleming's wild-cat schemes, he found it.

Fleming had written of the D.N.I.'s concern with the movements of the U-boats and the German fleet from Hamburg and Wilhelmshaven into the North Sea and the Atlantic. This was a constant headache for the British Admiralty, for these North German ports were impossible to blockade. The U-boat packs could come and go and there was constant risk that the German battle fleet would choose some unguarded moment to issue forth. Naval Intelligence at Whitehall had to do its best to find out what was going on, but this was difficult. We had our spies in Hamburg, but they were at best erratic, and the ports were beyond the range of normal aerial reconnaissance.

Different solutions were discussed, and it was Fleming who brought up the idea of the isle of Wangerooge. It was a typical Fleming plan. The island is an elongated sand-bank off the German coast, pointing out to the German Bight. Its sole inhabitants were fishermen and sea-birds, but it lay along the main channel out of Wilhelmshaven. Shipping from Hamburg and Bremerhaven used it as a landmark as they sailed to the North Sea.

'It ought to be quite possible to hide a trained observer there,' said Fleming casually.

'How on earth?' said somebody.

'It could work,' Fleming said. 'Those off-shore German islands are pretty bleak at the best of times. At this time of the year there'd be nothing there but miles of God-forsaken sand dunes. A trained man with binoculars and a radio transmitter . . .'

Somebody asked how he proposed to hide such a man under the noses of the Germans.

'Didn't you ever read the *Riddle of the Sands*?' Fleming replied.

The idea hung around as ideas do but Bond could see its possibilities. Unlike the other members of the department, he had worked as an agent inside Germany and knew how often the most daring scheme succeeded. Without Bond's interest the idea would have lapsed. Fleming, the potential thriller writer, liked to devise his daydreams, but for James Bond anything was better than this futile life in London. And, for once, Fleming was spurred to action.

It was the first time Bond had seen the practical side of Fleming. Every objection was politely swept aside, each difficulty calmly coped with. Fleming displayed an obsessive attention to detail, almost as if he, not Bond, were going. Bond, who lacked this sort of mind, could value it in others. Fleming worked hard. Within a day or two he had decided on the sort of clothing Bond should wear, the food that he should take, his weapons and his sanitary arrangements. The two men spent several afternoons at Brookwood, testing entrenching tools in the Surrey sandhills, and planning the living quarters Bond could dig for himself on Wangerooge. Experts were summoned to devise a form of shuttering to hold back the sand. Binoculars and periscopes were lovingly selected and Bond instructed how to use the latest model short-wave transmitter. Fleming performed all this with boundless energy. He was planning an adventure – Bond had merely to perform in it. The fact that his life would be at stake seemed almost incidental.

This did occur to Bond. Increasingly, it seemed as if he were simply taking part in some complicated game. He wanted action now – not suicide. His doubts, however, merely acted as a spur to Fleming. For the last few days Bond had been through a crash-course in identifying German warships and had been practising the final points in the construction of his shelter. Fleming explained arrangements for landing and retrieving him by submarine. This would take place at night.

'God willing,' said James Bond.

'My dear chap, it will go like clockwork. There'll be no problems for a submarine. No problems at all.'

'And if I'm caught?'

'You won't be. There are only a few fishermen around,

and they won't bother you.'

. It was too late to argue, and at the beginning of February, Bond joined H.M. submarine *Thruster* at Harwich at the start of a three-week Baltic patrol.

Secretly Bond had always dreaded submarines, which seemed like steel coffins, but he was excited by this new adventure. Fleming was there to see him off – a tall and somehow melancholy figure in his superbly cut lieutenant's greatcoat. There was a thin dawn drizzle from the sea. The submarine shipped moorings, the engines started. Fleming smiled wryly, raising a languid hand and Bond finally sensed how much he envied him his journey.

It was an exciting voyage. The Germans had anti-submarine patrols working from the Isle of Sylt: the submarine submerged by the Dutch coast and proceeded slowly northwards under water. There was a scare of enemy attack and only after dark did *Thruster* surface and pick up speed from her diesels. For a while Bond stood on the bridge with the Commander. It was pitch black with freezing sleet in the wind. The Commander pointed to the right, 'Emden's through there and Wilhelmshaven's further on. We'll reach your place by midnight.'

Germany seemed such forbidden territory that Bond was surprised at how easily he landed. Just twenty minutes later he was climbing into a rubber dinghy from the submarine and being rowed ashore. Two sailors helped with his equipment. No one spoke or showed a light; when Bond was safely in the dunes they left him. Bond had never felt so lonely in his life before.

Not that he had much time to brood. First light was due at eight. By then he would have had to have dug himself in, camouflaged his hide, and made himself secure before his first full day. He worked furiously. There was a fishing village just along the coast. His stretch of beach was theoretically deserted at this time of year, but he could take no risks. The dunes were covered with thick clumps of dense sea grass and sea holly – more than enough to give the cover he required. The fine sand too was simple enough to burrow;

as Bond dug he kept remembering himself as a small boy, building his sandcastles on the beaches of the Baltic.

Long before the dismal morning light reached Wangerooge, James Bond was ready. It had been easier than he expected, and he had excavated a sufficient cavity to hold himself, his stores and his transmitter. The walls were shored back with the aluminium planking specially devised by Fleming and the supplies department. The roof was driftwood, sand and grass. Thanks to Bond's weeks of training, his hide was virtually invisible. Bond had become a human mole.

He found a mole's life most unsatisfactory – boring and cramped and very cold. But he was busy. He had his specially constructed periscope binoculars to watch the sea. He also had his short-wave radio. The aerial was hidden in the dunes. He had prearranged times to speak to London.

During the first morning Bond could appreciate the accuracy of Fleming's thinking. Wangerooge was on the German navy's doorstep and there was a constant flow of inshore shipping – first the low crouching shape of German E-boats roaring their way home to Bremerhaven after a night patrolling in the Channel. Then came some coasters bound for Hamburg. And twice that morning Bond saw the quarry he was really after – two U-boats, grey steel whales sliding past so close that he could hear the throb of engines. He could see their numbers on the conning towers. Within two days they would be trailing Allied shipping out in the Atlantic.

This was exciting, but Bond found himself longing for a cigarette, someone to talk to, even a book to read. At times he felt a wild urge to leave his burrow and stroll across the sand. To console himself he munched biscuits and sucked malted milk tablets from his rations. Around six o'clock he made himself his first meal of the day – more biscuits, chocolate and a can of self-heating soup. Afterwards he thought that he had earned a double swig of brandy.

Like a large nocturnal animal, Bond crept from his lair when it was safely dark. The joy of stretching cramped limbs and sniffing the night air from the sea! For a while he worked, enlarging the burrow so that he could lie full length in it and sleep. He had an inflatable sleeping-bag and was soon comfortable. At 12.15 he called the Admiralty in London, using a simple code and prearranged wave-band, and reporting everything that he had seen. He would have liked a two-way conservation, even a word, with Fleming. This was too big a risk. He pulled the cover tight above his head, wound in the aerial, and slept.

He was awakened early by the roar of aircraft overhead. He raised his periscope and saw the grey-green body of a Dornier flying-boat passing some thirty yards away. He could see the pilot's face and an observer in the rear gun turret. There was a big white swastika on the tail.

The plane roared off. Bond breathed again, remembering there was a seaplane base at Cuxhaven. Three minutes later the plane returned. This time it seemed still closer, roaring along the surf-line of the beach. This was no training flight.

He watched the flying boat wheel like a big suspicious sea bird: then with a shower of spray it landed, and came taxiing towards the shore. It anchored. Bond watched four men climb into a black rubber dinghy. They rowed ashore, and then fanned out along the beach.

Fleming had been over-optimistic about the transmitter. The Germans must have intercepted last night's message and fixed its origin with accuracy. These searchers knew what they were looking for.

Bond thought he was lost. All he could do was lower the periscope and wait. Never had he felt so vulnerable and helpless. It seemed impossible that four trained German airmen could miss him. He could hear them calling to each other and even picked out certain words – 'English spy', 'radio'. One of them was mentioning a gun. Finally the four men seemed to give up. They had stopped ten yards from where he lay. One of them the leader, said, 'It's no use. No one could hide out here. Perhaps the bastard's in the village.'

Someone replied, 'But that's impossible. He'd have been spotted. He *must* be here.'

The first voice replied, 'Well, he's not, is he? We'll just have to wait. The Herr Colonel will be furious.' Bond heard them walk away – and then he breathed. Slowly he raised the periscope and saw the men climb back aboard the dinghy. There was the savage rasp of engines; the Dornier swept up and away.

Bond forced himself to think. The outlook seemed distinctly bleak. The Germans had been more efficient than anyone had guessed. True, they had not found him – yet – but it could only be a matter of time before they did. They were watching for him now. Once he broke radio silence they would find him, and there was no question now of summoning the submarine to take him off. Nor could he stay trapped in this hole for ever. Water would run out first – unless he went mad from solitude or claustrophobia.

Bond spent the morning trying to devise some method of escape – without success. Surrender in some form or other seemed inevitable. Bond shuddered at the thought of the remainder of the war inside a prisoner-of-war camp. Rather than this he would wait till nightfall, make his way up to the village, then steal a boat. It would be risky. The villagers must have been warned of him by now, but anything was preferable to surrender. Bond knew he must conserve his strength. He fed himself and slept.

It was late afternoon when he awoke. He was cold. He started to prepare the rations he would take with him that night for his escape. But first he needed to survey the beach. It was empty – so was the sea. Then he noticed something. Far to the right there was a ship approaching. There was the beginning of a North Sea mist, making it hard to identify, but as it came closer Bond was certain what it was. One of the outlines he had learned during his lessons on enemy shipping was of the high-speed ocean-going tankers – the Germans called them milch-cows – which the Germans had developed to refuel their U-boat fleets. This was one of them. Two E-boats followed it to give protection as it steamed off into the darkness.

For James Bond this changed everything. The tanker was

a first-class prize. Once the Admiralty knew its route, it could be shadowed: at some point out in the Atlantic there would be a rendezvous with several German U-boats.

It would be worth a great deal for the Royal Navy to be there.

Bond knew then where his duty lay. Whatever the risk, he had to radio once more to London – only then would he try to escape. And then he had an even better plan.

He waited until dawn to send his message. Reaction from the Germans came more swiftly than he thought. They must have been waiting for him to break silence. The Dornier returned, flying in straight above him. Things were working out as he expected. There was the same routine, the same men landing in the rubber dinghy. This time they seemed more determined than before. All of them were armed. His plan was working. He heard the first man shout when he saw the transmitter Bond had left. It was a hundred yards or so behind him, on the far side of the dunes. He had left a lot of other equipment there – enough to keep the Germans occupied for several minutes, minutes he needed for his getaway. He couldn't watch them now. He had to take a chance, waiting just long enough for the search party to be diverted. Then he made a break for it.

It was easier than he expected. The Germans were quite occupied. Bond could crawl in the cover of the dunes right to the beach. His limbs were cramped and hardly moved at first, but he forced himself. He was almost at the water's edge before they saw him, and he was in the dinghy and away before the shots rang out.

Bond had never rowed so hard in all his life. Luckily, the sea was calm, and, luckily, the German airmen were no marksmen. But there was still the problem of the flying-boat. The Germans would certainly have left somebody aboard – this firing from the beach must have alerted him. But Bond possessed one advantage. Whoever was aboard the plane had no idea of what was going on. The last thing he would be expecting would be for the English spy his comrades were out looking for to come aboard of his own free will. Bond drew along the side of the Dornier. There was an open door in the fuselage. Here he shouted out in German.

'Quick, you idiot, bring the first-aid kit. There's been shooting, somebody's hurt.'

'What?' said a voice.

'Quickly,' said Bond, 'somebody's dying.'

A German's head appeared. Bond had his gun out.

'Steady,' he said, 'don't move. I'm going to need you. It would be a shame to kill you.'

It was a terrifying takeoff. The aircraft roared and shuddered over the water. Some of the men on shore began to fire, and for a moment Bond thought the pilot would purposely crash the plane. Then the nose lifted and, reluctantly it seemed, the Dornier was away.

But even then, Bond's problems weren't over. The pilot was a surly individual – a heavily built, red-headed man. Bond had to keep his pistol firmly in his back as he ordered him to set his course due west for England and climb to 5,000 feet. For a while the man obeyed; then suddenly he shouted – 'Look out, Englishman. Fighter-planes.'

Bond glanced where he was pointing. He should have known better. The pilot's fist landed against his jaw, and in a moment the two men were grappling in the cabin, 5,000 feet above the North Sea. It was a vicious battle. The pilot was heavier than Bond, and in the moment of surprise, had knocked Bond's pistol from his hand. Then he kicked out with all his strength. Bond doubled up in agony. As he did so, his shoulder lurched against the Dornier's controls. The nose tilted and suddenly the world became a dizzy, flailing madhouse with the engines screaming and the aircraft diving steeply towards the sea. In desperation Bond tried one last wild blow against the man's throat. Against all the odds it connected. There was a gurgling noise. The man went limp. Desperately attempting to remember his prewar flying instructions and hoping they held good for German aircraft Bond reached for the controls, the plane responded and he managed to pull the aircraft up. But only just. By now it was almost down to sea-level. Bond saw the grey waves just below. He eased the Dornier's controls towards him, and slowly the big lumbering plane responded.

By now, Bond had no idea where he was, or how much fuel remained. He had picked up his pistol and kept the pilot covered in the seat beside him. At the same time, he held the plane on course for England, trusting in his luck and the compass to get him there.

Bond estimates that they had been flying nearly two hours when the attack came. The first he knew of it was the uncanny sound of bullets ripping through the fuselage behind him. And then, away to the left, he saw two British Hawker Hurricanes, in their green and brown camouflage, wheeling away before returning to the attack.

The Dornier pilot was quite conscious now.

'Bad luck, Englishman,' he said. 'Your own people will kill you after all.'

It looked as if they would. This time the fire was closer still. One of the cockpit windows shattered, and then the whole plane shuddered, and reeled sideways. Bond fought to hold it, but part of the tail was shot away. One of the Hurricanes returned, wheeling like a bird of prey around its victim. The flying-boat was now out of control, heading for the sea in a fast shallow dive. Bond struggled to keep the nose up. Then with a great thump they struck the water. There was a wrenching, tearing sound as the Dornier's back broke. The spray subsided and the plane began to sink.

It was the Dornier's red-headed pilot who saved Bond's life. He knew the escape hatch, and helped Bond through it to the roof. He also produced the rubber dinghy in which both of them spent the next two hours after the seaplane sank. An R.A.F. air–sea rescue launch finally brought them in to Harwich later that afternoon. The two parted more amicably than when they had first met.

Bond came back to Whitehall feeling jubilant, but not for long. True he had got the information of the German tanker through to the Admiralty, but there were delays and it was lost. And in the meantime the whole adventure had been criticized. Bond's old reputation as a glory-seeker was pur-

suing him, and Lieutenant Fleming had been reprimanded
for a scheme which put a British submarine at risk. Having
to be rescued by the R.A.F. was considered thoroughly bad
form, and Bond, though still officially attached to the D.N.I.,
was in disgrace. He was sent to work at their offices at
Penge. And it was here his great adventure ended.

But these early months of 1940, the secret-service world
was changing rapidly. Whole new branches were sprouting –
MI5 and MI6 were taking on fresh personnel. Fleming was
off to Canada. It was a bad time for Lieutenant Bond. He
was considered 'frivolous', and when he applied for transfer
to active service his request was swiftly granted.

* * *

Bond loved the Navy and the fourteen months he spent as a
sea-going sailor are among the happiest of his life. He
trained at Devonport and was seconded to destroyers. Just
before Dunkirk he joined his first ship, H.M.S. *Sabre*, as a
lieutenant. He was at Dunkirk. *Sabre* was bombed but still
managed to bring back three loads of British troops from the
beaches. After repairs, she went on convoy duty in the North
Atlantic.

It was a novel life for Bond. He had never known the daily
hardships of a serving officer, nor had he had to face the
cramped togetherness of life below decks in a narrow ship.
He was regarded as distinctly "odd". He was considered
something of an intellectual and a puritan. He was reserved,
swore rarely, and never discussed his women or his family.
The men found him meticulous about duties and they respected him, the old hands in particular. His fellow-officers
soon found that he was not a man for liberties. He had a
sharp tongue, a strong sense of *amour propre* and could drink
anyone beneath the wardroom table. He was admired and
popular but had no particular close friends. This used to
worry him. Everyone thought him self-sufficient, whereas he
was really nothing of the sort: his natural reserve, the life
that he had led, made him unfitted for close human contact.

Even so, life aboard the *Sabre* did a lot to thaw him out. One night ashore in Kingston, Jamaica, he became the hero of the ship. He was in charge of the liberty party. The men were due back aboard at midnight but there was a bar brawl with the crew from an American cruiser, so that Lieutenant Bond found himself in the middle of a pitched battle. Bottles and knives were being used. His men were getting much the worst of things. Bond was very calm, telling his men to get outside. Most of them did but a drunk heavyweight U.S. petty officer kept up the battle.

He had already knocked out several British ratings and threw a bottle at Lieutenant Bond. Bond saw it coming, ducked, then, grabbing the American, threw him across his shoulders. The man landed with a crash of broken glass against the bar. Bond hit him once as he tottered to his feet and the fight was over. Bond's men were safely back on board by midnight.

The incident worked wonders for Bond's prestige, and it was really after this that he began to feel that he belonged aboard his ship.

The shared dangers and discomforts of the mid-Atlantic helped Bond become more human, and he enjoyed his freedom from the tensions of the undercover world. Those lonely battles of the past were over. The enemy was open and straightforward, and he was fighting now with men he trusted. Bond preferred that. He became brawnier and put on weight. He could sleep anywhere and any time. For the first time for years he was devoid of worries or ambitions. Then it all changed.

*　　*　　*

During this time afloat, Bond lived a life of almost total chastity. This too was a relief. After his past involvements he enjoyed a pause from the demands of sex. There had been moments of brief indulgence in the Bahamas or New York, generally with married women who regarded the servicing of good-looking Allied personnel as essential patriotic war-work. Perhaps it was, but it left Bond depressed. He enjoyed sex, but not impersonally. He liked his women to be something more than animated text-books of the sexual act. He was also slightly prudish or, as he would have said, romantic. He liked to think that there was at least the possibility of love before he clambered into bed with anyone.

This attitude and long months of seaborn abstinence meant that by spring 1941, Bond was becoming vulnerable. His teenage cynicism was behind him, and as he became more human so it appeared inevitable that he should fall in love. He duly did – sentimentally and quite predictably with the sister of a brother officer. Her name was Muriel. Her brother was the second-in-command. Bond got to know her from her photograph in her brother's cabin.. The smile was Claudette Colbert's, and the nose Greer Garson's. The second-in-command assured Bond that she was 'a thoroughly good sort'. He was quite right. Bond met her briefly during leave that Easter. They saw a show together, had supper in a Corner House. Bond kissed her – that was all – but promised he would write. He did.

The photograph had flattered her. It was not quite Miss Colbert's smile – nor for that matter quite Miss Garson's nose – but she was a thoroughly nice, well nurtured, English miss. Daddy was army. The family lived near Pulborough in Sussex. She was twenty-two, pure as they used to be in those days, and she had never met anyone like Bond before.

Late that July, H.M.S. *Sabre* steamed home from the West Indies for a refit at Birkenhead. Bond had leave and travelled down to London with the 2i/c. Some three weeks later he was happily engaged. It was all terribly conventional – visits to Kent to introduce Aunt Charmian (she raised her eyebrows but said nothing), visits to Sussex relatives of Muriel, visits to London. Bond seemed happy. Muriel adored him, and for the first time in his life he was conscious of doing what Brother Henry always called 'the proper thing'.

It even seemed the proper thing when Bond, on one of their last nights together, rang up the Dorchester Hotel, asked for the manager, and ordered a double room. Muriel agreed, for after all, they were engaged and she was nearly twenty-three.

For the first time in his life with any woman, Bond felt nervous. She was quite lovely, and most understanding; they dined discreetly in the restaurant and prepared for bed. But the fact was that Bond simply had to have a drink. When he explained she understood quite perfectly. Daddy, she said, was just the same. She'd wait for him upstairs.

Bond was ordering his favourite martini – the bar, to his surprise, had Gordon's gin – 'And do make sure,' he told the barman, 'that it is . . . '

'Shaken, not stirred,' a voice behind him said. Bond turned, and there was Fleming.

Bond thought that he had aged. The sombre face had grown more lined, but otherwise he seemed exactly as Bond remembered. For some reason, he felt relieved to see him. Bond offered him a drink explaining that he was just engaged; Fleming roared with laughter.

At first Bond was angry, but Fleming's laughter was infectious. They drank. They talked. They had another drink. Fleming recalled the Wangerooge affair and hinted at the secret work his department was engaged in. Bond tried to talk about his life aboard the *Sabre*, but it all sounded just a little flat.

'Pity you left,' said Fleming.

Bond said nothing.

'Things have changed in D.N.I. We could do with you. The Admiral said as much the other day.'

'He did?' said Bond, and Fleming nodded.

'I think,' he said, 'that we should have a bottle of champagne to celebrate – our meeting, your engagement.' Champagne was all but non-existent in wartime London, but the barman was a friend of Fleming's. He produced a bottle of vintage Clicquot. Fleming become didactic, as he often did with alcohol.

'You should be back with us – not playing sailors.'

Bond argued, Fleming was persuasive, and it was well past

midnight before they parted. Muriel was fast asleep; Bond just a little drunk.

This time they trained James Bond thoroughly – first at a house in Hertfordshire at a course for saboteurs, then out in Canada. Bond was a prize trainee, winning high marks for fitness, unarmed combat, weaponry and personal initiative. In Hertfordshire he was given an A-plus mark and privately commended to the D.N.I: in Canada he gave a judo instructor mild concussion and took the range records at small arms and on the sub-machine gun.

The Canadian establishment was at a place called Oshawa, on Lake Ontario. It had been founded, late in 1940, by Sir William Stephenson as training ground for his American agents, and at the time it offered the most rigorous and thorough training of its sort anywhere outside the Soviet Union. Bond learnt a lot.

As an inventor in his own right – much of his fortune came from his prewar inventions in radio photography – Sir William was a technocrat of sabotage. It was from him that Bond became acquainted with the whole armoury of the modern agent – cyphers and electronics, explosives and radio and listening devices. The trainees used the lake for underwater exercises, and it was here that James Bond trained as a frogman, learning evasive tactics, underwater fighting, and techniques with limpet mines. Bond spent three months at Oshawa. When he returned to London D.N.I. had already received a confidential report, commending his success and ending with a single statement – 'The agent is a lethal weapon of the highest calibre.'

Had Bond known this, he would have been more wary when Fleming took him out to lunch soon after his return. Bond had enjoyed himself in Canada. Muriel had seemed a little sullen when he left – despite the *débâcle* at the Dorchester they were still officially engaged – but out in Oshawa he had found it hard to worry too much on her behalf. Now he was looking forward to some active service and Muriel agreed that it would be wrong to rush ahead with marriage. Fleming seemed relieved when James Bond told him this, for as he explained to Bond, there was 'an element of risk' in the small assignment the Service had in mind for him.

Fleming had chosen Bertorelli's Italian restaurant in Charlotte Street for their meeting – a change from Scott's: none of those silver tankards of black velvet, no grilled plaice. They had the *plat du jour*, an ambiguous wartime stew called *spezzatino*, and half a bottle of Valpollicella. It was a strange background in which to be asked to kill a man. Not that Fleming used the word 'kill'. He said, 'deal with'. It was all arranged and shouldn't be too difficult. But there must be absolutely no mistakes. There was a fearful lot at stake. Fleming poured himself the last of the Valpollicella and started to explain his task.

'The man's Japanese. He's called Shingushi and he's in New York. Officially he's with their consulate-general – he has an office on the thirty-sixth floor of a skyscraper on Lexington Avenue. But unofficially the man's a cypher expert – probably the greatest in the world. We've been studying him, and now we know for certain what he's up to. For several months we've known that the Germans have been getting detailed information of Allied shipping movements from New York, and it appears that this has been relayed from their friends in Tokyo. The question was how the Japanese were getting it. Now Stephenson's found out. The Japanese have been intercepting all our messages, to and from the Atlantic convoys, and little Shingushi has been busily decoding them.

Bond still remembers Fleming's cold impassive face as he sat there, chain-smoking his Morlands Specials.

'So what do *I* do?' said Bond.

'Dispose of him, dear chap. This is war. It must be done. One just can't be a softy in these matters. It will be like shooting an enemy in the front line – except that this little fellow must be worth a good three top-rank divisions.'

'Isn't there someone in America who can do it? Why bring me in?'

'America's not in the war but she is giving us a lot of help.

There must be nothing that could create a diplomatic incident. This must be what gangsters call "an outside job". Officially no one in New York will know you. If anything goes wrong, you're on your own.'

Bond could not refuse. This was the sort of operation he had trained for. He knew its logic, but wished it didn't have to seem quite so like cold-blooded murder. Fleming was smiling. 'I envy you New York,' he said. 'Take my advice and buy some shirts from Abercrombie's while you're there.'

Bond travelled light. He took no weapon and no identifiable possessions. There was a certain urgency about his mission so he was booked by air, flying to Lisbon where he caught the morning clipper to New York. It was a ten-hour flight – which gave Bond time to brood. But at the same time he felt that lift which always comes at the start of an assignment. Nothing could ever equal it.

Bond's sense of excitement was increased by his first sight of New York, for he loved the city. It was evening and all the sky-scrapers of Manhattan were glittering with light as if inviting him to some enormous celebration. After his nights in blacked-out London he was suddenly alive. He had to remind himself that he was here to kill a man.

He had booked in at the five-star Volney Hotel, because he heard that Dorothy Parker lived there. It had the right degree of comfort and respectability and Bond had the sense of being something of an honoured guest: it was a long time since he had known the luxury of a good hotel, the pile of towels in the bathroom, the well-made bed, the discreet air-conditioning. He rang for a double bourbon on the rocks, shaved and then bathed luxuriously. At 8.15 he rang Sir William Stephenson's private number.

As head of British Intelligence in North America, Sir William was a busy man, but he arranged to meet James Bond that night at 10.15 at Murphy's bar on 45th Street. Bond dined alone – off T-bone steak and ice-cream in the drug-store round the corner – and walked to his appointment.

Bond had never met the quiet Canadian before, but was impressed at once by his efficiency. He liked the down-to-earth approach of this small energetic man, the way he bought the drinks, asked Bond if he had eaten, and then got down to settling his task.

He made no bones about the difficulties. There had already been attacks upon Shingushi; the Japanese were thoroughly prepared.

'They're treating him the way they treat their Emperor. He's removed from normal human contact, guarded day and night. None of us have seen him. You're going to have your work cut out.'

Bond asked about Shingushi's private life. As far as Stephenson knew, he had none. He had his quarters in the Consulate. Only occasionally at weekends did Shingushi venture out, carefully guarded by security men, who hustled him inside an armoured limousine and drove him to a villa on Long Island. The Japanese had women there.

'What chance of getting at him there?'

'No hope in hell. The place is walled in and there's every possible burglar device. I know. I've tried them.'

Despite his pessimism, Stephenson did offer Bond some help – photographs of Shingushi, detailed plans of the Japanese consulate, biographies of some of the Japanese surrounding him. Bond thanked him.

'Tell me,' he said, 'how dangerous is this man, Shingushi?'

The Canadian finished his drink before replying.

'You could say that every week he lives, that man's responsible for several hundred Allied deaths at sea. That's how I'd think of it if I were you.'

Stephenson did Bond one further service. A cardboard box with the monogram of Saks, Fifth Avenue, was brought up to his room as he was having breakfast. Bond had been having trouble trying to explain to room service how he liked his eggs.

'Sure sah, you're meanin' sunny side up with double crispy rashers.'

For once, Bond had given in rather than try telling an American how to boil a three-and-a-half minute egg. He told the bell-hop to leave the parcel on his bed. When he opened

114

it he found a neat attaché case. Inside were the barrel, stock and telescopic sight of a folding high-velocity Manlicher sniper's rifle – plus twenty rounds of mint-new steel-tipped ammunition. There was no delivery note.

Bond had slept well, but the excitement of his arrival in New York had left him. His eyes smarted in the October wind, and for the first time he felt the effect of time lag from his journey.

It was Sunday. His instinct was to take the day easy, but he could not relax on an assignment. Despite all Stephenson's doubts about the villa, there was something to be said for seeing it. As a gambler, Bond had often benefited from outside chances; one never knew one's luck. Besides he had never seen Long Island at this time of year and could think of no better way of spending an empty Sunday in New York.

He took his dark blue Burberry and the small attaché case and called a cab to Penn Station.

There was a sense of holiday about the trip – the all but empty Sunday morning train of the Long Island Railroad, the glimpses of the tenements of the Bronx (what Fleming called 'the backside of New York'), and then the potato fields and duck farms of Long Island. It was all very different from Fifth Avenue. The villa was at the far end of the island – the name of the station immediately appealed to Bond. It was Sag Harbor. Here he descended.

Sag Harbor is a summer place – a few big old houses out towards the Sound, but otherwise a lot of summer property. Bond found its October melancholy appealing. He asked a porter for a cab.

Here Bond had his first real piece of luck.

'Where you going, mister?' said the porter.

'Lansdown Boulevard,' said Bond.

There was one cab, an old black Chevrolet. The porter waved to it.

'Another customer for Lansdown,' he shouted. 'You'll have to share,' he said to Bond. 'That's the only cab around this morning.'

Bond thanked him.

The driver was an old man in a cap. He drove a leisurely cab. 'All right for Lansdown Boulevard?' said Bond. The old man nodded. Bond gave him the number.

'Lady in the back going to the same house,' said the cabbie, opening the door. In the car was sitting a small middle-aged Japanese woman, dressed in black. Bond nodded to her; she nodded back. The journey passed in silence.

There are moments in an agent's life when he must accept whatever chance comes up. This was one of them. The journey took some fifteen minutes, and finally the cab drew up at the entrance to a private drive. There was a large, green painted steel door – each side of it a high brick wall. Beside the door a notice warned trespassers that there were 'electric methods to repel them'.

But the cab was evidently expected. There was an answering device beside the door. The cabbie gave his name. One of the doors swung open.

'No one around this morning,' said the cabbie.

The drive wound between trees and shrubbery towards the house. Bond tapped the driver on the shoulder.

'Here. This will do for me,' he said and gave a twenty dollar bill.

As Bond got out the woman took no notice. In her world whatever men did was strictly their own male business.

There was a bank of rhododendrons – a shrub which Bond detests, but which provided cover. He hid and waited twenty minutes. He saw the cab return, there was no outcry from the house. Now was his chance to reconnoitre.

The shrubbery continued to the right. Bond followed it. The ground rose slightly and from here he could see the house. It was like a fortress, a two-storeyed, concrete affair, the windows shuttered, the doors protected with iron grilles. It would be madness to try entering but Bond still had the feel that luck was on his side. He was content to wait, settling himself within the dank protection of the bushes. Here he took out the rifle, assembled it, fitted the telescopic sight and pressed ten silver rounds into the magazine.

The house puzzled him. There was no light within, no sign

of life. Bond lay very still; the rifle was becoming part of him. Then the rain started, a cold drizzle from the Sound: the hours ticked by. Twice he thought he heard a car, but still saw nothing. It was early afternoon before anything occurred. The rain had stopped by now, and suddenly the grille was pulled back from the big French windows facing the lawn. A white-coated servant stepped out, shouted something and a dog bounded out, barking and bounding off across the lawn. The servant called again and a small girl appeared, an ugly little girl of seven or eight in a bright pink dress. Bond watched her through the telescopic sight. She was laughing at the dog, and Bond could see that she had lost her two front teeth. She threw a ball and the dog went bounding after it. It was a mud-brown mongrel bitch with a tail like a feather duster.

Then a third person appeared. There was no mistaking him. There was the same large head and dumpy body that Bond had seen in the photographs, except that now the man was laughing. Bond moved the cross hairs of the sight to just below the grey breast-pocket of Shingushi's suit and squeezed to first pressure on the trigger. At that moment there was a gust of wind, bringing some leaves down from the lime trees on the far side of the garden. The dog chased them. The girl laughed, clapped her hands. Shingushi picked her up.

It was Bond's chance. Shingushi was squarely in his sights, but all that Bond could see was the girl's pink dress.

His finger failed to move, and the chance was over. Shingushi turned again, put the girl down and went back inside the house. The child followed, then the dog, wagging its stupid tail.

Bond waited but his luck had left him. Not until dusk did he risk scaling the wall and then he had to walk back to the station. It was nearly midnight before he was back at the Volney. Monday morning there was a telegram from London.

'Goods overdue. What news?', signed Fleming.

Bond skipped breakfast – always a bad sign – and spent most of the morning sitting on a bench in Central Park. Here he went over the whole affair. He thought about

Shingushi and the child – why did the wretched little man have to involve himself in such a dirty business? He also forced himself to think of sailors drowning in the North Atlantic, sailors perhaps from his own destroyer. Quite calmly then Bond made his decision. He no longer had the luxury of following straightforward orders aboard ship. He was a solitary man doing his best to fight a war. There was no point in being squeamish.

It was a bright autumn day; the Park was crowded, but Bond had never felt so much alone. He strolled out and down Fifth Avenue. New York no longer seemed exciting, but he ate a good lunch at Flanagan's Restaurant in Lower Manhattan and then rang Stephenson. There were still certain things he had to know.

That afternoon James Bond got down to work. First he met a man called Dolan, a fat Southerner with bright blue eyes. Dolan showed no surprise at what Bond wanted. All that he seemed concerned with was to double the $500 a day which Bond was offering. Rather than argue, Bond agreed.

Then Bond took a taxi to the building on Third Avenue, where Stephenson had hired him an empty office on the fortieth floor. Here he made sure of the view from the windows. Some sixty yards away stood the building containing the Consulate General of Japan – almost directly opposite were the windows of the thirty-sixth floor.

That evening Bond and Dolan took possession of their office: the long wait started.

It was a very simple operation. The main requisite was patience and Bond remembered how, as a boy in Kent, he had waited all afternoon with his air rifle for a rat to emerge from its hole in a barn. Now he and Dolan both had snipers' rifles and were waiting for Shingushi.

It was an endless business and Bond began to wonder whether it would work. Not that Dolan minded; every day that passed earned him another thousand dollars. He rarely spoke, drank endless cans of beer and belched in place of conversation. Bond soon detested him, but he was said to know his job. Bond hoped he did.

It was surprising how soon Bond picked up the routine in the Consulate – also the faces in that office opposite.

Only on two occasions did he see Shingushi – both around nine o'clock at night when he suddenly walked in to the main office, chatted with someone at a desk, then walked away. Bond understood how difficult he would be to kill. There could be no mistakes – only one shot, one chance. Another problem was that the windows of the building were all double-glazed and strong enough to deflect a bullet. This had to be allowed for.

Wednesday, a second telegram arrived from London – less polite this time. Thursday, Shingushi failed to appear. And by Friday even Bond's young nerves were beginning to fray. As usual, he and Dolan took their places in the room with the window open and the lights off. Bond had worked out that they were quite invisible to the Japanese. And, as usual, the two men sat in silence. Afternoon merged into evening. The lights went on in all the skyscrapers and soon New York was shimmering around them like a phosphorescent anthill. It was nearly nine, and the traffic below was thinning down Third Avenue when Dolan nudged him.

'Here he comes, the little bastard. Here comes our boy.'

Shingushi had come waddling in. Through his telescopic sight, Bond could see him blinking as he turned to a filing cabinet. This was the moment.

'Now,' barked Bond.

It was an eerie noise within the darkened room – Bond's voice and then the strangled thud of two silenced rifles firing almost simultaneously. Dolan fired first as arranged, for his shot had to break the double glass in the Consulate window. A split second later, Bond's shot sped through the hole straight to its target. Bond paused to watch the little Japanese keel over, then collapse. At this distance he barely seemed a man at all – more like a target on a range.

Everything went smoothly then, for Bond had rehearsed it many times – the swift dismantling and packing of the rifles, the locking of the office door, and in the street the car was waiting where Bond had left it. They drove towards the

Park, then stopped the car. Bond had Dolan's money ready in assorted bills, and as he paid him, Dolan's blue eyes smiled.

'Good shooting, Mr Bond. It's been a pleasure working with you.'

As he opened the car door he belched, then ambled off towards the Park. Bond drove away. He didn't feel like celebrating. Instead he sent a telegram to London, then dined alone, got moderately drunk, then bought himself a hundred-dollar whore. Her name was Rosemary. It was a pity she was wearing pink.

*   *   *

The Shingushi killing gave Bond a reputation that he didn't want. He was a fighting man – and not a murderer. Where there was any choice he always settled for assignments which involved direct confrontation with the enemy. This generally seemed possible, and 1942 was a busy year for Bond. He was behind the destruction of the big refinery at Brest in February. Two months later he was in France again, this time in Vichy where he posed as a commercial traveller and engineered the release of three Allied agents held in the local gaol. A few weeks later he was flown to Alexandria to take charge of countermeasures against the Italian one-man submarines which had already taken heavy toll of the Allied shipping in the harbour. This was a complex operation, for which Bond had been partly trained in Oshawa. But it was hideously dangerous. Bond organized and trained an offensive task force of naval frogmen who could work at night against the submarines, and several times they fought hand-to-hand combats with the Italian frogmen in the harbour. Casualties were heavy but the one-man submarines were beaten.

Bond was proud of his success – at the end of 1942 he was promoted Lieutenant-Commander and brought back to London – but he always feared that his reputation would involve him in a repetition of the Shingushi business. Early in 1943 it looked like happening. By a coincidence, Fleming was once again involved.

For some time Naval Intelligence had been having trouble with its Baltic circuit. This whole area was of great importance since it also covered the British convoys to Murmansk. Russia was now our ally – Germany was battling towards Leningrad and trying hard to close the Northern ports. But we were getting faulty information; agents were being caught, four in the last two months. With so much at stake, such wastage could not continue.

Fleming explained all this to Bond, but, as he talked, something about his manner made Bond uneasy.

'It looks as if you'll have to take a little trip,' he said. 'Sweden. You'll find it chilly after Egypt, but I'm sure you'll make the best of things. I'm told the Swedish girls are ravishing.'

'Whereabouts in Sweden?'

'Stockholm. Lovely city. There's a man called Svenson. I'm afraid we need him dealt with – rather your line of country.'

Bond raised his eyebrows but said nothing.

'He's one of ours – in theory. We trained him over here – you may have met him. He's a Norwegian – big, good-looking chap – ex-sailor. I had him set up in a Stockholm shipping agency for cover, but he's doubled on us.'

'You're sure?' said Bond.

'No question. It's the usual story – good work to start with, then too many women. We've had reports of heavy spending. Now we're having all this trouble with the circuit and it must be Svenson. The opposition got two of our best men last week and we know that Svenson was the only person who could possibly have betrayed them. He must be fixed – for good.'

'Couldn't you find someone else?' said Bond. 'I knew him.'

'Did you now? So much the better.'

Despite himself, Bond was impressed by the thoroughness of Fleming's preparations. During the next few days they spent a lot of time together and Bond could see that nothing had been left to chance. Fleming had assembled a complete biography of Svenson. He even had some clips of film taken during training. The two men ran them through in the private cinema behind the Admiralty. Bond recognized at once the ready smile, the lumbering good-nature of the big Norwegian.

'I'd have trusted Svenson anywhere.'

'That's been the trouble,' said Fleming grimly.

Finally Bond realized that he knew too much about this man he had to kill. It would have been better to have known nothing for knowledge causes pity and a sense of guilt. It is much simpler to destroy a traitor than a human being.

* * *

Perhaps it was his mood, but Bond found Stockholm an uneasy city. Behind its palaces and quays and calm good sense lurked a hygienic pallor that depressed him. It was a city of cold eyes and painless dentists. Any excess was possible in such a place.

Bond had officially his prewar role of diplomatic courier to the British Embassy. He had made a complicated journey to the north by British warship, then across the border and by train to Stockholm. He had no doubts about his mission. It was necessary, but it was no adventure. Instead of the usual excitement of a fresh assignment, he felt a dreadful heaviness. He was the visiting executioner.

Bond didn't want to meet his victim face to face. Stockholm was an impersonal city – the place for an impersonal death; the quicker now the better.

He had no difficulty finding Svenson. His house was in the old city, a gabled, yellow-painted house straight from the pages of Hans Christian Andersen. Svenson had his office here and private flat. From the café opposite Bond spent some time watching it. Business did not appear to be too good. During the morning he saw two people entering the house, both of them well-dressed Swedes in heavy overcoats. There was no sign of Svenson. Just before lunch the front door opened and a girl came out. From behind his copy of *Svenska Dagblat,* Bond watched her as she crossed the street and walked towards the café where he sat. She was tall, slender with the palest coloured hair that Bond had ever seen, a Hans Christian Andersen princess. He saw her enter the café, walk to the counter where she bought some smörgäsbord. Then Bond sensed that she was looking at him. Lowering his paper he looked back. The girl had violet eyes. Bond recognized the look she gave him – it was a look of fear and unmistakable suspicion. For just a moment he thought she would speak. Instead she turned away, collected her neatly tied package from the counter, and Bond watched her cross the street and enter the house again. She used a latch-key of her own.

Bond was still hoping Svenson would show himself. It was all he needed. But although Bond kept the house under watch most of the afternoon, there was no sign of him. Bond cursed the girl. She must have warned Svenson of the man watching from the café opposite. That hygienic operation Bond was hoping for began to seem unlikely. It looked as if he could not avoid personal contact with Svenson after all. He waited hopefully till nearly six. Then he telephoned.

A woman answered. She spoke Swedish. It was a young attractive voice and Bond imagined it must be the girl. He replied in German, asking for Herr Svenson. She said he was out, and had no idea when he was returning. Who was speaking?

'An old friend of his – James Bond. I'm staying at the Carlton Hotel on Kungsgatan. Perhaps he'd ring me. I'll be there tonight at eight.'

But Svenson didn't ring, and finally Bond tried again. This time the telephone was answered by Svenson.

At the first sound of that booming voice with its fragmented English, Bond was reminded of the man that he had known. Happy-go-lucky Svenson, great drinker, womanizer, and Norwegian patriot. He always had enormous warmth of personality – even now Bond felt it in the voice.

'James, this is wonderful, just wonderful. You of all people here in bloody Stockholm. I can't wait to see you.'

'I'm not staying long, and tomorrow looks impossible. Any chance of seeing you tonight? It's been a long time.'

'So it has – too long. But yes, of course. We must meet and have a drink or two at least. I can't have you leaving Stockholm without seeing you.'

Svenson suggested a café, Olafson's on Skeppbron – two minutes from the royal palace. Bond promised to be there.

He was, but Svenson wasn't. Once again Bond was armed and ready to complete his mission. But although he waited until gone eleven there was no sign of Svenson. Bond was almost relieved when it was clear that he would not come. It would have been a wretched business to have drunk with a man and reminisced about the past, then gunned him down. On the other hand it meant that Bond would now need to involve himself still deeper with his old friend to get a chance to kill him.

Bond didn't feel like food, but forced himself to eat some smörgasbord and drink sufficient snaps to numb his feelings. Then he set out again for the yellow gabled house in the old city. This time Bond walked. It was a freezing night, and Bond recalled that Stockholm was as far north as Alaska. But the stars were bright, the spires and roofs of the old city still glittering like some Arctic city in a fairytale. Bond cursed the city for its beauty.

When he reached the little square, the house was in darkness. This time Bond was careful to stay out of sight – Svenson or the girl might well be watching for him. Instead he tried the street behind the house. There was an alleyway, a wall, a window he could force, and he was in. He found a staircase and then, gun in hand, set out to explore. The house was silent. Bond's first thought was that Svenson and the girl had fled. Then he heard voices from above. Tiptoeing he reached a landing. There was a bedroom door with light beneath it.

Bond called out, 'Svenson,' there was no reply, but the light inside the room went out.

'Svenson, I'm coming after you,' he shouted, then kicked

the door in. There was a shot – a bullet hit the woodwork by his head, and spun off down the stairs. Bond was expecting this. He had dodged back and fired twice towards the source of the shot. This seemed as good a way as any now of killing Svenson. It would be less like murder – more of an equal fight.

Bond waited, holding his fire. He could see nothing in the room, but somebody was moaning. Bond paused in readiness to shoot again.

'Svenson,' he called softly.

'For God's sake hold your fire,' said a voice, Svenson's voice. 'Why are you doing this to me?'

'You know why,' said Bond.

'James, just wait while I put the light on. Don't you know you've hit her?'

Bond realized it was a woman moaning. The light went on.

Svenson was sitting up in bed. He was much fatter than Bond remembered and sat clutching the bedclothes to his chest. He was unarmed and white with fear. Sprawled across the floor lay the girl Bond had seen that morning. She was naked. Blood was pumping from a bullet hole below the breast. In her hand she still held a small silver automatic.

There was not much that Bond could do for her. The violet eyes were already closed, the knees drawn up against the slender belly. She tried to speak, then slumped against the floor. Bond knew that she was dead.

Svenson was trembling. *He* was moaning now.

'Let me explain,' he said. 'You are my friend, James. You must understand.'

'I understand too well,' said Bond.

It was a pathetic business. Bond had never witnessed the effect of total fear before. He would have liked to have shot Svenson where he lay, but couldn't. Instead he heard his terrified confession followed by the inevitable plea for mercy. Bond was revolted – as much by himself now as by Svenson. War is a dirty business: but some men's wars are dirtier than others.

When Svenson realized that Bond was quite implacable he begged him one last favour – to be allowed to shoot himself

– and Bond agreed. He took the gun from the dead girl, left one bullet in the chamber, and threw it on the bed.

'I'll wait outside,' he said. 'Get it over quickly.'

Bond waited several minutes but there was no shot. When he went back into the bedroom, Svenson was still lying in the bed. He had the girl's gun in his hand and fired at him, as Bond knew he would. Svenson's gun-hand trembled when he fired. Bond's didn't.

*　　*　　*

Bond was commended for the Stockholm mission. After Svenson's death there were no more casualties in the Baltic circuit – nor were there any diplomatic repercussions.

The Stockholm police apparently were satisfied that the death of Svenson and his mistress was a *crime passionel* by an unknown person. Such crimes are common in the north: the dossier was closed.

For Bond, the irony of the case was that it confirmed him in the last role that he wanted – that of a 'hard' man, a remorseless killer. But luckily his talents were employed on 'cleaner' assignments for a while. Towards the end of 1943 he was back in Switzerland, organizing the escape of two important Jewish scientists from Germany across Lake Constance. He had a period behind the lines in Italy, helping the partisans attack the big Ansaldo naval works at Spezia. Later he was attached to the naval task force liaising with the French resistance in the Channel ports before D-Day. But Bond's big assignment came at the end of 1944, during the crucial German offensive into the Ardennes.

This has long baffled the more attentive readers of Ian Fleming's books. For Fleming was involved in this as well, and mentioned the affair in passing, thus giving rise to Mr Kingsley Amis's pained query, 'what was a commander of naval intelligence doing in the Ardennes in 1944?'

Fleming himself did hint at the answer in his short story *From a View to a Kill* where he mentioned 'left-behind spy units' set up by the retreating Germans in the Ardennes. In fact these units at one point looked like becoming a menace to the Allies, and it was largely thanks to James Bond that this was averted.

Throughout the summer of 1944 there had been reports from Allied agents that the Nazis were preparing a full-scale resistance movement against an Allied victory. It was known that in Berlin an entire S.S. department, based in big offices off Mehringplatz, was concerned with nothing else. It was commanded by a full-ranking S.S. general named Semler, and already Goebbels was planning to ensure that the Nazi myth survived defeat in war.

Already he could see that a full-scale Nazi resistance movement was now the immortal Reich's best hope of immortality. And in London the Joint Chiefs of Staff set up a small committee to contain it. As something of a German expert, Fleming was a member. It was through him that Bond became involved.

During the autumn the committee's chief concern was the Ardennes. Nobody doubted that the Fuehrer's massive armoured offensive to win back lost German conquests here would ultimately fail. But our agents were reporting that one of the secret aims of the offensive was to gain time to plant a self-contained resistance set-up here for the future. It would have arms, underground headquarters and carefully disguised command points for its troops. It would include the so-called 'Werewolf Movement' but in addition have a fully equipped and trained 'secret army' to harass the advancing Allies from the rear. According to well-confirmed reports, the S.S. general from Mehrmgplatz was personally in charge, and Himmler had paid a two-day visit to the area.

Information had suddenly become crucially important, but no Allied agents had succeeded in penetrating the area. Nazi security throughout the battlehead was strict, with a virtual black-out of all information within forty miles of the salient. Fleming suggested Bond as one of the very few men who might discover what was going on.

Bond was summoned to a house in Knightsbridge where he was briefed by an owl-like man called Grunspan. He was

127

a former history professor from the University of Münich and one of the few Jews ever to have escaped from Auschwitz. Later Bond learned that it was here that he picked up his appalling stammer.

Bond did his best to listen patiently as he struggled to explain what he wanted.

'Commander Bond,' he said. 'We must have information we can act on. We know that Himmler plans this as a showpiece. If it succeeds it could provide a pattern for the future.'

'What do I have to look for?'

'The centre of this secret army.'

'Won't it be fairly obvious once we've reconquered it?'

'Obvious? My dear Commander, do you know the Ardennes? Perfect guerilla country.' He pointed to the map. 'Miles upon miles of forest. Why, you could hide the Wehrmacht there and nobody be much the wiser.'

'Where do you suggest I start then?' Bond asked.

'There's not a lot to go on, but perhaps you could start here – a place called Rosenfeld. It's now some twenty miles behind the front line and we know it was one of the places Himmler visited. We also know that there are strong concentrations of S.S. in the district.'

'And what about this S.S. general, Semler?'

'You're well informed, but I'm afraid he's something of a mystery man. We've no photographs of him – only reports that he's being tipped as Himmler's successor. Already he seems to see himself as something of a saviour of Nazi Germany.'

Just two days later Bond heard the rattle of German spandaus firing across the narrow no-man's-land to the west of a town called Haslach. He could see nothing, but the Armoured Corps captain with him pointed towards the line of woods where the firing came from.

'They've got their armour concentrated there. A division of Panzer Grenadiers, equipped with Mark Two Tigers – what you might call the cream of the cream. We know they're grouped back through the forest. We'll have to see if they attack again.'

For the past two weeks the armies had been locked in battle. On one side was the massive power of the Allies – on the other the desperation of a Wehrmacht launching its final bid to save the Fatherland. The German heavy tanks had broken the Allied advance, but now they in their turn were halted. This forest land was witnessing the power of steel and high explosive as the Allied armies picked up their momentum towards Berlin.

Bond knew that his mission was somewhere behind that line of forest. Rosenfeld lay five miles to the east. It was a daunting prospect to attempt to infiltrate the enemy's front line, but there seemed no alternative. That night James Bond was dropped by a low-flying British aircraft into a wooded area close to Rosenfeld. Rather than risk a parachute, he used a reinforced container known as a 'coffin' which had been invented to land men and arms for the French resistance. He landed safely, rolled clear, and did his best to hide the coffin in the undergrowth. Just at this moment hell seemed to burst around his ears. Bond had never been on the edge of an artillery bombardment before. The whole forest seemed to rock and the night was lit up with the flashes of the German guns firing back. Bond smiled to himself – the artillery were certainly on time with the diversionary cover they had promised. The shells were dropping half a mile to the west, but nobody was going to challenge Bond as he picked his way to his objective.

This was a wooded rise to the east of Rosenfeld. According to the photographs from aerial reconnaissance it commanded most of the village. Bond reached it and then did his best to conceal himself in undergrowth. The guns were still nagging at each other in the west, but finally they stopped; Bond started his uneasy wait for morning.

He had been luckier than he expected. For half a mile or so there was a gentle slope of scrubby heathland skirted by a road, which led to Rosenfeld. The edge of the wood where he was lying seemed uninhabited, but further to the left was a long line of entrenchments. Further on there was a coppice.

As he looked he could gradually make out seven or eight Tiger tanks concealed beneath branches and long swathes of camouflage netting. Mechanics were at work. Bond could faintly hear their voices in the still morning. Gradually the village came to life. Parts of it had been badly shelled, but it was evidently still full of troops. A dog was barking; smoke rose from mobile kitchens; through his binoculars Bond watched half a dozen grey-clad men saunter along the street for breakfast.

Bond spent the morning watching but saw nothing unusual. Troops moved through the village up towards the front. Two of the tanks moved off. Twice he saw Allied aircraft but their targets lay elsewhere. Then Bond noticed something.

On the far side of the valley was a hospital – a long, low, modern building. The flat roof had a large red cross – so did The walls. So far these red crosses had done their work. the hospital appeared unscathed. What had caught Bond's attention was the steady flow of lorries to and from the place. They had gone on all morning, and Bond started counting them. There were fifteen in slightly less than an hour. What hopital could need quite so much transport? There was only one way to find out.

There was a narrow bend in the road a mile or so back, and as the German army driver changed down to take it, he saw a figure in British army uniform leap towards the cab. That was all he saw of Bond as the door swung open and a jarring blow caught him below the ear. The lorry stopped. There was a brief scuffle in the cab, and three minutes later when it drove on there was a different driver in the German's uniform – James Bond. Propped up unconscious by his side was the German, now in British uniform.

Bond drove fast, with tyres screeching through the village and up towards the hospital. When he arrived he parked the lorry behind several others, slung the unconscious German over his shoulder and dragged him inside. From now on everything depended on how long he could sustain the bluff. It was the British uniform that did the trick. Bond began shouting about British troops being in the forest. Orderlies were running, an alarm was sounded and everyone was suddenly yelling orders. The unconscious man began to stir. The pandemonium increased, and Bond was free to slip away. He had seen enough.

Someone did ask where he was going. In a thick Hamburg accent Bond replied,

'I must just back my lorry up.'

But instead of backing it, he turned it and drove full pelt towards the village. Nobody stopped him and he abandoned it on the corner where he had ambushed the driver. Soon afterwards the bombardment started and Bond hid in the woods. He was hungry now and very tired. When darkness came he slept a while and after midnight started the hazardous trek back to the Allied lines.

It was ten days before the German panzers cracked and the retreat began. By then the whole German salient had been blasted by Allied guns. Much of the forest was a wasteland, but, to Bond's surprise, Rosenfeld appeared to have survived. Apart from shattered windows, the hospital on the hill appeared intact. Bond had made sure to be included in the advance party that occupied the village. He also made sure that his first call was to the hospital. It was full of German wounded and humming with activity. Some of the wounded men were lying on mattresses in corridors. A young doctor showed him round. Bond was accompanied by a British brigadier, an upright, very typical regular soldier with a moustache and double D.S.O. He was obviously impressed by what he saw.

'Can't help admiring Jerry, can you? They're an efficient bloody lot, even when they're beaten.'

Bond nodded, but said nothing.

'That doctor in charge – the tall one with the monocle. Couldn't take his eyes off you. Ever met the man before?'

'Yes,' said Bond, 'I have. Ten days ago. He was in uniform.'

'Uniform? What sort of uniform?'

'An S.S. general's. His name's Semler. Some people think

that he'll be Himmler's successor, but somehow, after today, I doubt it.'

It took the Allied field security three days to check the hospital. Some of the cases were quite genuine – so were the doctors. But a lot more of them were S.S. personnel. The cellars of the hospital were crammed with arms, and a command post had contact with Berlin and with resistance points throughout Germany. Thanks to James Bond the rising the S.S. planned from Rosenfeld Hospital never materialized, and without it the German Nazis were truly doomed.

7

Scandal

I had an idea that there had been some scandal hanging over Bond at the end of the war. Urquhart had mentioned what he termed 'a spot of trouble', and from chance remarks of Bond's I gathered that he still felt bitter over how he had been treated. When I asked him, his first reaction was to shake his head.

'Absolutely nothing,' he said briskly.

'But you left the Secret Service.'

'So did a lot of others. The war was over. I'd had enough.'

'Enough? Enough of what?'

'Oh, for God's sake. Can't we just leave it there? I was bored, you understand.'

'And that was all?'

I had not seen Bond furious before. It was quite daunting. The jaw clamped tight, the face went slightly pale. I sensed the violence just below the surface. He breathed deeply, checked himself and then said very softly,

'Just say that I was anxious for a change. And now, if you'll excuse me . . .' He rose abruptly, nodded me good-day and strode off to the hotel. It was to be two days before I so much as caught sight of him again.

During this time I had a chance to ask Sir William Stephenson about this period. He was distinctly cagey too.

'There was a row with M. He'd only just taken over as head of the Secret Service. There were mistakes on both sides, and Bond received a good deal less than justice. He should have got the decoration he was recommended for, but he was very stupid too. He made it difficult for M.'

'But how?'

Sir William smiled. He is a shrewd old man.

'It would be wrong for me to try and tell you. I'm afraid that's something you must get from Bond himself.'

I was not over-keen to bring the matter up again; in the event, it was Bond who mentioned it quite calmly of his own accord. This was two days later after dinner. He was sitting in the bar alone and called me over. He was quite affable and made no reference to our earlier *contretemps*. He even seemed eager to talk, and turned the conversation back to the war's end.

According to what he said, he had been uncertain what to do in peacetime England. Officially, he was still on the establishment of the Volunteer Reserve of the Royal Navy. Finding himself with a fortnight's leave, he went back to spend it with Aunt Charmian.

'I was hoping I could think things out. It was the one place where I thought that I could come to terms with myself.'

Instead he found this sudden contact with his family unsettling. Aunt Charmian was full of gossip; Henry was married now and in the Treasury. 'Just the place for him,' said Bond. A week or two before, Aunt Charmian had met Bond's ex-fiancée in Canterbury. 'She was looking very *settled*. She had two children with her – told me her husband was in fertilizers. She was most interested to know what you were doing.'

Later, Aunt Charmian talked about the Bonds. Grandfather Bond had died the year before – aged ninety-two – and Uncle Gregor had inherited the house in Glencoe. 'It should have been your father,' said Aunt Charmian. 'It would have suited him. Instead your uncle's drinking more than ever, and often talks of selling up the place.' Aunt

Charmian was horrified at the prospect. To his surprise, Bond found he didn't care.

Nor did he care about the past. In his old room he found a locked drawer-full of letters – most of them from Marthe de Brandt and other women long forgotten. There were some photographs as well. He burned the lot. The Bentley was still in the garage where he had left it at the beginning of the war; the tyres were very flat, the metalwork was rusty. Bond locked the garage doors. Wherever else the future lay it wasn't here. That night he told his aunt that he would probably be staying in the services.

'I'm sure that you know best,' she said.

As it turned out Bond's official transfer to the Secret Service wasn't simple. It meant a change in status from a serving officer to a peacetime civil servant. Bond's application was submitted early in February 1946. A few days later he was summoned to an office on the sixth floor of the Regent's Park headquarters to meet the newly appointed head of the Secret Service. This was Sir Miles Messervy, a former Admiral and secretary to the Joint Chiefs of Staff. Bond had never met him but knew his reputation. His enemies criticized his arrogance and inflexibility; his admirers described him as the most brilliant officer of his generation. As a man he was something of a mystery. All that most people knew of him was his initial – M.

Bond's first impression was unfavourable. Perhaps it was the pipe. (Bond had never cared for pipe-smokers since Eton – his housemaster had been a devoted Bruno Flake Cut man.) And there was something less than warmth in M.'s manner – no word of welcome, not even an invitation to sit down. The steely eyes surveyed him from the weatherbeaten face. Bond noted the closely cut grey hair, the tightly knotted tie, the neat arrangement of the ruler, blotter, shell-case ashtray on the desk, and, once again, remembered school. The last time he had felt such apprehension was when summoned by the head during the trouble over Brinton's sister. M. had the same headmaster's trick of staring at his victim hard before speaking.

'Commander Bond,' he said at last. M. had a cool dry voice. 'I have been looking at your records.' He tapped a thick, much-handled manilla file on his desk. Bond would have given much to read it. 'An interesting career. Experience like yours must be unique.'

Bond didn't like the way he said 'unique'.

'It remains to be seen whether we can use you. Things are changing fast, Commander. The postwar pattern of the service will be very different from what you are used to. What I propose is that you join us on probation. During this period I thought that you might like to go to America for us – on attachment to the Office of Strategic Services in Washington. They're expanding and are keen to pick our brains. They've requested someone with field experience and you've been highly recommended.'

M. relaxed slightly then.

'It's quite a chance,' he said. 'Be sure to make the most of it.'

Bond was uncertain whether to be pleased or not. He liked the idea of America and of working with Americans. But, on the other hand, he knew that this sort of foreign attachment was often a discreet way of disposing of unwanted personnel. He discussed arrangements with the young Sapper colonel M. had just brought in as his Chief of Staff. He was to leave at once and travel through New York to Washington where he would be officially on the staff of the British Embassy. He would have diplomatic status and allowances and the attachment was for a minimum period of three months.

'The Americans can't wait to see you,' said the Chief of Staff and grinned. 'Go easy on the Bourbon and those fresh young secretaries.'

Bond flew into New York in the spring. It was the first time he had been there since he killed the Japanese in the Rockefeller Center; the memory haunted him. He was twenty-five but felt immensely old. For ten years he had been at war, plotting and struggling and murdering his fellow men. Now it was over and he realized his soul was sick of it. The time had come to catch up on a lot of living.

In *For Your Eyes Only*, Fleming quotes Bond as saying that the best things in America are the chipmunks and the oyster stew. He saw no chipmunks during his few days in New York, but it was then that he discovered oyster stew – in the Oyster Bar on the suburban level of Grand Central Terminal. It struck him as the greatest dish since the *bouillabaisse* he ate with Marthe de Brandt in Marseilles before the war. He discovered other things as well. After the years of wartime London he was excited and appalled by the affluence of New York. He enjoyed shopping for objects that would give him pleasure – things had to work and either be extremely cheap or extremely luxurious. He bought a 25-cent Zippo lighter and the Hoffritz razor which he has used ever since. He also bought Owens toothbrushes, socks from Triplers, and an expensive set of golf clubs from A. and C. But what gave him greatest pleasure was to discover what he always called 'the greatest bargain in New York' – the 5-cent Staten Island ferry from the Battery.

It was the perversity of a puritan, loving and rejecting the richest city in the world – an attitude which Bond has always had towards America. During these few days in New York he stayed at the Stanhope, a five-star hotel opposite the Metropolitan Museum. Sir William Stephenson had recommended it. Its dignity and calm appealed to Bond, despite its cost. Similarly, he made great show of eating simply in the most expensive restaurants. As a friend of Sir William's and something of a celebrity, he was entertained extravagantly; but at Voisins he insisted on dining off vodka martinis, eggs benedict and strawberries. At Sardis he had scrambled eggs. When he flew on to Washington, Bond had the feeling that he had put New York firmly in its place.

In Washington the Embassy took care of him. This was a mistake. The last thing James Bond needed was to dine with the Ambassador or swap gossip on the city's cocktail circuit. Washington was not his city. After New York he found it formal and pretentious with too much marble and too many monuments. It brought out the worst in him. The Head of Chancery offered to take him round the White House. Bond replied that he'd rather see the Washington gasworks – end of conversation.

The one thing Bond was grateful for was his flat. The Embassy had lent him a ground-floor service apartment in a brownstone off N Street. Bond had never seen Georgetown before: almost in spite of himself he found that he was captivated by it. He liked its style, its easy elegance. Also, although he won't admit it, he clearly did enjoy the rich indulgent lives of the wealthy set who lived there.

For, socially and sexually, Bond was a success in George-town. He was invited everywhere. His arrogance and obvious dislike of politicians appealed to the masochistic instincts of his hosts – and, more still, of their wives. His British accent and his hard good looks seemed to guarantee him all the conquests that he wanted. He was quite ruthless, knowing and very cruel to women, a policy which, as usual, paid rich dividends.

Somewhat hypocritically, Bond insists that once again he was distinctly shocked by the eagerness of these rich American wives to go to bed with him. 'They had no self-respect. It was all too easy. There was absolutely no romance.' But this time, absence of romance did not stop him making the most of things.

Bond had work to do. It suffered. He claims that not until much later did he discover what a crucial period this was for American Intelligence.

Men like Alan Dulles and General 'Wild Bill' Donovan were hard at work revamping the whole U.S. secret service structure. The old Office of Strategic Services was about to be transformed into the all-powerful Central Intelligence Agency, the C.I.A. And several of the top men genuinely wanted to draw on Bond's advice and expertise. Bond didn't want to talk. He got on well with Donovan, and, in later years, Alan Dulles became something of a personal friend. But he still had a condescending attitude to most of the American secret servicemen he met. Some of them clearly were naïve and others inexperienced but Bond made the mistake of treating them all as something of a joke. He gave little and was particularly bored by the organizers of the O.S.S. who consulted him (unlike Ian Fleming who was in Washington a few months later and who compiled a detailed constitution for the C.I.A. for General Donovan). The simple truth was that in U.S. Intelligence circles, Bond soon made himself heartily disliked. He never had been a tactful man, particularly with anyone who bored him; within a few days of his arrival in Washington, he had begun to put the backs up of several men who mattered. His socializing made things worse.

There were several warning incidents. The first involved a young French diplomat. A former Vichyite, he had somehow got himself appointed to the French Embassy. At a small dinner given by a leading Georgetown hostess, he taunted Bond about the British in North Africa. There was a scene. Bond replied in the sort of French that is rarely heard in Washington, and when he hit the man the Frenchman fell, smashed an almost genuine Chippendale *escritoire* and needed his jaw pinning in three places.

A few days later there was another scene at a big reception for a famous film-star who had just made a film on the Normandy invasion. Bond arrived slightly drunk with a U.S. Navy captain. Both of them laughed a lot throughout the film, and afterwards Bond told the star to stick to Westerns – they were safer.

None of this mattered over-much. People who knew James Bond liked him and made allowances. The final incident was different.

This time there really could be no excuses.

As usual, the cause of all the trouble was a woman, but, for once, Bond was innocent. She was the wife of an influential Congressman, a rich pro-British democrat and friend of the Ambassador. He was in his fifties, his wife in her early thirties. 'She was,' says Bond, 'a hard-faced, predatory bitch.'

The husband had heard of Bond from Sir William Stephenson, and was anxious to meet him. He made a fuss of him, and invited him for the weekend to his house near

Albany. Bond went. He liked the Congressman and, as he had a private golf-course near his house, Bond was looking forward to a weekend's golf. He felt he needed it.

That night the Congressman got drunk, and the wife suggested Bond should sleep with her. Bond claims that he refused, 'but as things turned out it would have been much better if I had.'

The following weekend the Congressman again invited Bond. Bond declined: the man insisted. There was a golfing competition which he wanted Bond to join. Bond packed his brand new clubs and went. He felt safer in this genial all-male company. His host was charm itself, and Bond was relieved to see that the wife was absent.

If she had taken umbrage at Bond's refusal, so much the better.

But on Sunday morning she appeared. She had a Piper Cub and had piloted herself up from New York, landing on an airstrip just behind the house. Her arrival brought an air of tension to the place. She was difficult, rude to her husband, awkward with the guests, and after lunch Bond heard doors being slammed upstairs. Shortly afterwards the Congressman told Bond that he had sudden urgent business back in Washington and left.

For Bond it was an embarrassing situation. He had been planning to take the evening plane back to Washington from Albany, but the wife insisted she would fly him back herself. They seem to have had an eventful Sunday afternoon. There was more golf, a lot of drinking, supper round a barbecue and then, at ten o'clock or so, the last guests left and Bond found himself alone with his hostess. She began calmly to prepare for bed.

Bond tried to handle the situation lightly for he insists that he was still acting the gentleman, 'a fatal thing to do', and telling the woman that he liked her and her husband far too much to spoil things with a casual *affaire*. She was incensed at this. He kept his temper and said that he had to get back to Washington. Finally she said that, fine, she'd fly him there.

She was a skilful pilot, and it was only later that Bond was to learn just how drunk she was. At the time he thought she was doing her best to scare him. She certainly succeeded, but he was determined not to show it. He admits it was the most hair-raising flight he has ever lived through. They were following the main line of the Turnpike but losing height. Bond asked her twice about their altitude: she didn't answer. He asked again. This time she swore at him, shoved the stick forward and shouted, 'O.K, big boy – fly the bloody thing.'

Bond tried to grab the stick. The plane was a bare few hundred feet above the Turnpike. It stalled, the engine roared, and the plane fell like a dead bird. It landed in a field some twenty yards from the road and flared immediately. Bond seems to have been thrown clear. The first patrol car at the accident discovered him along the road. There was not much that anyone could do to save the woman.

It was a very messy business and this time nobody could hush it up. The press had something of a field day. Bond felt he had a duty to see the husband and at least try explaining what had happened. It was harder than he expected. Incredibly, the man had loved his wife, and Bond found it impossible to tell the truth. The Congressman was very bitter. So was the man from the British Embassy who had the task of dealing with the press. Bond told him the truth. This made the situation worse.

The diplomat, a Wykehamist, had disapproved of Bond from the moment he arrived. He thoroughly disliked him now that he was attempting to shift the blame on to a dead woman. Bond was a cad – as well as a diplomatic liability: his usefulness in Washington was over.

Coldly, the diplomat suggested Bond had better catch the evening plane to London. Once he had gone the Embassy would do its best to smooth things over. These things did happen, but in future Commander Bond might be advised to steer very clear of politicians' wives.

Bond says that he was sorely tempted to hit the man. 'He was so very smug, so very Foreign Office about it all.' The fact that he was right did not make it any better, although in fact James Bond has followed his advice religiously ever since.

Bond's disgrace was serious. He did his best to salvage what was left of his reputation by seeing M. at once: at least he managed to make sure that M. heard his version of events before anybody else's. But if James Bond was expecting a sympathetic ear from that old sailor he mistook his man.

M. said very little, but his silence made it clear what he was thinking. While Bond was talking he went on filling his pipe. He said, 'humph' once or twice, then lit up, puffed, and muttered 'most distasteful'. Finally he told Bond that he would be looking into the affair in detail. Bond would be hearing from him.

Bond had been hoping that things could somehow be glossed over and forgotten: he did not know the rancour of an outraged Wykehamist. A full report arrived from Washington along with all the newspapers. None was particularly flattering to Bond.

It was a bad time to have come unstuck. With the ending of the war, establishments were being pruned, and good men thanked for their services and given their bowler hats. Even his old ally, Fleming, was soon to leave Whitehall for Kemsley Newspapers. The whole style of the Secret Service was changing too. The new fashion was for what Bond sardonically refers to as the 'Dirty Mackintosh Brigade', the self-effacing, slightly shabby men whose subfusc image was so different from his own.

These were the men who called him 'Playboy Bond'. He claims that they were jealous of him – of the money that he spent, the women he enjoyed, the life he led. Above all, they were jealous of his past success. Now they could have their own back. They did so with a vengeance.

Bond understands that he had to go, but the way he was dismissed still rankles. He was kept waiting nearly a fortnight. There were reports on him which he had no chance to see, let alone answer. After his years as one of the stars of the department, he felt himself an outcast. Even the C.M.G., for which he had been warmly recommended, was withheld.

Finally M. did see him; he was at his frostiest, and gave Bond no chance to argue or defend himself. After considering the case he had decided that a board of inquiry would not be in the interests of the Service. Commander Bond must not feel from this that he was in any way exonerated. Words could not express the disapproval that he felt at his behaviour whilst on a delicate and most important mission. The Commander would leave the Service. This would be best for everyone.

Even as M. spoke, Bond found it hard to credit what he was saying. But the verdict had been given – the case was closed. There was no word of thanks for all that Bond had done, still less of regret or consolation: only the noise of M. sucking his dead Dunhill. Bond said, 'Thank you, sir.'

M. said nothing.

They did not shake hands.

It was an early summer morning; Bond walked down Baker Street after the axe had fallen, feeling a little dazed. The unthinkable had happened, but he was alive and still comparatively unscarred. According to the Paymaster he had £300 in his old account with Glyn Mills Bank. The sun was out, the first summer dresses in the shops. It was 1946, the first full year of peace.

Bond's spirits rose. By Marble Arch he noticed new leaves on the plane trees by the park. People were strolling past him, leading their ordinary, uncomplicated lives and suddenly Bond realized that he was one of them. He was no longer tied to a life behind a gun, no longer threatened with the fear of sudden death. M. had set him free and he could start a normal life at last. The idea was so exciting that he crossed Park Lane, entered the Dorchester and ordered a half-bottle of Dom Perignon to celebrate.

Bond began looking for a job. He was quite optimistic now that the time had come to settle down. He reviewed his assets – youth, good looks, and skill with languages. He was single and without dependents. But as he soon found out, these were assets which he shared with several thousand other young ex-servicemen.

He took job-hunting seriously and wrote endless letters that began, 'Dear Sir, I wonder whether . . . '. One in ten brought a reply. There were a few offers. A jute mill in Madras required a manager. A stock-broking firm in Mincing Lane required a clerk. A private eye in Marylebone needed investigators. . . 'most of the work's divorce-court stuff. You'll find it stimulating.' Bond thought otherwise.

A fortnight passed. Bond was rising late by now, skipping breakfast, then getting down to writing letters. He lunched alone, generally in a pub along the King's Road. The afternoons went on job-hunting. The rent on the flat in Lincoln Street was due. It was ten days since he had seen his current mistress, a snub-nosed secretary in the press department of the Ministry of Defence. Purely by chance he met a wartime colleague who was now working as chief security officer with Harrods: he offered Bond a job as store detective.

It was the last sad straw. That evening Bond decided to make money in the one sure way he knew – by gambling. Bond still enjoyed his wartime membership of Blades, although he hadn't been for several months. He put on his dark blue suit, arrived at nine, stayed clear of the bar (to avoid the embarrassment of having to buy drinks that he could not afford) and took his place in the great eighteenth-century gaming room. He had always played to win, but never before because he needed money. He was disturbed to find how much this spoiled the game: it even dictated his choice of an opponent. He found himself picking someone he would normally have avoided – Bunny Kendrick, a cantankerous old millionaire who was a bad but frequent loser. Bond played high. For more than half an hour he lost. Kendrick was delighted in the way that rich men are at such unnecessary strokes of fortune. When Bond was £200 down, he panicked – and it was then that he was tempted. He suddenly remembered an all but foolproof card-sharp's trick Esposito had taught him, a way of dealing himself a perfect run of cards. It would have been so very easy, and no one would have noticed – certainly not Kendrick. Bond was sweating, and this chance of cheating was so frightening that he almost left the table there and then. Instead he forced himself to finish playing and ended owing £80. It was the most wretched evening Bond has ever spent at a card table in his life. Next morning he decided he would ring the man at Harrods. But on that very day his fortune changed.

Bond was walking past the Ritz Hotel (he tended to walk everywhere these days) when he saw a small, familiar bald figure entering the large swing doors. It was a good three years since Bond had last seen Maddox. After the fall of France he had made his way to London, picked up a colonel's job with Military Intelligence and spent most of the war in the Middle East. Later he joined the Free French in Algiers and returned to Paris with the ending of the war. He was delighted to see Bond, and insisted that they had a drink together. Maddox showed all the signs of obvious prosperity – expensive highly polished shoes, a tightly cut check suit, the rosette of the *Légion d'Honneur* in his buttonhole.

'Consultant work,' he said when Bond asked what he did, 'at, shall we say, a somewhat elevated level. I work with various big French commercial houses, chiefly with connections throughout Africa.'

'And you enjoy yourself?'

'Have you ever known me not to? I have a family you know – two boys. We live just outside Paris at Vincennes. You must meet my wife.'

But Maddox was a wary husband. When his wife appeared – she had been shopping and returned earlier than expected – Maddox treated her with care. Bond could see why. She was lovely – a blonde, Parisienne with that particular sheen of beautiful French women who take their menfolk and their wealth for granted. Bond was amused to see that Maddox was careful *not* to press her to stay. Only when she had gone did he invite Bond to lunch.

Bond loved the grill room of the Ritz. It was like old times to be eating here with Maddox. He remembered the evening long ago, in Fontainebleau when Maddox had recruited him. Soon he was telling Maddox everything – the ups-and-downs of his career, the scandal out in Washington, and M.'s behaviour. Maddox sat in silence, staring at the park.

'James,' he said finally, 'I will be frank with you. I don't believe you'll ever change. When I recruited you I warned you that you'd never get away. The life you've led has made you what you are.'

'Thanks very much,' said Bond, 'but what do I do now?'

Maddox relit his large cigar and wreathed himself in smoke.

'I think,' he said, 'that you should come and work for me.'

* * *

Bond would have hated to admit how good it felt to be aboard the morning plane to Paris. He had his battered pig-skin case that had been with him on so many old assignments. Even to pack it had brought back a touch of the excitement of the old days: pyjamas, light blue shirts, and black hide washing-case. He wore the dark blue lightweight suit, the hand-stitched moccasins, the heavy knitted-silk black tie that virtually comprised his private uniform. He stretched his legs and watched the Staines reservoirs recede below the Viscount's wing-tip. Early though it was, he broke his usual rule and ordered a long cool vodka tonic. Maddox was paying for the trip. He could afford it.

He thought of Maddox. That wily little man wasn't befriending him again for fun although Bond had told him that his days of dangerous living were over. Bond wasn't giving up his dream of normal life as easily as that.

He had forgotten how much he loved Paris. It was his first time back since just before the war, but nothing had really changed – the same stale smell of Gauloises at Le Bourget, the drumming of the taxi on the cobbled roads, the barges on the river. He was remembering things that seemed forgotten. From the Place d'Italie the driver took the Boulevard St Germain. Bond was earlier than he expected and paid him off at the corner of the Rue Jacob. This was where he had lived with Marthe de Brandt – the little flat beside the Place

Furstenburg; it seemed so long ago that he could not believe that this was the same scarred brown front door, the same trees in the courtyard.

Bond's nostalgia deepened as he walked down the narrow street towards the river, then crossed the Pont des Arts. How sensible of Maddox to have settled here in Paris, and how typical of him to have chosen an office on the Ile de la Cité with a fine view of the river and one of Bond's own favourite restaurants, the Restaurant Jules, just round the corner. At Bond's suggestion this was where they ate, although Maddox had a table booked at the Tour d'Argent. Bond felt at home at last as he sat down at the marble-topped table in that crowded restaurant. They had *quenelles* and *boeuf gros sel*, apricot tart and camembert and splendid coffee. They had the faintly sour house wine in a heavy glass decanter, then drank their cognac afterwards in the little square beneath the mulberries. It was Bond's first day of positive enjoyment since he had left the Secret Service.

Maddox outlined the work he had in mind for him. Since the Liberation he had been working for a syndicate of big French bankers as 'security director', a title which appeared to cover top-level planning to protect the group's massive interests throughout the world.

Maddox was much concerned with anti-subversion and the control of sabotage. He wanted Bond to join him, 'as an adviser, nothing more. You'll have your base right here in Paris, and the job can be what you care to make it. You can travel, and I'll promise that you won't be bored. At the same time you can settle down a bit, make some money and decide what you really want to do with life. We might even find you a good-looking rich French wife. You could do worse.'

On that bright spring day in Paris, the offer seemed irresistible and, for the next four years, James Bond became an exile. He was a sort of mercenary, a soldier of fortune. With his command of languages he was at home in France, and anywhere else he happened to be sent. He had been well trained by the British Secret Service; as a non-Frenchman working for the French, he could be quite objective over their interests. He liked to think himself completely apolitical. Neither the demands of local nationalists, nor the antics of French politicians remotely interested him. He affected to despise them all. To him all politicians were quite simply 'clowns', some more ridiculous or more corrupt than others. He had a job to do. As he said to Maddox, it wasn't all that different from the store detective's job with Harrods, but it did have more scope.

There were great journeys which he loved, weeks spent travelling rough across Morocco or over the Sahara. He got to know Dakar, that scorching, fascinating melting-pot of France and black Africa. In Conakry, the capital of Guinea, he found a night club where the black hostesses wore nothing but full-length ball-dress skirts and long blonde wigs. In Timbuctoo he bought himself a 'wife' for fifteen sheep. He caught the spell of Africa – its size, its paradox, its mystery. He travelled up the Niger river, and got to know the tribes of Senegal. Here it seemed that he could live a cleaner life than he had known in Europe.

When he did come back, it was to Paris, to confer with Maddox in his elegant small office by the river. He never seemed to visit London now. He had given up the flat in Lincoln Street and finally arranged to have the Bentley repainted and restored and brought over from Pett Bottom. Resplendent in its polished brass and 'elephant's breath grey' paint, it now lived in a lock-up garage off the Rue Jacob. Bond lived nearby. He had a tiny roof-top flat behind the Place Furstenburg, 'more like the cabin of a ship than a gentleman's apartment' as Maddox used to say. So far the rich wife Maddox had promised had not materialized.

Professionally, Bond pulled off several coups which more than justified his salary. In Bamako he stopped the blowing up of the great barrage recently built by the French across the Niger. At Algiers airport he scotched an attempt to hijack a consignment of gold to the Bank of France. In Paris itself he had the task of handling a kidnapping. The son of one of Maddox's wealthy colleagues had been taken from his house near the Bois de Boulogne. Bond was convinced he

148

knew the kidnappers, and on his own initiative set out to find them. There was a risk of the child being killed. Bond knew that if that happened he would be blamed. Despite this he went ahead and bluffed the gang into believing that he was bringing them the ransom. They were holed up inside a block of municipal flats in Belfort. Thanks to his instant marksmanship, Bond shot two of them before they could harm the boy. The rest surrendered and Bond drove the child home in safety.

Through acts like these, Bond was becoming something of a legend. But it was a strange uneasy life he led. France was not his country. At times he felt as if life were uncannily repeating a perpetual pattern which had started with the wanderings of his family when he was 'a boy. He was becoming like his father, always on the move and always fighting other peoples' battles.

He was approaching thirty and knew quite well that he had settled nothing. He was still rootless and, despite a succession of fairly clinical *affaires*, still without lasting emotional attachment. He had begun to doubt if he were capable of one.

Like most compulsive bachelors, Bond was scared of women. Not physically – he was a vigorous and virile lover, and he enjoyed the routine of a seduction. It was an all-absorbing game that satisfied his vanity. His fear began when that other head was firmly on the pillow – worse still the morning after. Like all romantics, he was genuinely shocked when his women were revealed as human beings. Smeared morning make-up quite upset him and he disliked it if his women used the lavatory. Any demands, except overtly sexual ones, made him impatient.

With such an attitude to women it was not surprising that James Bond stayed resolutely single, especially as his habits were becoming more and more confirmed with age. His 'cabin' up among the roofs of the Rue Jacob possessed a monk-like quality, his mistresses were becoming more and more alike. They were all beautiful, all fairly young, and married or divorced. They enjoyed sex as much as he did but they all stuck by the unspoken rules of the game – pleasure but no extraneous demands, sentimentality but no sentiment, passion but no comeback from the world outside. Bond secretly preferred them to leave shortly after making love. (Since they generally had husbands, they invariably did.)

All this seemed satisfactory; had one met James Bond one might have congratulated him on having solved his problems and made the transition from war to peace better than most. He finally had money and success, work he enjoyed, a style of life most men would envy. But Bond was human and by that strange perversity that dogs all human beings, the very things that should have left him happy left him dissatisfied.

He loved settled families, especially with happy, well brought-up children – the Maddoxes, for instance. He used to visit them a lot, and 'Uncle James' became the children's hero. He always brought them presents, and remembered their birthdays. He used to tell them stories, show them card-tricks, carry them pick-a-back around the garden. People who saw him with them used to think what a splendid father he would make. He also admired faithful wives (indeed, deep down, they were the only women that he *did* admire). This was one reason why he fell in love with Maddox's wife, Regine.

Soon after his arrival he had attempted to seduce her. She had been perfectly good-natured about it, even taking care to protect his precious vanity.

'Darling James,' she said, kissing his hand before replacing it where it belonged, 'you're too good-looking for me now. A few years ago it would have been different, but now. . . '

Bond tried to replace his hand. She firmly repelled it.

'Besides, I'd probably just fall in love with you, and think what trouble that would cause.'

And so, instead of sex, they dined at Maxim's.

Within a day or two, Bond had convinced himself he was in love with her. The role suited him. It did not stop him chasing other women, rather the reverse. Depending on his mood he would be seeking consolation or revenge. But he had an air of sadness now which was irresistible – to everyone except Regine.

She remained resolutely what Bond used to call his *'Princesse lointaine'*. They were friends. She used to recommend him books to read and remind him when he needed a haircut. He bought her scent and told her all about his different women. It was the sort of friendship that would have gone on for ever – but for her husband.

There was something ironical about an old rake like Maddox becoming jealous of James Bond, especially when Bond was technically quite innocent. Perhaps Maddox understood this, perhaps he knew that mental infidelity was worse than any physical *affaire*. For several months Bond did not realize he knew. Then there was trouble.

Everything went wrong that summer. Bond had been going through one of his periodic hates against the French – their rudeness, narrowness and general meanness. There was a running battle with his concierge. Several assignments had been unsatisfactory, and suddenly Paris seemed impossible – crowded and hot and full of tourists. Maddox had been increasingly irascible. Bond began counting the days off to his holiday. Maddox was very much concerned with trouble in Algiers. The local nationalists were already starting their campaign against the French: the French were getting worried. There had been small-scale riots, bomb attacks and killings. Maddox, and many like him, saw them as portents of disaster round the corner. Much of the trouble was that already it was clear that the local *gendarmes* in Algiers could not contain the unrest. There had been raids on banks owned by the Syndicate. Several employees had been killed, but there had been no arrests. Then, in July, the manager of the main branch in Oran was gunned down and several million francs were stolen.

It was a disturbing case, seeming to create a pattern for the future. If it went unchecked there would be more killings, more armed robberies to finance the violence and subversion. Maddox was much concerned and visited Oran in person. When he returned he discussed it with James Bond.

'The *gendarmerie* are useless. None of them realize that

this is war. The only answer is attack.'

Bond was surprised at Maddox's vehemence – it was unlike him. Bond asked what he meant.

'I mean that we must teach the Nationalists a lesson. In Oran I found out who was behind the raid – a man called El Bezir – a Communist and head of the local F.L.N. commando.'

'You told the police?'

Maddox began laughing. Bond felt suddenly uneasy.

'The police? James, you're getting softer than I thought. Since when have the police in Algeria done anything? I want you in Oran. I've a man there called Descaux. He has his orders and you'll work with him. I want this El Bezir man dealt with.'

For once Bond tried to duck the mission, but Maddox was insistent. When Bond reminded him that he was due to go on holiday, Maddox exploded. Finally, reluctantly, Bond said that he would go.

In fact he liked Oran. At this time it was relatively peaceful, and the city with its port, its great bay and the mixture of the French and Arab worlds was still part of the old North Africa. It had great atmosphere and charm. French legionaries from the Sahara lounged in the outdoor cafes of the Rue Maréchal Lyautey, sipping their Pernods and smoking their issue Bastos cigarettes. The Arab city of the kasbah seemed to Bond part of the oriental world that he remembered from his boyhood. The only drawback to the mission was Descaux.

Bond met him the first evening he arrived, and disliked him instantly. He was a strutting, loud-mouthed little man with thick eyebrows meeting above the nose. He talked a lot about 'teaching the blacks a lesson' and soon made it clear to Bond that this meant assassinating El Bezir. He had it all worked out. There was an empty shop beneath the flat where El Bezir was living. They would drive in at night, plant half a hundredweight of gelignite beneath the flat, set a short time fuse, then drive off.

'You'll kill a lot of innocent Algerians,' said Bond.

'Innocent Algerians – are there any?' said Descaux.

Bond's first reaction to Descaux was to fly back to Paris and resign. He was sickened at the idea of such squalid murder. Then he realized this was impossible. However he behaved now, he was implicated. Descaux would go ahead without him; when the gelignite exploded Bond would still be responsible for the deaths that followed. Suddenly he realized that Maddox must have known the situation when he sent him to Oran: then, for the first time, Bond felt angry.

He had one hope, a man called Fauchet. Bond had known him briefly in the war when he was with the French Resistance. Now he was in Oran as head of the intelligence branch of the French *Sûreté*. He was a barrel of a man with small, shrewd eyes – a Corsican and very tough. Bond called him that night and asked certain questions. Fauchet promised the answers by next morning.

Bond realized the need for caution. Descaux was armed, and obviously suspicious. Next morning, when he called on Fauchet, he discovered why.

'I've been on to Paris for you,' said the Corsican. 'They rang me back an hour ago. Quite a character, this friend of yours.'

'They know him then?' said Bond.

'I'll say. Descaux's an alias of course. Real name is Grautz – German father, Belgian mother. During the war he worked with the Vichy secret police, and for the Gestapo. There's still a lot against him on the file – torture of suspects, murder of hostages, alleged involvement in the mass executions at Nantes in 1943.'

Bond looked grim. 'And this man El Bezir?'

'A nationalist, an intellectual, but something of a moderate.'

'Any connection with the bank raid?'

'Absolutely none. We've got two men inside who've just confessed. We've even got the money.'

Bond felt that he was beginning to understand.

'What about this man Descaux?' said Fauchet. 'We'd better pull him in before there's trouble.'

'No,' said James Bond. 'Leave him to me.'

Bond knew the cheap hotel where Descaux was staying. There was a garage at the rear. He had no difficulty entering, and in the old Citroën van he found the gelignite, the timing apparatus Descaux had boasted of. It was a primitive affair, but certainly sufficient to destroy a building. Bond was examining it when Descaux entered, with a gun.

Bond could have shot him first. He didn't, because he had other plans and there were things he needed to find out. Descaux disarmed him, tied him up – the knots were very tight – and then, methodically and lovingly, beat him up. Again Bond could have stopped him, but again he didn't. There was no other way of getting him to talk. Then, finally, when Bond's face was pulped and his body limp from kicking, Descaux stopped – the orgy over.

'That was on orders from your boss,' he said.

Bond mumbled some reply.

'He really hates you. Still, you've yourself to blame, you stupid bastard. Playing around with his wife like that. You should have known better with a man like Maddox.'

Bond stiffened. Up to that moment he had never guessed the truth. Now that he did, everything was clear. Maddox had simply used the El Bezir affair to get even with him. The fact that the Algerian was innocent didn't matter. Maddox wanted Bond destroyed – and didn't mind how.

'He's got it all worked out,' said Descaux gloatingly. 'You're going to take the rap for tonight's little caper. When our black friends are blasted to their Maker the evidence will point to you. He's a clever little man, your Mr Maddox. He's seen that I'm completely in the clear, but as for you the evidence would guillotine the President of France.'

Descaux opened the garage doors and climbed aboard the Citroën. Bond heard him backing out, then listened for the bang. He had already fixed the timing apparatus on the bomb and it exploded, as he knew it would, three minutes later. Descaux was killed, a lot of glass was shattered, and it took several hours to fill in the crater in the road. No one else was hurt.

But as for Bond the bitterness went deep. Fauchet looked after him, and helped clear up the case. Bond made sure that nothing backfired on Maddox. Bitter though he was, he couldn't have that on his conscience. Instead he cabled his resignation to Paris and asked a friend to close his flat and ship the Bentley back to Aunt Charmian. A few days later, when his face was healed, he left for Kenya. He was through with Europe.

For several months he stayed in Kenya. During this time he worked for an American who made wild-life films for television. Bond enjoyed it, but there was trouble with a woman. Nairobi was a small place. Bond moved again – first to Mombasa, and then, when the money started to run out, on to the Seychelles. Living was cheaper there. Girls were easy. Nothing worried him. He stayed here several months, bumming a living as he could. It was restful to have reached rock bottom and to be free of loyalties and duties. No one could use him or betray him. Bond was content.

It is hard to know how long he might have stayed here. Places like the Seychelles, dead-end paradises, seem to be full of potential James Bonds. For a while he helped a man prospect for treasure, then he worked for an American millionaire who was searching for rare fish. Fleming retold this episode, changing the time and names and certain key facts, in a short story which he called *The Hildebrand Rarity*.

It was a gruesome business. The millionaire was killed – to this day full responsibility for his death remains uncertain – and, for some while, Bond lived with his widow. She was rich. She loved him. And as Bond says, 'I was past caring what I was by then. If I was a gigolo, at least I was paying for my keep.'

Then, once again, chance intervened; Ian Fleming arrived in the Seychelles. He was travelling for the *Sunday Times* and writing about the buried treasure of an eighteenth-century pirate. He said he was appalled to see how Bond was living. No one should waste their talents and their life like this. They talked a lot together and Fleming said that during the time that Bond had been away, there had been changes in the Secret Service. Why not come back?

Suddenly Bond found that he was missing London, missing the old life, and the excitement he had known. It was too tempting to resist. When Fleming travelled back to London, Bond came with him.

8

007 is Born

Bond had enjoyed talking about the Seychelles. Now that he had dealt with the scandal of the Washington affair he could apparently relax and during these few days we had slipped into one of his inevitable routines. We would meet every evening after dinner. Sometimes he brought Honey with him, sometimes not. (To my surprise, the two of them appeared to be becoming quite a cosy couple. I wondered if Bond realized.) And then, without much prompting, he would begin to talk. He liked to have his bottle of Wild Turkey bourbon, and his cigarettes (I was relieved to see that he was off the de-nicotined Virginians and back on the Morlands Specials – one more good sign). He was becoming more precise and less self-conscious, particularly now that he began explaining how he made his prodigal's return to the Secret Service. It was an ironic story and he told it well.

I had not realized the role that Ian Fleming played in this. I knew, of course, that long after he left Naval Intelligence for journalism, Fleming had maintained his contacts with the secret-service world. What I didn't know was their extent, and how he acted as an unofficial talent scout for the department. I can see now that this would have been a role that suited him. He knew the top brass of the Secret Service personally, M. included, and the range of his acquaintanceship was quite phenomenal. He was a dedicated human catalyst, a great one for knowing exactly the right man for any job. This was one reason for his effortless success as a journalist – I can remember how he always knew the one key person for a story when he was writing his weekly column on the *Sunday Times*. He obviously used his talents in the same way for the Secret Service – particularly with Bond, although it must have taken all his skill and tact to organize.

One of the most exclusive dining clubs in London is the so-called Twinsnakes Club. Fleming has mentioned it, much to the chagrin of some of its more straightlaced members. It meets once a year, generally at the Connaught Hotel, and consists of the most distinguished members, past and present, of the British Secret Service. They dine extremely well and, when the port is circulating, one of their members reads a paper. The standard is traditionally high. In the past their numbers have included Buchan and Charles Morgan, as well as the heads of the profession. The famous story of *The Man Who Never Was* originated with a paper which was read here. This year it was Fleming's turn. He chose for his subject, 'The ideal agent – a study in character'.

Fleming described a man called X. He was in his early thirties – good-looking, something of a womanizer, adept at games, tough, dedicated, socially acceptable. He had sufficient glamour to take him anywhere, and was the perfect man of the world. As Fleming said, 'The grey-faced, anonymous operators that are now in fashion have their limitations. How can they hope to penetrate the topmost echelons of politics and commerce and society where the decisions matter?'

But at the same time, X was enough of an outsider to maintain complete integrity. He was what Fleming called 'his own man' – slightly cynical, entirely without social or political ambitions, and, of course, unmarried. 'A red-blooded, resolutely heterosexual bachelor,' was how Fleming put it.

In the discussion there was general agreement with Fleming's thesis – most of the argument was whether a man like X could possibly exist. M. in particular seemed convinced that he could not. Fleming heard him out, and then said quietly, 'Oh but he does. You've even met him. His name is Bond.'

Even then Fleming must have done a lot of delicate persuading behind the scenes, for M. had not forgotten Washington. But two days later M.'s secretary, the cool Miss Moneypenny, rang Bond to say that M. would like to lunch with him at Blades. Slightly puzzled, Bond accepted, and, soon after, Fleming rang. He admitted having fixed the lunch, but said that he thought Bond should 'make his number with the old fire-eater'.

'I've had a word with him, and I think I've cleared up that misunderstanding over Washington. You have to make allowances you know. M.'s a Victorian. He was married – they were quite devoted – and ever since she died he's been faithful to her memory. Rather touching, but it means he's sometimes sensitive about sex and marriage.'

'You're telling me,' said Bond.

'But he's a fascinating character. Extremely complex. Works like mad, of course, and a real hard nut. And yet a marvellous man to work for once you know him. Those who do won't hear a word against him.'

'I'll believe you,' Bond replied.

'Oh, and a few words of warning. This time, when you meet him, don't admit to knowing any languages too well. M. has two phobias in life – men with beards and people who are fluent in foreign languages. On no account call him "Sir".'

'I wouldn't dream of it,' said Bond.

'And let him choose the wine.'

'Oh God,' said Bond.

*   *   *

It was uncanny to be back at Blades. Since that evening when he lost £80 to Bunny Kendrick, Bond had allowed his membership to lapse. But Prizeman, the hall porter, remembered him, welcoming him back as if it had all been yesterday.

'Commander Bond. Nice to see you. Sir Miles is expecting you in the dining room.'

Whatever qualms Bond had at meeting M. again were lulled by the prospect of that splendid room. Here Robert Adam had approached perfection – his architecture still embodied an ideal of eighteenth-century calm and certainty. Against such a background the grimy subterfuges of the secret-service world appeared unthinkable. It was even hard for Bond to think of this solid gentlemanly figure in the dark blue suit as the antagonist of cruel and dedicated men in Moscow and Peking waging a war that never ceased.

M. was genial. The eyes were twinkling now. Reluctantly, Bond had to admit that he had a certain charm; he talked about his recent salmon fishing on the Test.

'A Scot like you must know more about salmon than I do,' said M.

'Haven't fished for years,' said Bond.

'Oh no, of course. Golf's your game.'

Bond nodded. Somebody, probably the Chief of Staff, had been giving M. a swift run-down on his hobbies – Bond wondered how much else he knew. They chatted briefly about golf, although M.'s ignorance about the game was evident. Bond thought that, after all, he had a kindly face: if there was such a thing as a typical old-fashioned sailor's face, M. had it.

M. scanned the menu (without spectacles), and ordered soup and steak-and-kidney pie. After the talk of fishing on the Test, Bond was ready for the Club smoked salmon, but at the last moment something told him that it wouldn't be appreciated. He had the same as M.

'And how about a little wine? I'm sure you have some preference.'

But Bond said, no, he'd rather have Sir Miles's choice. M., positively beaming now, ordered the wine waiter to bring out a carafe of his favourite Algerian, 'the old Infuriator of the Fleet, you know' (Bond wondered briefly who else at Blades could possibly have drunk it).

When it arrived M. brushed aside the wine waiter's

suggestion that he ought to taste it. Instead, he filled their glasses, and then drank with gusto.

'I think,' said M. 'it's time that you rejoined us.'

It all seemed very casual, rather as if M. were asking him to renew his membership of Blades.

M. clearly relished steak-and-kidney pie. Bond admired his digestion and the no-nonsense way he piled his plate. Most men of his age, he thought, would have been worrying about an ulcer or their arteries.

'Fleming's not been giving you any idea what we have in mind for you?' said M.

Bond felt the steely eyes were watching carefully. He shook his head.

'As you have probably gathered, things have changed a lot since you've been away. The so-called "Secret War" we're fighting has been hotting up, in all directions. The opposition keep us on our toes, and we have had to regroup accordingly.'

Bond nodded. There was a silence broken only by the champing of M.'s jaws.

'It's an unpleasant fact of life that in our business we sometimes have to kill our enemies. The opposition makes no bones about it. I take it that you've heard of Smersh?'

'*Smiert Spionam*', said Bond.

M. glanced up quickly.

'Quite,' he said. 'Well as we know, for two years now they've run their training school outside a place called Irkutsk. They have a special course in what they are pleased to call "liquidation". They also have a section specially devised to cope with all assignments which have a so-called "assassination element". You'll have to read the dossiers on it back at Headquarters, but the point is that this is a threat which we must face. We can't be squeamish. A few months ago I formed a section of our own to deal with it. It's called the double-O section. I think it might suit you.'

'You mean,' said Bond, 'that you want me to be part of our own murder squad?'

'Nothing of the sort,' said M. gruffly. 'That may be the

way they do things over there. We don't, thank God. But we must be prepared. This is a crisis, and we're fighting for survival. We need men like you.'

Bond had promised to let Fleming know how the lunch went. Accordingly he went along to his office in Grays Inn Road to tell him.

Fleming's office was a funny place, more like a down-at-heel country solicitor's than an important London journalist's – partitioned off with reeded glass, an anteroom outside with Fleming's black felt hat, briefcase, and a copy of the *New York Review of Books* on the small table.

Bond told him of the 00 section.

Fleming nodded. 'Yes, I know about it. Great news.'

'But I can't take it.'

'Can't take it?'

'I've had enough of killing.'

'But, my dear chap. This is ridiculous. You're being offered an élite position in the top rank of the Secret Service – something most agents would give their back teeth for. How can you think to turn it down?'

'I've told you.'

'And so you're willing to go on with the sort of wasted life you were living in the Seychelles? Bumming along, living from hand to mouth unless you find a fat rich widow you can marry. James, I hate to see you living in this way, it's no life for you. This is one thing you do superlatively well. You must continue. If you don't you're sunk.'

And so Bond finally rejoined the Secret Service. Thanks to M.'s interest he was earmarked from the start for service in the 00 section, but it was soon made clear to him that he had to earn this status. His record was impressive but he had to prove that he was still up to scratch. He also had to train in the most gruelling school for secret agents in the world. He had a lot to learn if he would catch up on the years that he had been away. But it was reassuring to be back. Once he had made the decision to return, he soon forgot his doubts, and, for the first time since the war, he had a sense of purpose and a job that he believed in. He also felt relieved at being back inside what Fleming called, 'the warm womb of the Secret Service'. Loner though he was, Bond needed the security of an organization and a settled context for his life.

He had three months of hectic training – three months in which he worked harder than ever in his life before. First came the tests of his physique and basic skill in combat. Most of these took place in the extensive cellars under the 'Universal Export' building by the park beneath the remorseless eyes of the world's top experts in human stress and self-defence. At first he was stiff and felt his lack of training, but he knew his body could absorb the work, and within days he was feeling fitter than he ever had. The doctors testing him passed him as 'fit for all assignments'. Then came the urgent days on the ranges checking him out for weaponry – small arms, machine-guns, rockets and the diverse tools of his appalling trade. He spent three afternoons with Richmall the armourer choosing the private weapon he would carry. The ·32 Beretta was his own choice; its compactness, neatness and rates of fire appealed to him in preference to more cumbersome automatics. As Richmall said, 'The main thing is to have a weapon you're at home with.' Bond agreed.

Bond's mind was tested, and then trained as well. The preliminary tests were frightening and meant to be: periods of solitude to check his breaking point, sessions of interrogation by the hardest experts in the game, and, finally, the so-called 'torture chamber' where for three days and nights a succession of cold, faceless men set out to break him. The purpose was to discover his 'pain threshold' and then fix his 'co-efficient of resistance'. Both were extraordinarily high.

After the first month, the emphasis was changed, and Bond spent several weeks at a house near Basingstoke learning the basic new technology of the secret war. There was a whole new expertise to master: cyphers and cypher machines, systems of drop-outs and controls, planning and methodology. The gadgetry of espionage was now formidable with electronics and computers on the scene.

During these weeks, Bond must have owed a lot to his inheritance from Andrew Bond. His mechanical aptitude was high; so was his mental stamina and concentration. He had the sort of brain that could absorb practical detail swiftly and, once again, his grades were excellent.

Then followed further weeks in London, weeks during which Bond stayed at an hotel in Bloomsbury and went before a succession of Civil Service boards. A few of them amused him – most of them were tedious, but as Fleming told him when he saw him, 'The Civil Service is a sacred institution. You mustn't hope to hurry it'. Bond was patient, and was finally officially informed that he was appointed as a Grade V Civil Servant with attachment to the Ministry of Defence – normal pay-scale (£1,700 p.a. rising by increments to £2,150 maximum), pension benefits, and certain allowances 'in the event of active service'.

Then and only then was he given his own permanent niche in 'the Secret Service Vatican' as he describes the Regents Park Headquarters – a small, cream-painted fifth-floor office with a Grade V Civil Service dark brown carpet, a Grade IV Civil Service desk, and a shared secretary, the delectable Miss Una Trueblood. When Bond was given his official pass he felt that he had earned it.

Then came a period of virtual idleness. He had had no word from M., nor for that matter had he seen him since their lunch at Blades, but he began to settle in. It was a strange place. There was a total ban on talking 'shop' of any kind and also a clear taboo on any sort of gossip with his colleagues. Not that he saw many of them. He was aware of the inhabitants of other offices around him. From time to time he saw them – in the corridor, or eating in the staff canteen. They would nod as if they knew him, and usually that was all. The one exception was M.'s Chief of Staff, Bill Tanner. He was a humorous, wary man who seemed to guard the secrets of the whole department. Bond sometimes lunched with him. They found they had a common interest in cars – Tanner was proud of his elderly Invicta – and a common enemy in the department's head of administration,

Paymaster Captain Troop, R.N. Retd.

Fleming, who had had his own battles with the Paymaster during his time in N.I.D., described him, cruelly but accurately, as 'the office tyrant and bugbear' of the Secret Service. Tanner's description was less charitable, and one of his pastimes was to bait the wretched man unmercifully. Bond soon joined in, compiling lengthy memoranda over soap and paper-clips and typewriter ribbons. It passed the time.

More important for Bond's future was the discovery now of his 'comfortable flat in the plane-treed square of the Kings Road', a stroke of luck for which he was to be everlastingly grateful. It was some years now since he had lived in the flat which Fleming had found him in Lincoln Street, but he felt his London roots were here and wouldn't have considered any other part of London. The flat was at number 30, Wellington Square. It was on two floors, and his first reaction was that it was far too big for him. But his Uncle Ian had died recently: to his surprise, Bond had inherited nearly £5,000, and suddenly it seemed sensible to spend the money on the one luxury which Bond had never known – a comfortable establishment in London.

He asked Aunt Charmian's advice – she was the one woman on whom he could rely for a disinterested opinion. She was all for it, 'but who'll look after you?' she said.

Bond hadn't thought of that.

'You'll have to have a woman,' said Aunt Charmian.

Bond groaned.

'I know just the person. Remember May McGrath? She's been working for your Uncle Gregor ever since your grandfather died. The other day I heard that she can't stand it any more, and, frankly, I don't blame her. She's no cook, I know, but she's a conscientious body. Perhaps I'll write to her.' And so James Bond acquired both a flat and 'his treasured Scottish housekeeper'. Life was quite definitely looking up.

He gave a lot of thought to the flat once he had signed the lease. It was typical of him to plan it all minutely. There was a lot of work to do. When it was finished the whole place reflected Bond's personality.

It was a genuine bachelor establishment, for Bond had virtually ruled out marriage now that he was working for the Secret Service. Also it had to run like clockwork, whether he was there or not. May had her private quarters on the lower floor, next to the spare bedroom. Bond had a stylish sitting-room on the floor above with two long windows facing the square. His bedroom adjoined it, the kitchen was behind.

Like le Corbusier's definition of an ideal house, this was quite simply Bond's 'machine to live in'. The arrangements and the décor were extremely Bond. The sitting-room was positively Spartan – certainly no female hand had put its gentle touch here: dark blue chesterfield and curtains, battleship-grey fitted carpet, green-shaded reading lamp and, on the walls, a somewhat faded set of 'Riding School' prints Bond had once acquired in Vienna. He didn't care for them particularly, but as he told Aunt Charmian, 'they are the only pictures I possess and they fill the space as well as any others.' As Fleming noted, there was no television.

The kitchen was altogether homelier. Long and narrow, 'like the galley of an expensive yacht', it had been carefully planned by Bond, who took a secret pleasure in equipping it. There was a lot of stainless steel and fitted-cupboard space, an air extractor, a large Frigidaire, complete with deep-freeze cabinet, and an elaborate drinks cupboard. He took some trouble finding his dark blue and gold dinner service. It was Minton, and its simple opulence appealed to Bond. Once he had set up the kitchen Bond took great care telling May exactly how it was to run – 'Breakfast is most important. I lunch at the office, and generally I dine out too. When I'm at home I'll eat some sort of snack, unless there's company. If there is I'll take care of that myself. Please make sure that there's always a supply of fresh unsalted Jersey butter, whole-wheat bread, smoked salmon, steak and caviare.'

This was not just a reflection of Bond's basic taste in food. He was remembering May's limitations as a cook. As Aunt Charmian said, 'May is more Glen Orchy than Cordon

Bleu.' But he did find that she could organize his breakfast with the absolute precision he demanded – the two large cups of de Bry coffee brewed in the Chemex percolator, the jars of strawberry jam, the Cooper's vintage Oxford, and the Fortnum's honey. He also soon discovered an unsuspected virtue in the worthy May. She was the only woman he had ever known capable of boiling an egg exactly the time required for perfection – three and a third minutes.

The one place in the flat where Bond did allow himself some self-indulgence was in furnishing the bedroom. He bought a king-sized double bed from Harrods – 'if you like women, cheap bedding is a false economy' – blue and gold wallpaper, and a thick, fitted Wilton. But one of his more perceptive mistresses described the room as 'just like a boy's bedroom, with its knick-knacks and a place for everything'. On the dressing table was a pair of silver-backed brushes that belonged to his father, and by the head two photographs of women – his mother and Marthe de Brandt.

Bond's early efforts at home-making were interrupted by a summons from the Chief of Staff. It was July. The plane trees in the square were thick with leaves, and Bond was feeling restless.

'Hope you're not planning to seduce anyone important during the next week or so. M.'s on the warpath,' said the Chief of Staff.

Now that James Bond was meeting M. again he felt nervous: as he waited in his anteroom he thought about the power M. wielded and how this whole lethal complex of the Secret Service rested upon him. 'Hideous responsibility – rather him than me!' thought Bond. The signal light above the door glowed red. Bond entered.

M. was benevolent at first, congratulating Bond on his performance during training.

'I'm more than pleased. We discussed you at this morning's meeting of department heads. It was agreed that you should be seconded to the 00 section. The 007 number has been vacant for some time. From now on it will be your official code name in the Service.'

Bond felt a certain triumph, but before he could thank M., the old sailor made a gesture of impatience.

'Now down to work. It's high time you began to earn your living, 007. Do you know Jamaica?'

'During the war my ship called there briefly – I always wanted to go back.'

'Well, now's your chance. I want you out there straight away. Frankly, I'm worried. We've been receiving very odd reports from our head of station there – a man called Gutteridge.'

'Odd, in what way?' asked Bond.

M. put his fist against his chin and frowned. How could he explain to Bond that he was personally concerned for Gutteridge? He knew the effect the tropics had upon a man. He also knew better than accept second-hand reports about an agent's drinking habits, but there was more to it than that. M. liked the man – they had served together for some while before the war. When somebody like Gutteridge began to send the kind of reports he had been lately, it was his duty to investigate. But it was difficult to explain to Bond that his first assignment with the 00 section might be no more than checking on a head of station's drinking problem.

'Chief of Staff will let you have Gutteridge's reports for the last few months. I suggest that you familiarize yourself with them before you go. I have a hunch that something's going on – something that could be very dangerous. I'd like you to prove me wrong.'

There was a pause as M. began searching for his matches; when he found them, Bond waited as he lit his pipe. Bond was reminded of the garden refuse burning in the park outside.

'One further thing, 007; while you are there, please make allowances for Gutteridge. He has his peculiarities like all of us.'

Bill Tanner seemed amused when Bond described the interview with M.

'Peculiarities – I'll say. I wondered if you'd get this job. Rather you than me, although I wouldn't mind a week or two in Jamaica, even with Gutteridge thrown in.'

Ever since the German booby-trap he was defusing had exploded in his face, the ex-Sapper colonel had suffered with his health; periodically the surgeons still excavated pieces of shrapnel from his body. Lately the sheer pressure of work in the department had been building up, and Bond could see how much this tense young man required a break. As Chief of Staff he was harder worked than anyone in the department.

'What's wrong with Gutteridge?'

Tanner pulled a face.

'Frankly, I'm sick to death of him. The man's a lush. He's been around for years, but just because he happened to have served with M. before the war, he's sacrosanct. And *I* have to deal with him, not M. Just work your way through these and you'll see what I mean.'

Tanner reached behind him for a large, untidy file. It was marked 'Station K – Top Secret'. He handed it to Bond, and shook his head.

'Read 'em and then do me a favour. Just put them you know where and pull the chain.'

That evening was one of those rare occasions when Bond ate at home, entirely alone.

May seemed concerned when he announced that he would be quite happy with a tin of soup and scrambled eggs.

'Ye'd be feelin' a'right?' she said.

Spencer Tracey was on at the Essoldo and she had been looking forward for some time to seeing him. Bond knew this quite well and, when he had teased her sufficiently, insisted on scrambling the eggs himself. Bond had a range of what he called 'basic survival cookery' which ensured that he could always manage on his own yet eat, if not in luxury, at least with a certain style. He felt this was essential for any bachelor. His favourite included *steak au poivre* (his secret here was to use Madras black pepper from Fortnums, leaving the raw steak in it overnight), kidneys in red wine with parsley, grilled country sausages from Paxtons, and, of course, scrambled eggs. His *oeufs brouillés James Bond* were cooked slowly and mixed with twice the amount of butter he had ever seen a woman use. Before serving, he liked to add a generous dollop of double cream.

This was what he had now, after a tin of Jackson's lobster soup. He ate off a tray in the sitting-room. It would have been hard to tell which he enjoyed more – the food or his self-sufficiency. When he had finished he had a generous glass of bourbon, lit a Morlands Special and, by the solitary light of his green-shaded reading lamp, got down to reading Gutteridge's report.

He soon saw what had upset the Chief of Staff. Few secret-service field reports rank as great literature, but Bond had never read anything as long-winded and bizarre as these. His first reaction was that the Chief of Staff was right – Gutteridge must have entered his decline. He had a recurrent obsession with the politics of the Jamaican labour unions. Nothing wrong with that. But it was obvious that, mixed up with this, poor Gutteridge also had a major persecution complex. His particular concern seemed to be that Communists were infiltrating the main unions. Much of his information was convincing – detailed accounts of union leaders who had been terrorized into changing their allegiance, stories of intercepted messages from Havana, estimates of how funds from Moscow had been deployed to purchase votes.

But, at the same time, Gutteridge included details of a conspiracy whose major aim was his destruction. There was a so-called 'Goddess Kull' who cropped up on a number of occasions. He was none too coherent here, but she was described as 'the incarnation of all evil' and also as 'the great destroyer'. She had her followers and Gutteridge seemed to think that they were after him. One report described how Kull's devotees were howling for him in the night.

It was well past midnight before Bond had finished reading. By any standards the reports were odd and his first reaction – like the Chief of Staff's – was that what Gutteridge needed was a transfer, preferably to a clinic. But as he prepared for bed he wondered. There was something eerily convincing about these reports, and alone there in the flat Bond could feel something of that sense of fear of the strange man who had written them in the far-away Jamaican night.

Tomorrow Bond would be seeing him. It would be interesting to find out who was right – M. or the Chief of Staff – and, as Bond checked his Beretta and fixed a hundred rounds of special ammunition into the concealed compartment of his suitcase, he wondered how many of them he would be firing in the line of duty.

*   *   *

Bond reached Jamaica in the evening, which is the best time to swoop down upon that gold and dark green island. After the cold and regimented gloom of Heathrow, full of that passive misery which brings out the worst in our island race, Bond felt the first joy of the tropics. Kingston, that wonderful, rachitic city, seemed even noisier and smellier than he remembered. He passed the bar, Louelle's, where he had knocked out the U.S. petty officer, and smiled to himself. It seemed a long, long time ago – what a clean-cut young fellow he had been then in his lieutenant's uniform, and how simple life had seemed.

Miss Trueblood had originally booked him into the Wayside Inn, an air-conditioned luxury American hotel, but at the last moment Bond remembered Durban's, once the most fashionable hotel on the island and now a splendid relic of the old Jamaica. Bond loved its enormous rooms, its old-style bar and its verandahs, and secretly enjoyed the feeling that it would not last. He had cabled Gutteridge to meet him here.

Gutteridge was late. When he did stagger in, Bond could only wonder how he had survived so long. The once good-looking face was red and puffy, the well cut suit was stained and baggy at the knees. Bond could not bear drunks, but there was something about Gutteridge that roused his sympathy. This was how secret-service life could burn you out:

171

in Gutteridge he could almost see a mirror image of himself one day. When Gutteridge suggested they should have a drink, Bond agreed. He even forced himself to listen sympathetically as the man rambled on – about his money troubles and the wife who left him and the slights he had to bear from other British residents.

'The island's being ruined fast, my friend. As for the British, we're right down the drain. Everyone with half a brain must know what's happening, everyone that is except the idiots in Government House – and no one cares.'

Gutteridge drained his glass, but now the drink was sobering him. His rheumy eyes were bright.

'I care though. It's my job to care, and I won't let them get away with it. This business of the unions – I keep warning M.'

'That's why I'm here,' said Bond.

'Listen,' said Gutteridge. He grew suddenly conspiratorial, peering around the empty bar, then drew his cane armchair closer still to Bond. 'There's a man called Gomez – he's directing the campaign. He's Cuban. Used to be a colonel in Batista's secret police. God knows how many men he killed – then he switched sides, trained for two years in Moscow, and now he's here. He works entirely by terror. Jamaicans have opposed him and been murdered. Horribly. Now all he has to do is threaten. No one will talk about him, so the police are powerless. But he already virtually controls the island through the unions. Soon there will be a blood-bath. Then . . . ' Gutteridge raised his hands then let them fall limply into his lap.

The man might be a drunk, but Bond found him convincing.

'And what about the Goddess Kull?' he asked.

Gutteridge smiled wanly.

'Ah. You've been reading my reports. That's good. She is this man Gomez's creation. I've told you he is a clever devil. He knows the people of the Caribbean and has studied all their superstitions and their fears. He has been smart enough to link his reign of terror with the cult figure of Kull,

172

the destroyer. The murders have apparently been done in her name, or by her followers. They have not been pretty.'

'But who is Kull?' asked Bond.

'She appears in many local legends. One of her names is the Black Widow, after the spider of that name who kills her mate by having him make love to her. It's a recurring theme in countless primitive cultures and clearly draws on a universal male fear. Anthropologists have called it, I believe, the *vagina dentata*, the toothed vagina.'

Bond poured himself another drink, but Gutteridge, cold sober now, was obviously enjoying his pedantic role.

'A fascinating subject.'

'I suppose it is,' said Bond.

'Elwin has written of it at length among the Assamese and there have been familiar studies from South America and New Guinea. The origin lies in the primitive male dread of the dominating female. But it invariably takes the form of a Goddess whose devouring genitals destroy her victims in the act of love.'

'You have been threatened too?' said Bond.

Gutteridge nodded.

'Several times. Gomez wants to keep me quiet, but I don't think he's too concerned with me. Just at the moment he has bigger fish to fry.'

'Like what?' said Bond.

'Now that he's got the unions, he's turning to the employers, particularly the rich ones. During the last few days several have been threatened by the Goddess. Either they do exactly as they're told, or Kull will deal with them.'

'But that's ridiculous,' said Bond. 'It's one thing to terrorize uneducated poor Jamaicans. It's quite another to try it with people who can defend themselves.'

'You think so?' said Gutteridge quietly. 'I suggest that first thing tomorrow you call a man called Da Silva. Mention my name. He's one of the biggest merchants in Jamaica, and he's an educated man – Oxford, I think. Go and see him, and then ask him the same question.'

Da Silva was a small neat man with heavy spectacles.

Bond put him in his early forties. He was of Portuguese descent. His people had come to Jamaica originally to trade but had settled in the eighteenth century; now they were part of the commercial aristocracy of the island. He was sharp, well informed and spoke with a faint American accent. When Bond rang him, he immediately suggested lunch, and picked him up from the hotel in a pale blue Chevrolet sedan. As they drove out from Kingston then forked right to take the panoramic road towards Blue Mountain, Bond could appreciate the splendour of the island – the heady lushness of the big plantations, the rich houses in the hills and the long blue vistas to the far horizon.

Da Silva's house lay at the far end of a drive of flowering casuarina. Almost despite himself Bond was impressed by so much luxury – the low white house, the shaded pool, the emerald lawns fragrant with hibiscus and bougainvillea. Da Silva suggested they should swim and afterwards, as they lay by the pool sipping iced daiquiris, he introduced Bond to his wife, a deep-bosomed, long-legged blonde from Maryland. For a while they chatted, about the current crop of tourists to the island, about New York and London and several friends they found they had in common. There was a faint pause in the conversation.

'Tell me,' said Bond. 'Who is the Goddess Kull?'

It would have been hard to find two human beings more different than Gutteridge and Da Silva, but Bond realized that they had one thing in common – fear. Da Silva's wife looked anxiously at her husband, then rose and said, 'I must be seeing to the lunch, darling. If you and Commander Bond would please excuse me.' As she walked off Bond thought that, scared or not, Da Silva was a lucky man.

'How much did Gutteridge tell you?' said Da Silva. Bond repeated the gist of last night's conversation. Da Silva listened gravely and then nodded when he finished.

'He's done his homework thoroughly, for once, and he's absolutely right. It's hard to know exactly who's involved, for nobody will talk. Men who have worked for me for years suddenly stop work without an explanation. One of my foremen was murdered just last month. I've done my best to fight against this evil and to carry on. Now I'm not sure.'

'Why not?' said Bond.

'Because I've just received a summons to the Goddess Kull myself.'

There, amid so much luxury and peace, Bond was inclined to laugh. It was one thing to imagine simple Jamaican labourers being terrorized by this primeval cult. But for a sophisticated, wealthy man like Da Silva to be taking it so seriously was quite different. Bond told him so. Da Silva shrugged.

'This is a funny island. And remember that I've lived here all my life. Things happen here that no outsider would believe, and recently we've been collecting all the backwash of the political upheavals on the mainland. We're living on a knife-edge.'

'A gilded one,' said Bond, looking across the lawns towards the house.

'But just as dangerous.'

Over lunch Da Silva and his wife discussed the threat with Bond. She was emphatically in favour of leaving the island.

'It's too risky staying. It'll be hard to give up the house, but at least we'll have our lives and we can start again in England or the States.'

Da Silva, on the other hand, obviously hated the idea of abandoning everything he owned.

'It would be cowardice,' he said.

'Cowardice is sometimes sensible,' replied his wife.

Bond asked about the form the threat had taken.

'My invitation to the Goddess Kull? I'll show you,' said Da Silva. From his desk he produced an envelope addressed to him and bearing a Kingston postmark. Bond opened it. Inside, on a page torn from an exercise-book, someone had scrawled in red ink:

Da Silva. Her Reverend Majesty and thrice-feared Goddess Kull desires you and calls you to her sacred bed on Friday the 18th at midnight. You will arrive alone at 307

175

Tarleton Street. Tell nobody and fail not. Kull is insatiable for those that she desires.

There was no signature, but at the bottom of the page was printed the obscene symbol of the *vagina dentata*.

'Charming,' said Bond. 'And where is Tarleton Street?'

'In the middle of the Kingston red-light district. 307 is a night club known as "the Stud-Box", but the whole area is a warren of bordellos, massage parlours and God knows what. You remember what Ian Fleming wrote about the stews of Kingston – they've been there for centuries and "provide for every known amorous permutation and constellation". The police are wary of going near them.'

'A good place to choose as the centre of a terrorist campaign,' said Bond.

Friday was two days away, and Da Silva finally agreed to let Bond know what he decided. In return Bond promised to say nothing. That evening Bond had a call from Gutteridge who was sounding strangely sober. He had discovered something. He would rather not explain over the telephone, but he suggested Bond hired himself a car and drove over to his house first thing next morning. He lived in a beachside bungalow at Montego Bay – he could even offer Bond some breakfast and the swimming was the finest in the world.

So Bond rose early and drove along the switchback coast road with the early morning sun glittering on the unbelievably blue waters of the Caribbean. A faint breeze – what Fleming called the 'Doctor's Wind' – was carrying in the fresh scent of the ocean, and Bond felt Jamaica was the nearest place to paradise that he had ever seen. It was hard to think of fear and cults of darkness in a world like this.

Montego Bay consists of several miles of pure white sand. Gutteridge had a former beachcomber's hut here, a tumbledown place of driftwood and ships' timbers where he often stayed to escape the noise and rush of Kingston. Bond found him pottering about outside, looking quite different from the drunken ruin of the night before. Coffee was bubbling on the stove and Gutteridge produced a full

Jamaican breakfast – mangoes and paw-paws and delicious yams.

'It's like a nature cure,' said Bond. Gutteride grinned.

'The island has its compensations,' he replied.

Over more coffee Bond told him of his visit to Da Silva. When Bond suggested working with the police, Gutteridge shook his head.

'Quite useless. If they make a raid on Tarleton Street, they'll find nothing. The Goddess and her friends will have vanished by the time the Law arrives. She's an elusive deity.'

'What's your suggestion then?' said Bond.

'I'm not sure,' said Gutteridge, 'but you see that white house on the point? I've discovered who is living there. Look through this telescope.'

Hidden behind the canvas awning of the hut, Gutteridge had installed a powerful Nikon telescope with zoom attachment. Bond crouched to look through it. It took a while to adjust and at first all he could see was a stretch of terrace and a small stone jetty.

'Move it to the right,' said Gutteridge.

Bond did. A red-striped mattress moved into vision. There was a woman lying on it.

'Try the zoom,' said Gutteridge.

Bond swung the small milled lever and the woman's face grew towards him. It was a face that he was never to forget. She was a golden-skinned brunette with the almond eyes and full lips of a Eurasian. The nose was small and delicate. So was the chin. She was laughing and Bond realized that she was one of the most beautiful women he had ever seen. She was completely naked, and, as Bond watched, she rolled onto her belly. A fat man with a moustache had been sitting on a canvas chair beside her, smoking a cigar. Bond saw him rise and then start rubbing her with sun oil. She continued laughing, even when he slapped her bottom. Bond could see the sunlight glinting on his rimless spectacles – the face was large and white and round.

'Who's the lucky man?' said Bond.

'That's Gomez,' Gutteridge replied. 'He's just moved in. I

don't know who the girl is. I don't envy her. But our friend Gomez is clearly feeling very confident to take a place like this.'

Bond spent a long time at the telescope. It wasn't often that he had the chance of studying an enemy and he was interested to see that he had several visitors. One was a tall bearded negro with dark spectacles. He and Gomez talked intently for a long time – the girl, Bond was interested to see, took no notice. Nor did she respond to any of Gomez's other friends. They were an uncouth-looking lot. Bond put them down as small-time local criminals and strong-arm men; Gomez appeared to give them orders. From time to time a servant in a crisp white jacket appeared with drinks – for Gomez only. The girl lay silently reading a magazine. Then Gomez finished his cigar, rose from his chair and walked off towards the house. The girl still took no notice. Bond saw her yawn, turn on her back, then slowly oil her thighs, her belly and her splendid breasts. Then she appeared to go to sleep; Bond suddenly desired her.

It was illogical and dangerous – Bond knew that. But there was something in this splendid girl stronger than any logic. Bond carefully surveyed the house. The dark blue shutters were all drawn, the door was shut. There was no sign of life.

'I think,' said Bond to Gutteridge, 'it's time to take a closer look at Señor Gomez's establishment.'

It was approaching midday and the sea lay heavy with the heat. Bond swam slowly, relishing the freshness of the water on his body. The terrace lay a mile or so away and he was careful to swim out and then approach it from the other side. He was quite close before he had a chance to see it clearly. When he did, he saw that the girl had gone. The red-striped mattress was where she had left it, but the terrace was deserted.

Bond paused, uncertain whether to risk going closer. Then, suddenly, one of the upstairs shutters opened. A man leaned out and started shouting and a few seconds later the doors on to the terrace were flung open too. Four or five men rushed out. Gomez was with them. They were shouting, and Gomez had a gun.

Bond ducked instinctively and swam off under water, but when he surfaced and looked back he realized that none of this hullabaloo was meant for him. The shouting continued. Gomez was shooting to the right and when Bond looked he could see why. Several hundred yards away there was the girl from the terrace. She was splashing frantically and circling her was the swiftly moving black fin of a shark.

Bond swam faster than ever in his life before. At least he had a knife – he had Gutteridge to thank for that – and as he reached the girl the shark was already turning in for the attack. Bond could see its pallid underbelly glinting below them in the water and as the great fish shot up towards them, Bond struck at it. As always at the point of greatest danger, his mind was curiously clear. He shielded the girl with his body and kicked hard – the shark veered off, trailing brown clouds of blood behind it. Before it could return to the attack, Bond heard more shouting. Gomez and several of his men had launched a rubber dinghy from the terrace. Within seconds they were hauling Bond and the girl aboard and heading back towards the house.

If Bond was expecting gratitude, he was mistaken. Gomez's first words were to ask him what he had been doing.

'Saving your girl-friend from a shark,' he said.

For just a moment the small pig-like eyes glared through enormous pebble lenses. Then he appeared to realize what Bond had done. The big face relaxed.

'Excuse me – the shock. I have to thank you – and on her behalf as well.'

Bond turned towards the girl. Her eyes met his.

'Glad to have been of service,' he said softly. 'Perhaps some time . . . '

'I am afraid it's useless talking to the girl,' said Gomez sharply. 'She's deaf and dumb. Totally. But I am sure she's grateful.'

'Not a great deal of use,' said Bond to Gutteridge. He had

walked back along the beach. 'He wasn't having me inside the house, nor was he letting me near the girl. They whisked her inside very fast, and somehow I don't think we'll be seeing much of her.'

'A pity,' said Gutteridge, and smiled, 'she might have been quite useful.' Bond nodded ruefully.

'Perhaps we should see about her later. For the moment we must think about the problem of Da Silva and his appointment with the Goddess Kull tomorrow night.'

Da Silva was 5ft 8in and Bond was 6ft 2in. Their colouring was different, so were their profiles. Despite this, Gutteridge and the make-up expert from Police Headquarters somehow succeeded in turning Bond into a reasonable facsimile of the Jamaican.

'Try keeping in the shadow,' said the make-up man. 'You've got his accent pretty well, and with those spectacles of his you should get by.'

Bond hoped that he was right, especially when he found himself driving Da Silva's Chevrolet into Kingston late that Friday night. The police had been alerted now, and Gutteridge was working with them. But the whole plan depended upon Bond's being able to penetrate Gomez's defences without rousing his suspicions. It was essential now to find the Goddess Kull.

He had no difficulty in finding Tarleton Street. This part of Kingston was awake – the remainder of the city slept. There was a throbbing rhythm to the night. Pleasure was cheap here. Eyes seemed to watch from every doorway and, as he parked the car, Bond thought he saw faces in every shadow.

He did his best to hunch his shoulders and disguise his height.

'Mr Da Silva,' said a voice. 'Glad you could come along.'

The girl was young, her bottom waggled in its sequined dress. In easier circumstances Bond might have been tempted. But as she took his arm, he was grateful for the reassuring bulk of his Beretta in its shoulder holster.

'We're having quite a night,' the girl said in her best

comehither voice, 'hope you're all ready to enjoy yourself.'

There was a small bar crammed with people. Somewhere behind, a steel band dinned to a frenzy. She led him through the dancers and down a corridor.

'Hold it,' said somebody and Bond was blindfolded. Strong arms gripped him now and he was being dragged down stone steps and then along a tunnel. He could feel water dripping on his head. Then there were more steps and Bond felt himself entering a room. The arms released him.

'O.K.,' said a voice, 'take his blindfold off.'

After the darkness, Bond's eyes blinked. There was an unimaginable scene before him. He was in a cellar with a high vaulted roof. It was lit by burning torches and at first sight Bond thought he was in some sort of church. More than a hundred men and women were standing before him like a congregation, and at the far end of the cellar was a raised platform with candles burning. The air was heavy with the scent of burning joss sticks and of marijuana. Along the platform was a row of skulls.

'Welcome,' said a voice. Bond recognized the owner as the tall bearded negro he had seen with Gomez at the house on Montego Bay. He still wore his circular dark spectacles, but was now dressed in priestlike robes.

'Welcome,' the others in the room responded.

'We are all here to worship Kull, the great Destroyer,' chanted the negro.

'Indeed we are,' the audience replied.

'The brotherhood of Kull demands obedience. Those who deny her must make love to her.'

At this a shudder seemed to pass through the congregation. Some of the women moaned.

'Kull, Kull,' they cried.

'And you, Da Silva, will become one of us. You will not oppose us. You will swear homage to the Goddess Kull, or share her bed with her.'

As the man said this his voice had risen to a crescendo, and suddenly Bond saw the wall behind him opening. A throbbing wail of music started. The congregation sank on its knees. As the wall slid back it revealed a room behind with an enormous golden bed. On it lay a naked woman.

'Kull,' moaned the congregation. 'Hail to thee Kull, thou great destroyer.'

Suddenly the music ceased.

'What is your answer?' shouted the priest of Kull. And Bond stepped forward.

'I will make love to her,' he said.

There was a hideous silence as Bond walked towards the goddess. As he stepped across the platform he took off Da Silva's spectacles and revealed his full height. He and the girl recognized each other and the wall slid to behind him.

Gomez was in the room and several of his henchmen. One held a long machete. Two of them were armed. But Bond's gun was faster. It thudded twice and then the man with the machete was on him. Bond leapt at him, the butt of his beretta smashing against his hand. The machete clattered on the floor; the man lay whimpering in the corner of the room. Then Gomez grabbed at the machete. He had the strange agility of many fat men, but as he lunged, Bond aimed a blow at him that caught his spectacles. Bond ground them underfoot, leaving the Cuban to thresh blindly at him with the machete. Bond hit him once behind the ear and all was over.

Gomez, that ruthless killer, had died as he lived – violently. The man who had attempted to control the Caribbean through his black reign of terror would terrorize no longer. The fat, myopic master of the Goddess Kull was dead.

But Kull still lived. So did her followers. Bond could hear them chanting in a frenzy in the room outside as they waited for the sliding doors to open. This was the moment that they longed for – the moment they would witness the appalling sacrifice of one more victim to her lust.

Bond looked towards the girl. She was still lying on the bed. To Bond she appeared more beautiful now than when he saw her through the telescope, and he wondered how much she understood of what was going on. How much had she ever known? She smiled. He moved towards her and as he touched the bed some hidden mechanism made the doors start to open. Bond took her in his arms.

There was a hush outside. Kull's congregation waited and the doors drew back. Then somebody cried out. It was a cry of fear. A miracle had happened, for Bond had moved. He had embraced the Goddess Kull and lived. The cry was taken up, and for a moment Bond feared the worshippers would lynch him but the Goddess had her arms around him. She smiled at him. Kull the insatiable had been satisfied. The congregation started to applaud.

At this point there was a great commotion at the rear of the hall. Gutteridge and several policemen from the Jamaican special branch had suddenly arrived – following the small homing 'bleeper' Bond had hidden in the heel of his shoe. Despite the sudden change of heart of Kull's worshippers, Bond was relieved to see them. Kull's reign was over.

But this was not the last that Bond saw of the girl. As Gutteridge explained, her legend still lived in the fears of many of the people who had feared her for so long. To show that it was over, Bond spent several days with her, touring the island, and although she was deaf and dumb this hardly seemed to matter. She had loved Bond ever since he saved her from the shark and to this day his memories of the Goddess Kull are over a gentle, silent girl with golden skin and the few days he spent with her beside Montego Bay.

9
Casino

There was one point which I had been avoiding – Bond's relationship with M. The time had come to ask about it. Had M. really been, as Fleming wrote, the one man Bond had 'loved, honoured and obeyed'?

I chose my moment carefully before I asked him. I wanted no more outbursts like the other day's. But after dinner he was in a mellow mood, and when I broached the subject he started laughing.

'Let's be quite honest about all this,' he said. 'The truth is that old Ian always liked to make me look something of an idiot. As I'll tell you later, there was a reason for this, and a good one. But he also liked to pull my leg and it amused him to describe my dog-like devotion to steely-eyed old M. Of course, he overdoes it dreadfully. Sometimes I think he makes me sound just like some bloody spaniel wagging my tail whenever M. appears.'

'Didn't you?'

'Did I hell! As I'm trying to explain to you, it wasn't like that at all. Back in 1951 we were all working very hard indeed and M. just happened to be the man in charge. He also happened to be extremely good at a hideously demanding job.'

'And did you ever argue with him?'

He paused to light a cigarette. I had noticed that he often did this when he wanted time to think of his reply.

'Sometimes. Of course I argued. But the trouble with arguing with M. was that he was usually right. Particularly back in the early fifties. You must understand that we were really fighting for our lives and M. was the one man who could save us. Kidding apart, he was incredible. He's never had the credit he deserves; during those few years he brought us from rock bottom to considerable success. He was a very tough effective little man. In my book, nobody can ever equal him.'

Now that James Bond had started talking I realized that we were in for another of his late-night sessions. It was extraordinary how much his talk depended on his mood. Tonight he was obviously relaxed. The morose, heavy look had gone entirely. He leaned back, called to Augustus for his customary bottle of Jack Daniel's Bourbon, and cheerfully began explaining the situation M. had had to face in 1951.

This was the year that Bond returned from Jamaica, and as he says, he found himself 'quite suddenly in the front line of the secret war'. Things were hotting up. Smersh had moved onto the offensive and the British Secret Service was doing its best to meet the challenge. There had been losses, even in the 00 section. In January 1951 008 was found dead in a parked car fifty yards inside the Western zone of Berlin; three weeks later 0011, passing through China on the so-called 'Blue Route', failed to make contact in Hong Kong; and in the last few days 003, one of the most experienced agents in the section, had been dragged from a blazing car outside Belgrade. He would live – for a while at least – but his days of usefulness to the Secret Service (or to anybody else) were over.

For M. these losses would have been acceptable had they been matched by firm achievements: these were lacking, and M. was jealously aware of the activities of those hard brains directing Smersh from their drab headquarters on the Sretenka Ulitsa. Smersh was a contraction of two Russian words meaning 'Death to Spies'; for M. it had been living up to its forbidding name too well for comfort. Hardly any of the West's attempts to penetrate the security of the Soviet had worked.

The British network inside Russia was something of a joke, whilst the two major secret war campaigns launched by the West in the last few months – against Albania and the Ukraine – had foundered ignominiously. M. was under pressure. He was directly accountable to the Prime Minister and, as one recent writer put it, that wily politician 'was not disposed to be too impressed by the denizens of the secret-service world.' Not surprisingly, the lines on M.'s weather-beaten face were rapidly becoming something of a battlechart of the secret war. Fortunately he knew better than to lose heart at incidental set-backs. He knew that whilst in ordinary war it is the last battle that counts, in the secret war there could never be a final battle, only the ceaseless ebb and flow of murder and betrayal. M. had no illusions about the trade he followed. But it was a necessary trade. As long as he was in command, he would make certain it continued.

Bond was the sort of man he needed. M. realized this for certain after the Jamaica business, just as James Bond accepted that his life from now on lay with 'Universal Export'. For the Secret Service gave him an all-demanding cause to which to dedicate his life. It gave him a pattern and a purpose. Without them he would founder.

He also knew the way he needed his assignments. They were his chance to prove himself; without them Bond would have been stifled by the order and emptiness of his 'normal' life. Danger was as necessary to him as ever. It was the one form of escapism that could make life tolerable, and in the spring of 1951, the gods, and M., were smiling on James Bond. He was kept busy. Life was very good.

Within a few days of his return from Jamaica, he was off again.

'Another holiday?' Miss Trueblood asked as Bond walked back from his brief interview with M. She could tell from the expression on his face that he had work to do. He asked her to arrange his airline tickets.

'Which country this time?'

'Greece,' he replied. 'M. thinks I need a holiday.'

She groaned and said it was a good thing she wasn't envious by nature. Bond gallantly suggested she came with him; for just a moment it seemed as if that cool suburban blonde was tempted.

'A thousand pities you're engaged,' Bond said hurriedly.

The cover M. suggested was one that Bond enjoyed – that of a wealthy young enthusiast for underwater swimming anxious to combine a short holiday in southern Greece with some underwater archaeology. Q Branch had a rush job to equip him properly, but they worked fast, and Bond spent the afternoon checking the equipment he would take: a Cressi Pinocchio diving mask, a Heinke-Lung, a Leica underwater camera. It all fitted into a large blue holdall for the journey, but Bond also had a suitcase specially prepared by Q branch. It was a type that he had seen before.

'It'll fool the average customs man,' the quartermaster assured him, 'and anyhow, in Greece they're not too fussy with foreign tourists. You'll be all right.'

'What if someone drops it?'

'Safe as houses,' said the quartermaster.

Finally Bond collected the latest large-scale Admiralty charts of the southern coast of Greece, along with an imposing wad of travellers' cheques and currency.

'You've forgotten the Ambre Solaire,' said Bond.

'I thought you'd like to buy your own,' replied the quartermaster.

* * *

Bond left next morning on the midday flight to Athens, taking some trouble to maintain the image of the easy-going pleasure-seeker. He wore an open-necked blue shirt, a lightweight linen jacket and read Ernie Bradford's *Guide to the Greek Islands*. In Athens he was already booked into the luxurious Mont-Parnes Hotel, and a car from the hotel was there to meet him. He made sure his luggage was in order before being driven off. The hotel overlooked the city; once he had checked in he relaxed, swam in the pool, and then enjoyed his first Martini of the day. It was nearly five before he changed and took the hotel bus down to the city.

He had been given an address – the Anglo-American bookstore in Amerikis Street. He found it without difficulty and asked for an assistant called Andréas. Bond introduced himself, and Andreas, a small courtly man with a magnificent moustache and Brooklyn accent, was very helpful, recommending several books on classical Greek art and southern Greece. Bond asked if they could be delivered to the Mont-Parnes. Andreas said certainly, and promised to bring them up in person that very evening.

On leaving the bookstore, Bond took his time and wandered through the city. There was no great risk, but he had to know if anyone was tailing him. No one was. There was a golden sunset and the evening's first sea breezes were giving the stifled city a chance to breathe. The Acropolis was silhouetted against the sunset like some plastic tourist symbol; outside the café in Giorgiades Square where he stopped for a drink there were oleanders growing out of cut-down U.S. petrol cans. Bond felt that in different circumstances he might like Athens – but he doubted it.

That evening, Andreas, like all Greeks everywhere, was late. Bond had already dined when he arrived with his neatly parcelled pile of books. Bond thanked him, offered him a drink, and they sat together on the hotel's splendid terrace drinking retsina and watching the lights of Athens shimmer up the valley. Andreas was a determined talker who enjoyed the chance of showing off his very personal command of English. It wasn't every day he was invited for a drink at a luxury hotel, and he was out to make the most of it. Finally Bond steered the conversation round to southern Greece and Andreas mentioned a small port. He described it lovingly – the market-place, the eighth-century Byzantine church, the beauty of the local girls. Andreas hinted that he was something of a connoisseur of indigenous Greek sex.

'And the ship?' Bond asked. He had a limited capacity

for general conversation and was anxious for a full night's sleep. Andreas seemed disappointed at the directness of his question.

'Oh, she arrived last night, at precisely the hour I told London that she would. She is called *Sappho*, after our famous poetess. You know the poems of Sappho, Mr Bond?'

'Not intimately.'

'A pity. She was, of course, what you would call a Lesbian. Perhaps that puts you off?'

'It does. This ship – how big is she?'

'6,000 tons deadweight. A common looking coaster, I'm afraid. Registered in Alexandria. The captain is a Syrian called Demetrios. A good Greek name, Demetrios.'

'How long before she leaves?'

'Two days earliest – more likely three. They have to load her carefully. With that sort of cargo it is not wise to hurry. Too much hurry – Boum – food for the fishes, Mr Bond.'

'And the police? What are they doing while all this goes on?'

Andreas took a long draught of retsina – then sucked at his moustache.

'Officially, they must arrest the ship and then impound the cargo. That is our good Greek government policy. That's what our prime minister would tell your Foreign Office in London. But, between you and me, they act like your Lord Nelson. They put the glass eye to the telescope.'

Finally, Bond did get his sleep, and next morning he rose early, breakfasted, and packed. The ferry Andreas had recommended left at nine; but, being a Greek ferry, it was nearer ten before it hooted bravely, struggled out from the Piraeus and headed south. Bond was managing to hide considerable impatience behind a thin façade of cheerful tourism. The sun was hard and very hot. Islands floated past upon an amethyst horizon – Aegina, Poros, Hydra, then in the afternoon, Velopoula. Bond sipped ouzo, nibbled stuffed vine-leaves and felt mildly sick. The boat reached its destination in the evening.

It was not hard for Bond to find the *Sappho*. This was a

small town and the docks were not extensive. The ship was exactly as Andreas described her, ungainly and rather rusty, flying an Egyptian flag. Nor had Bond much more difficulty making out her cargo. There were some packing cases stacked along the quay – crated machine guns always have a certain look.

Bond booked at the hotel Andreas had recommended. It was a cheerful place with several goats tethered in the courtyard, a one-eyed barman and a terrace set with ancient trellised vines. It overlooked the sea. With nightfall oil-lamps were lit and fireflies darted through the air. Bond ordered dinner, gingerly, and told the barman he was staying several days to try the underwater fishing.

'We got a lot like you,' the man replied, scratching his eye-patch, 'but most of them come later in the season. We do have one man here though now, a real expert. You must meet him.' He shouted something in Greek. A small boy answered from the office.

'No,' said the barman. 'You're out of luck. But when he comes I introduce you.'

That evening Bond ate one of the six best meals of his life – *kedonia* (small clams) then octopus with wine and onion sauce and spring lamb simmered with herbs. He drank the ice-cold local white wine. It was very good. He had nearly finished and was sitting, smoking a cigarette and watching the lights from the night fishermen winking across the bay, when a large man in a red-and-black check shirt sat down at his table. He had dark eyes, a swarthy face, a small grey wart beside the nose, and something that instantly appealed to Bond – a sense of life, of openness and warmth such as one rarely meets. He spoke English of a sort and for an hour or so he and Bond talked – about the fishing on that splendid coast, the hazards of the rocks and tides and the excitements of the underwater world. He was a great enthusiast and he was full of stories – of the deep wrecks which he had plundered, of coral beds where rare fish swam, and of the riches which he hoped to find. They drank a bottle of the local wine together; it was years since Bond had formed such an instant friendship with anyone. As the man got up to go, he shook hands with Bond, and promised to take him swimming early next day. He explained he was a sailor and that his ship would soon be sailing.

'I'm often here these days, and they all know me. My name's Demetrios.'

Somehow Bond managed to avoid him all next day although the barman told him later that he had been asking for him. And somehow the little town had changed from the night before. Suddenly Bond found it dirty and oppressive. He couldn't wait to leave, but there was work to do, with the *Sappho* still in harbour. The barman told Bond she would be sailing on next morning's tide.

Bond had his instructions; they were not too difficult to follow. For the remainder of the day he rested, then got ready his equipment. Q department had done a clever job on the suitcase. With the linings of the top and bottom of the case removed, it was a simple task to screw together the two halves of the limpet mine. Bond set the timing apparatus as instructed – on a twenty-four-hour fuse. At dusk he set off from well along the coast, swimming out strongly on the evening tide. The sea was warm and faintly phosphorescent. He had the mine strapped firmly to his belly and he swam deeply, surfacing from time to time to take his bearings. The starlight seemed to filter through the waves, fish glided past and he swam on determinedly towards his quarry. He wondered if Demetrios were yet aboard.

When Bond turned in towards the harbour only the keenest lookout would have seen the thin line of bubbles that he left behind him. The *Sappho* had no lookout; Bond decided it would be most effective to fix the mine amidships. It was easier than he expected. The strong magnet on the mine dragged it towards the hull; as it thudded home Bond remembered the same sensation from his training sessions on the lake in Canada during the war; he was sorry that this was no training session.

Bond was back in the hotel before midnight. He asked the barman about Demetrios.

'Ah, the captain is back aboard his boat. He is sailing early, but he asked me to tell you he will meet you here a week from now when he returns. He promises to take you swimming.'

Bond thanked him, had a drink and went to bed. Next morning he rose early, caught the ferry he had come on, and was back in Athens in time to catch the night plane on to London. When he arrived it was gone two o'clock. He took a taxi from the airport to his flat and was so tired that he slept solidly till nearly ten. At the office people seemed surprised to see him back so soon.

'Successful holiday?' Miss Trueblood asked with just a touch of malice in her voice.

'Hope so,' Bond replied. 'Pity you weren't there, nice people Greeks. There was a man called Demetrios. You'd have liked him – rather your type.'

'And what's that, pray?' she asked.

For a while Bond told her about him – his looks, his sense of life, his love of the sea.

'Will you be seeing him again?'

'No,' he said. 'No, I don't think so.'

For the remainder of that day, Bond had long sessions with the men from S Branch. There was a great deal to discuss and it was gone seven before he got away. He walked down Baker Street to take the underground; by the station he paused to buy an evening paper. He saw that it was carrying the first reports of the sinking of a suspected gun-runner 200 miles north-west of Limassol. According to one source the ship, the *Sappho*, had been carrying arms and ammunition for the EOKA terrorists in Cyprus. The cause of the sinking was so far a mystery and there were no reports of survivors. Bond got on the escalator, then took his train to Leicester Square.

* * *

After the Greek affair Bond had been hoping for a real holiday, a rare opportunity to relax. Aunt Charmian had been unwell, and he had been planning to take her off for a few days in the South of France.

'Leave?' said M. querulously when Bond raised the subject. He made the word sound curiously obscene. Bond thought it hardly wise to remind him that officially he was entitled to a statutory four weeks off a year, plus compensatory days for weekends spent on duty – not that he ever claimed them. Not that anybody did with M. around.

'I thought that you realized the pressures we are under, 007.'

Bond held his ground, knowing quite well that in August M. himself had his customary two weeks' fishing on the Test. M. grunted. Later that afternoon Miss Moneypenny brought Bond an official leave slip for three weeks at the beginning of July. M.'s small meticulous signature was at the bottom.

Bond enjoyed being with his aunt. She was less demanding than any of his mistresses and he was glad of this chance to pay her back a little that he owed her. They stayed at a small hotel at Cap d'Ail. He hired a small brown Simca and drove her along the coast. For the first and only moment in his life, Bond was acting as a tourist guide, and actually enjoying it. He found it easier than he expected although, to tell the truth, he had a somewhat specialized itinerary. Luckily Aunt Charmian appreciated it. And, luckily for her, she had the Bond digestion and iron head for alcohol. She was a very tough old lady.

Bond told her he was going to corrupt her. She said it sounded very nice. They began with baccarat at Monte Carlo. Bond lost several thousand francs. She won, triumphantly, and then insisted on paying for dinner with champagne and all the trimmings at the Hôtel de Paris.

When they drove to Marseilles in search of low life, it was Bond whose pocket-book was stolen in the market-place, and Aunt Charmian who, once again, paid for dinner. When Bond took her to visit one of the toughest, and most foulmouthed, secret agents he had known in the war – a man called Reynard who had run an escape route over the

Pyrenees and was now producing scent at Vence – Aunt Charmian scored her greatest success. She drank Pastis with him, spoke better French than Bond thought possible, and laughed at Reynard's most improper jokes. Bond felt a shade embarrassed until Reynard told him what a splendid aunt he had, loaded her up with more scent than she had used in her entire life and kissed her strenuously on both cheeks.

'Why did you never tell me what nice friends you have?' she said as Bond drove back.

They still had another week to go when there was a call from London. Chief of Staff was on the line – appropriately apologetic.

'Crisis,' he said. 'M.'s shouting for you. Someting right up your street.'

'Isn't there someone else? I'm still on holiday.'

'It's you we need, James – no substitute will do. You should be flattered.'

'Humph,' said Bond.

'Tomorrow then,' replied the Chief of Staff. 'And, by the way, my love to the little woman.'

'The little woman, as you call her, is my aunt.'

'Auntie all right?' said Chief of Staff next morning as Bond strode past his desk in the outside office on the sixth floor of 'Universal Export'. After the late-night flight from Nice and then the struggle to get Aunt Charmian safely back to Pett Bottom, Bond was not amused.

'Nuts,' he replied as the red engagement light flashed above M.'s office door.

The brief interview that followed is described by Fleming at the beginning of *Casino Royale*. Bond now admits that whilst he was put out by M.'s indifference to his holiday – there was not even an apology for having to bring him back – he was secretly quite flattered by the assignment against Chiffre. Chiffre was a Russian agent who had embezzled the Party funds belonging to the Communists in northern France. He was now trying to re-coup by gambling. Bond was specially chosen to challenge him and beat him in the casino – thereby inflicting a genuine defeat upon the

Communist network on the Continent. Every agent thinks himself indispensible, but it is rare to have the fact confirmed. He was agreeably surprised to know that his reputation from the Roumanian job before the war was still remembered.

In fact the so-called *Casino Royale* affair was in some ways Bond's favourite assignment, certainly at the beginning. His morale was high, his health and confidence impressive, and, once he found himself back at Royale-les-Eaux, he started to enjoy himself. The little town had hardly changed. (Fleming perhaps exaggerates the efforts of the rich Paris syndicate to modernize the place, backed with their expatriate Vichyite funds. The money didn't last.) Indeed, for Bond, the town possessed considerable nostalgia. He vividly remembered old Esposito's brief triumph here in 1937, and the whole battle against Chiffre in the casino seemed like an echo of his fight with Vlacek.

This was the one assignment which possessed a touch of prewar glamour, and, as Bond admits, he made the most of it. As he says, 'it was a self-indulgence to bring over the Bentley and it was really too conspicuous for comfort.' But it had recently been fitted with its new Amherst Villiers supercharger and Bond was keen to try it out on the long French roads. It was like old times too to link up with René Mathis and to work with him, so that these few crammed days at Royale-les-Eaux seemed like a return to the lost exciting days of James Bond's youth.

It was this mood of deep nostalgia which must explain some of Bond's strange behaviour during the assignment, particularly with Vesper Lynd. True, she was pretty, but there had been many pretty women in his life before. Why was he taken in by her and why, to make matters worse, did he even think of marrying her when he knew that secret-service work and marriage never mixed? Why, if he had to choose a wife, should an agent as experienced as Bond have picked the one girl in the place who was a Russian agent?

As tactfully as possible I asked Bond about this, but he was quite open-minded on the subject. He readily admitted his behaviour had been strange. Indeed he found it hard to justify himself. His only explanation was that subconsciously he must have known that Vesper Lynd was working for the other side and that, in some perverse way, this became part of her attraction. Right from the start he knew that their relationship was doomed, and just because of this he felt doubly attracted. He talked of marriage because, deep down, he knew that it could never happen.

'It's difficult to explain these things. One isn't always all that logical, and the sheer pressure of my sort of life sometimes does make one act most oddly. It's really pure escapism, but one can get in the most frightful emotional tangles if one isn't careful.'

I asked him how he really felt when he reported back to M. that Vesper Lynd had been a double agent, and then added that laconic epitaph, 'the bitch is dead'.

'Oh, hideously upset. Fleming makes me sound quite horrible. In fact I blamed myself for the poor girl's suicide and was most dreadfully cut up. She was just one more woman who had loved me and had died. That sort of thing is very difficult to live with. That's why I spoke so bitterly, but Fleming seemed to think that I was blaming her.'

Bond may have been 'cut up' by Vesper's death but the cruel logic of the secret-service world demanded it. Alive, she would have spelt the end of his career. Dead, she enhanced it, and the fact is that the Casino Royale affair added enormously to Bond's reputation. It helped to establish him inside the department, and, for the few weeks after his return, Bond was free to bask in his success.

It would be nice to say that Bond spent this time mourning his dead beloved; but the truth is that he was secretly relieved to return to the calm routine of life in London. The flat retained its reassuring sense of order. On his first morning back May was there, rocklike and unambiguously sane, with breakfast and his copy of *The Times*. Everything was in its place: the brown boiled egg, the Minton china and the whole-wheat toast. The hum of the morning Kings Road traffic came through the windows, and, as Bond poured his coffee from his Chemex percolator, he realized that he was free. Nothing had changed, and he was duly grateful.

On his first morning back in Headquarters, Bond paid a brief routine visit up to M.'s office on the sixth floor. As usual, M. was fairly noncommittal. Always wary of bestowing praise, he seemed concerned with Bond's damaged hand (the Russian killer had carved his trademark, a Russian S for *Spion* on the back of it). 'Better make sure we get the plastic surgery fellows going on it,' he remarked gruffly. 'Can't have a member of the 00 section with an identifying mark like that.' But later in the day Bill Tanner informed Bond that 'the old man's really very pleased with you. I had to listen to him singing your praises to Head of S,' and, before Bond left the office, M.'s secretary, the formidable Miss Moneypenny, brought him a brief note recommending him for three weeks' further leave at the end of August.

Bond spent it in Provence. Early that spring he had heard that Maddox had died, and that Regine had bought a maas a few miles inland from Montpelier. Bond had written to her. She had replied inviting him whenever he could get away. And so he spent his leave with her. It was a happy time for both of them. They remained friends, not lovers, and for the children he was the 'Uncle James' that they remembered from their days in Paris. She told him that Maddox had died sad and embittered with the world. Apart from this, they never mentioned him.

When Bond returned to London, there was the usual backlog of routine work in the office to catch up on. Paymaster Captain Troop had been busy in his absence and there were several courses to attend. There were also lengthy sessions with the plastic surgeon to repair his hand – a painful, tedious business, although Bond had a brief *affaire* with the surgeon's receptionist, a gentle but ultimately boring girl called Cecily.

Then in November came the clash with Mr Big and the destruction of his extraordinary gold-smuggling racket from the Caribbean. Fleming described this in his book which he entitled – overdramatically for Bond's taste – *Live and Let*

Die. It was another big success for Bond, particularly when the Treasury solicitors made good the British claim to half of Mr Big's treasure in gold bullion. Thanks to James Bond a sum approaching £5 million sterling reached the British Treasury.

'I'm glad to know I'm paying for my keep,' Bond said to M. when he heard the news, but M. was not particularly amused. When it suited him, M. could be very stuffy over money. It was not a subject to be discussed by gentlemen.

10

Vendetta

'I was becoming just a little over-confident,' said Bond. 'It's a real danger in our type of life. When you have the sort of lucky run that I'd had you tend to think it will go on for ever. This is one reason why old M. was always grudging in his praise. He wasn't quite as sour as Ian painted him, but he was worried, and quite rightly, that one would start getting what he used to call a "superman complex".'

Bond was explaining how it came about that just as the tide of real success seemed to have set in for him, he found himself facing a real catastrophe. Few people realize that during 1952, James Bond was nearly driven from the Secret Service for good.

It was from M., soon after he returned from dealing with Mr Big, that Bond got the first inkling of the trouble to come. This was quite early in 1952 and M. was still worrying about that damaged hand of his. Despite the plastic surgery, the scar still showed. (Fleming was to notice this later. As he said, the hair grew crookedly on the skin that had been grafted from Bond's shoulder.)

'Dreadful pity,' M. said when he saw the scar. 'It should have been avoided.'

'How?' replied Bond.

M. shrugged his shoulders. 'It isn't good for you to have

this sort of trademark on you. What was it that Russian said to you when he killed Chiffre?'

'He said he couldn't kill me because he had no orders to from Smersh. He also said this was probably a mistake.'

'Exactly,' M. replied. 'They must have slipped up badly not to have realized your 00 rating. They're pretty certain to try to correct their error. We must be careful.'

Bond took little notice at the time. M. was passing through what Bill Tanner called 'one of his fusspot phases' and Bond was busy. This was the period when he acquired those 'three married women' Fleming wrote about. I asked Bond about them. He explained that he chose his mistresses carefully – just as he had done before the war in Paris. They were all beautiful, all women of the world, and all of them were in their early or their middle thirties.

'For me this has always been the most attractive age in women. Naïve young girls, however pretty, soon bore me silly. They make such demands – on your time and on your patience – and they invariably have one fixed, romantic end in view. Marriage. Whereas with older women things are different. You get intelligence and understanding and a clearly defined relationship. That's most important. No entanglements. I always made sure that we understood each other perfectly. Right from the start I told them there was to be no question of threatening their marriage – rather the reverse. There was to be no jealousy or possessiveness either. We would be civilized and we would enjoy ourselves.'

'And did you?' I asked.

Bond's eyes narrowed and he smiled.

'Perfectly,' he said.

'And were their husbands ever any trouble?'

'Not if the wife was sensible. It was really up to her to see that her husband's *amour propre* was not offended. Most English husbands are so busy making money or being with their friends that they're secretly relieved to have their wives kept happy by an expert.'

At this period Bond's three married women were an impressive trio, and he went to great pains to ensure that none of them suspected the others' existence. This was apparently quite a problem of logistics. One lived in Hertfordshire, was married to an aged merchant banker, and wrote historical romances. Bond used to meet her every Tuesday in his flat – when she had done her London shopping. The second was married to a prominent Conservative M.P. Bond saw her Thursdays – and whenever the House had an all-night sitting. The third one was Bond's 'weekend woman' as he called her. Bond knew her husband. He was a rich insurance broker and a member of Blades. The passion of his life was sailing – which he did from Friday night to Monday morning. As his wife loathed boats and was sea-sick, Bond really made it possible for him to continue his hobby – and his marriage.

The only trouble with this variegated sex-life of James Bond's was that his women occupied almost all his leisure – and at a time when the work-load of the whole department was increasing steadily.

But then, in April, M. again brought up the subject of Chiffre's killer, the man described by Fleming as 'the murderer with the crag-like face.' Thanks to the efforts of Department S, he had been identified. His name was Oborin and he was one of Smersh's top professionals. M. seemed unusually disturbed.

'It looks as if my fears for you were justified, 007. I don't wish to alarm you, but we must be prepared. From a report we've just received it seems as if last summer's failure to destroy you caused a major incident in Smersh headquarters. Our old friend, Colonel General Grubozaboyschikov (M. pronounced the name with alarming fluency) ordered an inquiry and Oborin pleaded that there had been an administrative error. General G. was furious – I can understand how he felt – and at one point it looked as if Beria would be involved. Contrary to British practice, 007, a failed Smersh operator normally pays for failure with his life. But we now know for sure that Oborin is very much alive. I'd give a great deal to know why. I may be wrong, but it could be that Smersh is giving him one last chance to make good his mistake.'

The idea of becoming a special target for Smersh did not disturb James Bond unduly. Experience had given him a firm (and not unjustified) faith in his powers for survival. Besides, had he ever let the fear of personal reprisal from his enemies worry him, he would have left the Secret Service long ago. But he did start to take precautions – carefully garaging the Bentley at all times, avoiding fixed routines, and never going anywhere without the reassuring weight of the Beretta in his shoulder holster. Between assignments life went on as usual. Then something odd occurred. One of the Sunday papers carried a front-page story on the sinking of the *Sappho*. It was sensationally written and suggested that the British Secret Service was involved.

When Bond read it, he was in Berlin, checking on a threatened bomb attempt on British Military Headquarters. This had turned out to be a hoax, but with the British Foreign Secretary currently touring Germany, it could not be ignored. Bond and a group of highly trained personnel had wasted a lot of time and energy on the case. To read about the *Sappho* in such circumstances did not improve Bond's temper.

Back in London next day, Bond discussed this with the Chief of Staff, who, like Bond, was puzzled by the article. He had already seen the editor and warned him against carrying a big follow-up story. What disturbed the Chief of Staff was that somehow the paper had got hold of Bond's name and were all set to publish it, along with a photograph.

'Where did the paper get its facts from?'

'Nobody knows,' replied the Chief of Staff.

There were more disturbing incidents. Now that the Chief of Staff was warned, he was able to cope with them. Newspapers are usually cooperative in helping to avoid trouble to the Secret Service. But it was clear that a campaign had started, to expose James Bond. His name was mentioned in the foreign press. There was a photograph, luckily not very good, in a German magazine. If this continued he knew his usefulness would soon be seriously curtailed. Knowing this,

M. took good care to hold him back from active service for a while. The scare subsided.

It was late that autumn before M. summoned Bond again. Bond was excited at the prospect of a fresh assignment; M., on the other hand, appeared unusually subdued. He called him 'James' – always a bad sign, this – and spent some time digging at the bowl of his pipe with the tip of a naval-crested paperknife. Outside the rain was falling on the park. M. and the room were grey.

'I am about to do what no one in my position ever should,' he said at last. Bond wondered what was coming.

'I am going to leave the decision over an assignment entirely to you. If you accept it – fine. If you refuse, we both forget and never mention it again.'

'That sounds very fair,' said Bond and looked at M. M. did not meet his eyes. When M. continued he spoke loudly and impersonally.

'Four days ago we received a message via Station H in Finland. Apparently a Colonel Botkin of the K.G.B. is anxious to come over. I need hardly tell you how extremely rare it is to have a member of the K.G.B. make such an offer, so I told Station H to go ahead and arrange the terms. They arrived this morning. He wants the usual guarantees, money and so forth – nothing out of the ordinary – except for one thing. He insists that he will surrender to one person only – you.'

Bond lit a cigarette. This also was unusual in M.'s office.

'Any reason?' he said dryly.

'He claims he met you in Berlin two years ago.'

'He didn't,' said Bond.

'We know he didn't.'

'So why so keen on me?'

'I think we both know why,' said M. 'That's why it must be your decision.'

'You think this so-called Colonel will be Oborin?'

'We're pretty sure. Our information makes it clear that Smersh is giving him one chance to correct that mistake he made at Royale-les-Eaux.'

'But isn't it too obvious? Isn't it clear that everybody here will smell a rat?'

'Of course,' M. said quietly. 'That's what our friends in Smersh are counting on. Unless I'm very much mistaken, this is a private challenge issued from Oborin to you. That's why it must be your decision.'

M. wouldn't let James Bond reply immediately and Bond spent a sleepless night. On the one hand he knew the risks he would be running if he went to Finland. Smersh would not be leaving much to chance, nor would their killer. Bond would be facing almost certain death. On the other hand there was something to be said for meeting a challenge of this sort head-on.

Luckily Bond was not a worrier. He used to repeat a saying of his aunt's, 'Worry is an extra dividend one pays to disaster in advance.' This he had no intention of doing, so finally he made his decision, closed his mind to it, and slept. Next morning he told M. that he was going.

M. nodded thoughtfully.

'I thought you would,' he said.

*   *   *

Bond enjoyed his first afternoon in Helsinki. He was expecting a drab icy little city. Instead he found that this whole portion of the eastern Baltic was enjoying its own version of an Indian summer. Birkin, the head of Station F, met him at the airport. He was a tall, much-decorated naval commander with a distinctly ghoulish sense of humour. He wore a monocle, a red cravat and sponge-bag trousers.

'Well, old chap,' he said, 'I trust you've packed your bullet-proof pyjamas. Looks as if you'll need 'em.'

'It's definitely a set-up then?' said Bond.

'Frankly, the whole thing stinks. I told M. as much. Clearly he thinks the 00 section needs a little thinning out.'

'And this man Botkin, from the K.G.B. – you've never seen him?'

Birkin shook his head and grinned.

'Not on your life. We've just made contact through intermediaries. A lot of unofficial traffic passes in and out of here you know. No, I've not seen the bastard, but he is very anxious for a look at you.'

That evening Birkin insisted on taking Bond out to dinner.

'Least that I can do in the circumstances. Could be your last good meal on earth. Besides, it'll be a chance to give you your instructions, if you're really going through with it.'

They went to Smourazi, traditionally the best Finnish restaurant in the city. It was just opposite the old cathedral, a prim grey building with a dome like a symmetrical bald head. The restaurant was crowded but the guests were mainly Swedes and somewhat solemn. Bond drank a lot of snaps and found the clientele improving. Birkin insisted on traditional Finnish food – *kalakukko* (Finnish fish cakes), Karelian steak (beef and mutton roasted together), and *poronkieltä* (reindeer tongue). Bond found it disappointing. Birkin ate with relish.

'The point of Finnish food is that it gives you stamina. You need it in a place like this. Pity you're not staying longer.'

Bond thought he would require something more than Finnish food to keep him in Helsinki.

'Before we finish off the snaps,' he said, 'just tell me how I contact Colonel Botkin.'

Birkin took his time explaining the arrangements. In the process he chewed reindeer meat, and drank still more snaps. The plan was basically quite simple. Bond was to go to Kotka, a seaport and the last big town before the Russian border. There he would take a motor-launch – Birkin explained, at length, the trouble he had taken getting it – and sail for a tiny island some ten miles from the frontier. The rendezvous was fixed for four o'clock next afternoon. Botkin would be there – and, if all went to plan, Bond would bring him back – 'or vice versa,' Birkin said.

'Exactly,' Bond replied.

According to Birkin, the great virtue of getting drunk on snaps was that it left no hangover. Bond found this theory optimistic but not accurate. He woke in his hotel feeling much the worse for wear. The only consolation was that Birkin looked even worse than he did after breakfast when he called to drive him off to Kotka.

'Must have been that reindeer tongue, old boy,' said Birkin. 'Can't always trust it.' James Bond nodded.

It was an impressive drive. Most of the way the road kept to the coast with views of pine woods, islands, and the pale blue sea. Birkin told him there were seven thousand islands between Stockholm and the Russian border.

'So how do I find the one I'm heading for?' said Bond.

'Easy,' he replied. 'Just stick to the bearing that I'll give you, and you can't miss it. You'll know when you've arrived. A big German battlecruiser called the *Lublin* was sunk just by the island during the war. They've never shifted her and she's still full of dead Germans. She's on the main channel through to Leningrad. Her superstructure shows for miles.'

Kotka was reached by lunchtime. It was a small bright modern town clustering round a glass works and a mammoth paper mill. The air smelt resinous. It was a crisp autumn day; Bond felt revived. Birkin had screwed his monocle firmly into his eye and proudly showed James Bond the motor-launch that he had hired for him.

'Cost us a dreadful lot of money. I only hope M. doesn't query it.'

'I'm sure he won't,' said Bond.

For Bond there was something of a schoolboy treat about the voyage. He was alone in charge of a small blue boat chugging its way across a tranquil sea. Behind him Kotka belched smoke from its paper mills. Ahead of him lay island after island with lonely buoys marking the sea-lane on to Leningrad. At first there was a yacht or two, and some of the islands seemed inhabited. But soon all sign of human beings ceased. He was alone except for the sea birds and the impatient chugging of his engine.

The sun sank early and the dusk was gathering when he saw the *Lublin*. Her masts were standing like a far-away lopsided tree on the pale horizon. Bond steered towards her.

The island lay just half a mile beyond, a chunk of rock, crowned with a scalp of pines.

There were two wooden huts and a small jetty, but no sign of life. Bond steered towards the jetty, tied up and jumped ashore.

He was early and explored the island. It was empty, but, to his surprise, one of the wooden huts was open. He looked in. It had been roughly furnished – chairs, table, blankets on a trestle bed. Bond drew his gun and entered. There was no one there.

Time ticked by and no one came. Bond watched the sea for sign of Botkin's boat, then darkness fell. It started to get very cold. It was a temptation to move into the hut and wait. Bond resisted it. Instead he lit an oil-lamp, plumped up several cushions under the blankets to the rough shape of a sleeping man, then left the hut and hid up in the pine trees, gun in hand. It was the longest night of his life. The cold grew bitter, until his hand froze to the steel of his gun. A bell-buoy by the wreck tolled in the darkness. And all the time the light burned on in the deserted hut. Somehow Bond kept himself awake.

The luminous face on his watch showed nearly three when the men arrived. He counted eight of them. They had approached so silently that they had the hut surrounded before he realized that they were there. One of them called out in English, then they rushed the hut, firing as they went.

Bond had an advantage from where he was and fired at them from the rear, trusting in darkness and confusion to mask his movements. There were shouts, several of the figures seemed to fall and Bond dodged between the trees keeping to the shadows, then staying very still. Some of the men had flashlights, but they soon realized that there was no point searching for him in the darkness. Somebody shouted from the hut, and the men with flashlights moved towards it.

Dawn came late, and suddenly the island was thick with men. There was more shouting now, and Bond could hear the trampling of undergrowth. Then he saw the searchers – Russian sailors working across the island in a line. They found him easily. There seemed to be no point in trying to resist. Three of the sailors grabbed him and as they brought him to the jetty Bond saw a face he recognized, the 'crag face' he had glimpsed beneath its mask at Royale-les-Eaux the night that Chiffre was killed – Oborin, his private enemy from Smersh.

There was no sign of recognition in those hooded eyes, but there was a brief command. Bond spun round. Oborin's right arm lifted and a blow like a steel bar caught him below the ear. A fountain of bright scarlet jetted through his brain – then total blackness.

It seemed like centuries later when he woke. He was in a small, white painted room lit by a steel grille light screwed to the ceiling. There were no windows. The floor was iron. There was a steel bulkhead door. Bond tried it. It was firmly shut.

His whole body ached and the pain in his head caused him to faint. When he came to, the bulkhead door was open. For a while Bond lay where he was. Then a voice said, 'Good morning, Mr Bond. It's good to see you.'

'Where are you?' Bond asked.

'All in good time,' the voice replied, and Bond realized that it was coming from a loudspeaker hidden by the light.

'First, I must introduce myself. I am the man who is going to kill you, Mr Bond. As you know, I slipped up at Royale-les-Eaux. This time there will be no mistake.'

'If you're so keen on killing me, why not last night?' said Bond. 'You had me at your mercy.'

'It would have been too easy,' said the voice. 'Besides, I have my orders. My masters want you back alive. That's why we had to have that little pantomime last night on the island, and that's why you're here.'

'But where is here?' said Bond.

'I thought you realized. You are aboard the *Lublin*. It is good that these old warships still have their uses and that all those sailors did not die in vain. She is a useful outpost for my country. We converted her when we still occupied this part of Finland during the war. She was originally an observation post to give warning of attack on Leningrad. We had much equipment hidden on her. There is an air-lock well below the waterline so that a submarine can relieve her crew. That's how you are due to leave, sometime this afternoon. The submarine is on her way.'

'Why is the door open then?' said Bond.

'A good question. I'll do my best to answer you. Feel under your left armpit, Mr Bond.'

Bond did. To his surprise he found his gun was there.

'Examine it, please.'

Again Bond did as he was told. The magazine had been reloaded after the shots he had fired last night.

'Now do you understand? My orders are to bring you back alive, but just for once I don't intend to follow them. You've caused me too much trouble, Mr Bond. I want to kill you. And to have that pleasure, I'm giving you a chance. Not a very big chance, but a better one than you'll get in Moscow. We are alone here on this wreck. The sailors who brought you here have gone. You have a gun. Use it, Mr Bond. Escape.'

There was a loud metallic click. The voice switched off. Bond lay where he was, planning what to do.

His cabin was evidently below the waterline, and from where he lay he could see a brightly lit corridor with steps at the far end. Somewhere along that corridor or up the steps, Oborin was waiting. It was the perfect killing ground, the carefully set-up site for a private execution. At first Bond thought he had no chance, but then he realized that Oborin's whole scheme for killing him depended for its certainty on one thing – light. If he could only plunge that corridor outside in darkness he might just have a chance. Everything depended now on whether the corridor lights and the light inside his cabin were on the same electric circuit. With luck they would be.

He used one precious bullet to shoot out the light. The glass cover shattered, and, although he cut his fingers, he managed to unscrew the base of the light bulb from its socket. He had a small stainless-steel comb. He insulated one end with its plastic holder then thrust it hard into the socket. There was the flash of a short-circuit – the lights in the corridor outside went out.

Bond hurled himself towards the steps and as he did so, two shots whistled through the darkness. Bond grabbed the steel rung and hauled himself up. A third shot caught his arm. And then he fired, instinctively. There was no real target – only a darker patch against the surrounding darkness. But Bond had practised in exactly these conditions in the cellars beneath Regents Park Headquarters. He heard the cough of his Beretta followed by the eerie twanging of a ricochetting bullet in the darkness. But with his second bullet there was no ricochet.

Bond stood quite still and listened. There was a cough. Bond fired again directly at the sound. He heard a thud and then a stifled groan followed by the choking sound of someone fighting for breath. He fired twice more. The choking stopped. Even then, Bond took no chances but waited several minutes more. There was no noise now but the sound of his own breathing. He fired again and then moved slowly forward until he reached the body. He nearly stumbled over it. The murderer with the craglike face was very dead.

It took Bond some while to find his way out. He was in a corridor with a steel ladder at the far end. Groping his way up he found a bulkhead door. He wrenched it open and found himself out on the tilting deck of the *Lublin*. The Russian had been right – the wrecked battleship was quite deserted. So was the island. At the jetty Bond could see the small blue boat he had arrived on still tied up where he had left it. There was something lifeless and depressing in the scene. Bond thought of the drowned sailors for whom this rusting warship was still a communal coffin. It was time to go before the Russian submarine arrived.

But first he had to make sure that the *Lublin*'s usefulness was over and forced himself down past Oborin's body to explore the ship. The Russians had sealed off a section of the hold and carefully installed their radio equipment, quarters for a crew and a whole range of electronic monitors. There was the air-lock where the submarine would dock and deep in the hold Bond found what he was looking for – the *Lublin*'s sea-cocks. These required all his strength to turn. He heaved and then he heard the rush of water. He took one last look round at this hidden watcher's world – then gratefully got back on deck.

The Baltic was colder than he had ever thought water could be. After his dive from the *Lublin*'s stern he swam the half-mile to the jetty, but he was nearly caught by cramp within the icy waters. Luckily, there were still blankets in the hut. He dried himself on them, then swathed himself and climbed aboard the boat. The engines started. There were two jerry-cans of fuel. He swung the blue boat's bows out to the open sea. As he passed the *Lublin* the great rusting monster seemed to lurch. The stern and barnacle-encrusted rudder rose from the water as the ship tipped further on its side and settled in the mud. By the time the Russian submarine arrived, Bond was safely back in Kotka.

'Well, bless my soul,' said Birkin when he saw him. 'Somehow I never thought that *you'd* be back.'

*　　*　　*

Bond was hoping that the death of Oborin would have settled his private score with Smersh, and for a while it seemed as if it had. Winter began – the ceaseless business of Bond's department seemed to increase in volume. There was a three-day visit to Cairo at the end of November. A British businessman's life was threatened by a group of extremist Arabs and an important trade agreement hinged on his safety. Within three hours of his arrival in Cairo, Bond knew the names of the would-be assassins and by that evening all of them had been persuaded to leave town. He also had a trip to Washington confering with the C.I.A. about an anonymous threat to the life of the U.S. President on his forthcoming tour of Europe. Both these assignments passed off without a hitch. Then came Bond's visit to Milan.

This occurred during the annual Trade Fair. These international affairs with entries from both sides of the Iron Curtain tended to become a field day for the Secret Service. Bond was quite used to them, and on this occasion he had to keep his eye on a technical adviser from a British electronics firm who was suspected of illicit contacts with the East. For Bond it was very much a routine operation. For cover he had arranged to be attached to a British firm of turbine engineers and duly took his place, complete with dark suit and exhibitor's lapel badge, on their stand. He knew enough to talk convincingly about turbine generators, and also managed to observe the man he wanted. In fact, nothing happened: the man was either innocent, or else aware that he was being watched. And Bond was free to enjoy the exotic pleasures of Milan. He liked the city. Unlike so much of Italy, it made no attempt to thrust culture and antiquity down his throat, and he enjoyed its zest and its prosperity. He liked the Milanese too – with their large fast cars and pampered women – and ate well, drank wines like Inferno and Lambrusco, and in place of his customary vodka martinis found himself enjoying what he called 'musical comedy drinks' – Campari sodas and Americanos.

During the four days of the Fair he had a double room at the Hotel Principe e Savoia. He approved of this as well. The hotel was solid and discreet; the barman poured generous measures and knew all the gossip of the city. It was in the bar too that Bond met the girl who saved his life. She was called Melissa. She was English, recently divorced and staying in Milan to meet her Italian lover. He was delayed in Rome; she was obviously lonely. Bond gave her dinner at one of the finest restaurants in Italy – Gianino's in the Via Sciesa where they ate artichokes and *osso buco alle milanese* – and spent the night with her. After the *grappa* and the gorgonzola this seemed the perfect ending to a perfect evening.

Luckily, they chose her room. At 4 a.m. the hotel was shaken by an explosion. Bond's empty double room was totally destroyed. As the *carabiniere* told him later, the bomb had been put underneath his bed.

'Fortunately,' said Bond, 'I sometimes sleep in other people's.'

The *maresciallo* from the *carabiniere* laughed, but before he left Milan, Bond sent the girl a golden bracelet with his heartfelt thanks; on this occasion he felt justified in charging it to his expenses.

But Bond was more disturbed than he let anybody see; especially when he had to give a personal report upon the incident to M. M. had nodded and said little. A few days later, May found a parcel in the post addressed to Bond which worried her. Something was loose inside it. Bond rang Scotland Yard; their experts later found that it contained sufficient thermite to have blown his head off. Again, M. was informed of what had happened.

Then came the final incident. Bond had been dining with his favourite married woman at the White Tower Restaurant in Percy Street. He had the Bentley and, as he drove her back to Chelsea, he noticed a small grey Austin in front which refused to let him pass. He hooted and flashed his lights, but the car stuck to the middle of the road. Bond swore. He was impatient to get home, and then, just by the exit from the park, the car jammed on its brakes and swung across the road. Another car was double-parked ahead and, as Bond struggled to avoid it, there was a rattle of machine-gun fire. The Bentley skidded to a halt. Bond was unhurt, but the woman beside him had been hit. Bond spent the next half hour seeing her safely into St George's hospital, and then coping with the police. There was a lot of coping to be done, and the evening ended, shortly before midnight, with a hurried conference with M. at the Regents Park Headquarters.

It was the first time Bond had known him appear at such an hour, but the Chief of Staff had summoned him from home. Both of them looked grim when Bond appeared.

'And how is the woman, Chief of Staff?' said M.

'The hospital say they've just removed the bullet from her pelvis. She's been in pain but she will live.'

'Thank God for that,' said M. 'And her husband – did you succeed in quietening him down?'

'Extremely difficult,' said Chief of Staff. 'Until I rang you, he was threatening to see the Home Secretary.'

'Just tell me one thing, 007,' said M. 'If you must have these affairs of yours, why on earth do it with an M.P.'s wife? Isn't life difficult enough without bringing in the House of Commons?'

'I thought,' replied Bond stiffly, 'that my private life remained my own.'

'Private life?' M. snorted. 'When will you learn that while you work for me you *have* no private life.'

By next morning, things had calmed down, but M. still took a gloomy view of James Bond's future in the Secret Service.

'We must face facts, James. This is a vendetta. Since you killed Oborin, Smersh have been out to get you. They have made you a marked man, and won't rest until they have totally destroyed you. It is a situation I have faced occasionally before. And I am afraid there's nothing to be done about it, James. I have no alternative but to suspend you from the 00 section, and get you some foreign posting until it all blows over. We'll have to discuss a suitable place for you. Where do you enjoy? The Bahamas? Strangways needs to be replaced in Jamaica – will that suit you?

Bond appreciated the attempt at kindness. But in a way it made the situation worse.

He knew that he was finished, just as he was getting into his stride. Smersh had beaten him – and he would never know whether the feud would rest. He would always be waiting for the bullet in the night, the poisoned cup of coffee. After the Vatican, Smersh possessed the longest memory in Europe.

Those next few days of semi-relegation were perhaps the bitterest of his life. He had to hand in his Beretta, that battered but efficient friend of many an assignment. And he no longer had that special status, that sense of being part of an élite. The way that everyone appeared so understanding simply made it worse. He began the melancholy business of packing – there seemed nothing else to do. Prepare expenses, close the files, make sure at least that everything is left in decent order.

He would store the Bentley when it was repaired – he couldn't bear the thought of selling it. And there would be no trouble subleasing the flat. He would have to pick his moment to tell May that he was leaving. He had never thought of her as a sensitive woman. One of her virtues was that she had always kept her life and worries quite apart from him, and left him free. She never varied.

But she seemed to know that there was something wrong. 'P'raps ye'd be liking me to mix ye a drink?' she said. Normally Bond prepared his own, but tonight he was grateful to the loyal old girl.

'An' by the way a friend of yours telephoned. The name of Fleming. Very polite an' nice he was. Asked you to call him back – a Victoria number. I've left it on your desk.'

11

Superbond

Bond still doesn't know why he called Fleming back. He was not in the mood to talk to anyone – least of all anybody as demanding as Ian Fleming. Besides, Fleming was a journalist. But when he did, that drawling voice from the far end of the telephone was strangely sympathetic.

'Met your managing director out at lunch today. I'd heard about your previous spot of bother in the office, and he filled me in on your threatened change of employment. I had an idea which quite appealed to him. It might be something of a solution. He's coming to lunch with me at Blades tomorrow to discuss if further. I think you ought to come as well.'

Bond had always envied Fleming's ease of manner when he talked to M. for, like many others in high places, M. had a soft spot for Fleming. This helps explain Fleming's own somewhat puzzling status at this time. Officially, he was a journalist who had had nothing at all to do with intelligence work for more than six years. But, unofficially, he was one of that handful of men who had M.'s confidence and whom he would consult. From the way they were talking when he arrived at Blades, Bond realized that M. had told Fleming all about him.

M. seemed on his best behaviour – with Fleming there, he

was no longer quite the steely martinet of 'Universal Export'. And Fleming was clearly buttering him up, as only Fleming could. He had already checked with Miss Moneypenny to make sure that they had M.'s favourite table – in the far corner of the room away from what he called 'the noise and scrimmage' of the younger members of the club. The chef had been alerted to provide M. with one of his favourite delicacies – a marrow-bone served on a special eighteenth-century silver dish. 'Hope the "Infuriator's" up to scratch,' said Fleming as he filled his glass. M. beamed. Bond recognized the Fleming treatment.

'James,' said M. pleasantly. 'Ian and I have just been having quite a little chat. I can't say he's converted me, but he does have a very interesting – I might say startling – proposition. As it concerns you personally I'd value your views on it.'

Something about the tone of voice made Bond wary. M. was being far too kind for comfort.

'You may recall,' continued M., 'that little piece of most successful deception we were responsible for in 1943. I believe Ewen Montagu wrote about it afterwards. He called his book, *The Man Who Never Was*. The idea was to trick the enemy by having the dead body of a British officer complete with certain documents washed up on the coast of Spain. The body was quite genuine – some poor fellow or other – but the uniform and documents were carefully prepared by British Intelligence. Ian here has this interesting idea that we could use you somewhat similarly – but by standing the whole idea on its head.'

'I don't follow you,' said Bond.

'I hardly thought you would,' said Fleming, butting in. 'We're not proposing to use your corpse or anything like that, not yet at any rate. My idea is simply this. In the Montagu story, the resources of the Secret Service were used to convince the Germans that a mythical man was a reality. Now I suggest that we should do the opposite, convince the opposition that a very real man is in fact a myth – or at least dead.'

217

Bond looked at Fleming. Fleming paused to savour the last mouthful of the club smoked salmon. Bond to this day remembers the strange smile, half cynical, half mocking, on his face.

'Go on,' he said.

'From what M. tells me, you have the honour, or misfortune, to have become Smersh's number one human target in the West. M. proposes to give in to Smersh, and have you posted to Station K in Jamaica in the hope that this will save your life. Now, I don't like being pessimistic, but I just don't see this working. Remember Trotsky and the ice-pick? Smersh destroyed him in the end – although in fact he had retired to Mexico City. I wouldn't give you any greater odds than Trotsky.'

Bond had stopped eating. He had passed his adult life facing the imminence of death. Even so, there was something chilling in the offhand way this gentlemanly Englishman predicted his demise.

'So what do you suggest? Perhaps M. would like to keep me under lock and key inside the cellars at Headquarters for my own protection.'

M. smiled a wintry smile. Fleming laughed.

'Nothing so drastic. No, I think that we should simply try convincing Smersh that you don't exist any more – better still – that you never existed. That you are a genuine man-who-never-was.'

'And how do we do that?'

'By making you a character in fiction.'

'Thanks very much. I'd rather take my chance with Smersh.'

M. cleared his throat.

'Ian's idea may seem a little, shall we say, original, but it might work. Whatever happens you won't lose by it. What he proposes is that he should try his hand at writing one of these cloak-and-dagger thrillers about you. Make it as real as possible. Name you, describe you as you really are, and base it all on some genuine assignment. But at the same time he would try to make it sound like something out of Buchan.

Sufficient fiction to make everybody think he's made the whole thing up. It'll take some doing, but if Ian here can pull it off everyone, and that includes our enemies in Smersh, could well end up convinced that you are now as real as Richard Hannay.'

'But Smersh *know* that I exist. They have me on their records.'

'They know that somebody from the British Secret Service did the things you did. If Ian's idea works, they won't believe that James Bond did them. Bond will have become a character in fiction.'

Possibly the Infuriator was as strong as M. had always claimed, but by the end of lunch, everyone was sold on the idea. Fleming was talking airily about the possibilities for the future.

'It could be the perfect cover. You really would be able to get away with anything. It could become a classic exercise in pure deception.'

'And M.,' asked Bond, 'he would be included?'

'Of course. That would really worry all those gentlemen in Smersh.'

At first M. demurred, but Fleming knew exactly how to flatter him.

'The book had better be damned good,' said M.

'It will be,' Fleming said.

* * *

'I'd never realized,' said Bond, 'just how hard old Ian worked – when he wanted to. I'd always thought he was a very lazy fellow. He liked to give one that impression; that tired way he had of talking, the long lunch hours, and so forth. But once he started on the story that became *Casino Royale* I was dealing with a very different Ian.

To begin with we spent a fortnight, – on and off, up at his brother's place in Oxfordshire – an ugly red-brick house set in a beech wood. There was a golf course down the road. We played together quite a lot.'

'Who used to win?'

'I'd say we were very fairly matched. Neither of us was what you'd call a stylish player. I had a stronger drive: Ian was more cunning. We enjoyed it as a relaxation and for the rest of our time there we worked very hard. During the war you know he'd been an expert at interrogation. Well, he interrogated me – every detail of that wretched casino business until I'd had enough of it – what was I wearing, How did I feel at such and such a point, why I did this and failed to do that?'

'And about the girl?'

'Yes, that as well. He was always very keen on dragging out what he used to call "the interesting bits". I thought that he was what they used to call "a gentleman". I should have known better.'

But the real point about this whole operation was the care he took. He was a very clever devil, and he had it all worked out. He took more trouble with Casino Royale than with any other book – there were several versions before a final one was agreed on. Fleming left not a single thing to chance. Even the publisher's reader used to work with him in Naval Intelligence. And he took extra special trouble over the style and those touches that would convince the men at Smersh – and particularly some Englishmen advising them in Moscow – that it all *was* a piece of fiction. He had been reading Sapper, Buchan and that sort of thing since boyhood so it wasn't difficult, and a lot of what he slipped in the book was really quite a joke – details like Chiffre's concealed razor blades, and those hairs he always had me placing on door handles. We used to make them up and laugh at them. But I had no idea quite what was coming. Don't forget that I was very much in hiding. Smersh was quite definitely out to get me. Most of this period I was existing with an armed guard on the door, in one of the special flats we used to have behind Headquarters. It didn't help one's sense of judgement or reality.

This was around Christmas time at the end of 1952. Ian had just gone off with his notes and his typewriter to his house in Jamaica – Goldeneye. I remember how he came back at the end of March, with his manuscript, and how excited everybody was – M. in particular. I couldn't see a copy for a day or two. But when I did I nearly went through the roof. I was so appalled that I sat up all that night reading it. The facts were right, in essence, but he'd really gone to town on me. I still think he overdid it. There was no need to make me such a monster, such a cardboard zombie, such a humourless, idiotic prig.

That's what I told them all, at any rate when we had our meeting. Ian was there and M., and head of S, and quite a lot of top brass from the ministries. And, in fairness to Ian, I must say that all of them were most enthusiastic. There is a great deal of the schoolboy in the senior civil service mind, and Ian had got their tastes exactly. M., I might add, was secretly delighted at the way Ian painted him. And Ian made great play about the way the book would have to appeal to one man in particular – Guy Burgess. We knew by then that Burgess was advising Smersh on English matters, and Ian said, quite rightly as it turned out, that if we could once convince the wretched Burgess that this hero was completely fictional, we were home and dry.

I tried various objections, but they wouldn't really listen to me, and, as M. said, 'This book is your one and only hope for a future in the service, 007', There wasn't much that I could say to that.

They did agree to toning down some of the sexier passages with poor Vesper. I really didn't care for them. M. backed me, I'm glad to say. Ian was very cool and authorish about them, but as M. said, 'there's no need to descend to the level of pornography, particularly as the girl is dead.' And, as you know, it went ahead.

*　　*　　*

The operation was, as Urquhart told me at the start, a classic in its way, a daring piece of pure deception against a cunning, very ruthless enemy. Even Bond admits that its success was due entirely to one man – Ian Fleming. Just as his conception was original enough to fool the Russians, so his whole execution of the books must surely rank as something of a work of genius. He seemed to know exactly how to marry fact and fiction and his whole concept of the fictional James Bond had just the right amount of fantasy to fool a clever enemy.

But whilst one is finally able to give Fleming a little of the credit he deserves, one should not forget the role the Secret Service played in the deception. The few men in the secret played their part superbly, even to getting an advance copy of the book to Moscow (via an ex-colleague of mine on the *Sunday Times*) and making sure that Burgess read it. Similarly, on publication day in London, there had to be elaborate precautions to make sure that none of the reviewers gave the game away. (In the event, the only one who nearly did was someone on the *Yorkshire Post*. Nobody seems to know how he was dealt with.)

And, of course, it worked. By all accounts, even Fleming was a little shaken by the way the Russians, the reviewers and the general public fell for Bond. Some months later, M. received a blow-by-blow report of the rumpus the arrival of that first copy of the book caused at Smersh headquarters. Burgess, apparently, was full of it. To start with, General Grubozaboyschikov took some convincing, but Burgess had underlined some passages from the book and read them, there and then, translating into Russian as he went.

When he had finished, the directorate of Smersh was silent. Who had slipped up? What idiot had first been taken in by the famous British sense of humour? All eyes were on the General.

'Where does this character called James Bond come from then?' the General asked.

'I'd say,' said Burgess, 'that he was Sapper from the neck up and Spillane from the navel down.'

The General said he hadn't read Sapper or Spillane, and Burgess, according to the report, replied that it was time he did.

Of course there was more to the deception than this one successful meeting, and the book required a careful follow-up to be effective. This was apparently where friend Urquhart comes on the scene. He was quite right when he told me he had worked with Fleming in the war. In fact (I should have guessed it), he was a failed romantic novelist who worked with Sefton Delmer's famous 'Black Propaganda' deception against the Nazis. So, in a sense he was the ideal character to place in charge of what Bond calls 'the nuts and bolts' of his affair. He had a lot to do.

From field reports it was soon clear that Smersh was baffled. They seemed to have called off their operations against Bond. M., in his turn, had given Bond instructions to lie low. (For several months after the publication of *Casino Royale*, Bond was in Tokyo, loosely attached to Station T and studying the Eastern network. He liked the women and the food, picked up a smattering of Japanese, and generally enjoyed himself. Not even Fleming now knew where he was.) But Urquhart was kept busy covering up Bond's tracks in London. He took a lot of trouble, and was extremely good at it. Some of his tasks were fairly obvious – like moving Aunt Charmian from Pett Bottom and sending May off to Scotland for a month or two. He also had an eye for detail, arranging such *minutiae* as erasing all records of Bond's membership of Blades and carefully removing his file from the secretary's office at Eton.

On the whole, Bond's few friends in England proved easier to deal with than he thought. Urquhart saw each of Bond's three married women, and told them just enough to keep them silent. He was a good psychologist, and did the same with other key acquaintances. And the strange thing was that as the books about James Bond became more popular, people who had known him seemed to forget that he *had* once existed. As Bond puts it, 'I was beginning to get absorbed into the character of "James Bond, the Secret Agent of the Fleming books". It became rather spooky, and I would sometimes wonder whether James Bond was real myself.'

But the main thing about the operation was that it worked. During his whole time in Japan, Bond had heard nothing of a threat from Smersh. On his return to London, M. confirmed that the manhunt by the enemy was over – for a while at least.

'You owe your life to Ian Fleming,' M. said when they met. 'Don't forget it.'

'Somehow I don't think I'll be able to,' said Bond.

Discreetly, Bond resumed his duties. There were a few barbed comments from the Chief of Staff, but on the whole Bond's role in the Fleming books was treated as a private joke in the department. It made no difference to his work. By now May had returned from Glen Orchy, Bond resumed residence in Wellington Square and the Bentley emerged from storage. Then, late that autumn, Fleming told M. that it was time to be thinking of a fresh James Bond book.

To do M. justice he was a little taken aback at first.

'You've written the damn book. It did its job magnificently. Surely that's that?'

But Fleming argued that he ought to keep the myth of James Bond's fictional personality alive. (He also gave M. more than a hint of what an excellent job the books were doing for the image of the British Secret Service. M. was beginning to be concerned with 'images'.) The upshot was that Fleming was given permission to describe Bond's last big assignment before all the trouble – the battle in the States with Mr Big. Fleming wrote this early in 1954, and from the start Urquhart was worried that it gave too much away. True, Fleming did 'trim it down a bit' as Bond puts it. But, as usual, he got his way with M. over the parts that mattered, so that the story is in fact one of the fullest and most accurate accounts of all Bond's published adventures. Fleming entitled the book *Live and Let Die*.

But long before it appeared that autumn, Bond had resumed the very active service he was used to. Indeed, 1954 provided one of his busiest years to date. This was partly due to the mounting pressure on the 00 section, and also to a quirk of M.'s. M. always had been, in Bond's words, 'a thorough-going slave-driver'. Hard with himself, he felt he had a right to be hard with others. He also thought that men respond to pressure and that more agents are destroyed by slackness than by the enemy. Around this time this attitude of M.'s grew worse. Bond himself agrees that there was an odd streak in him – he refuses to call it sadism – but M. had certainly inherited the attitude from the old navy that men need to be broken. He was almost happy when they did.'

Throughout 1954 it seemed as if M. was determined to see how much work James Bond could bear. More and more inter-departmental work was thrust on him as well as regular assignments for the 00 section. (For the purpose of the fictional James Bond, Fleming has emphasized his hero's hatred of all office work. Bond denies this and insists that he is, in fact, a competent administrator. From what little I could judge of him during these weeks I would agree.)

There was a constant round of courses, training sessions, and straightforward practice to keep his skills up to the mark. This is another point that Bond makes. In the books, his success appears so effortless that people forget that a top-flight agent is always learning, training, picking up fresh techniques to go one better than the enemy.

'The assignments are quite simply the tip of the iceberg. Underneath are weeks and sometimes months of training.'

Scarcely a day went by without Bond firing some weapon, either on an open range or in the cellars under Regents Park. Sometimes he spent weeks at a time mastering some new technique. His mind became a strange encyclopaedia of special knowledge – on poisons, on explosives, on changing fashions in subversion. His body was maintained in top condition like an athlete's. The whole routine built up towards the various assignments which were the point and purpose of his being.

During this time there were a lot of them. Most were routine – people to be protected, and sometimes silenced; enemies destroyed; attacks repulsed. As a professional, Bond always prided himself upon the speed with which he worked.

'It's a trade, you know. One likes to take a pride in craft-manship.'

As usual, Bond is being over-modest when he speaks like this. Some of his operations at this time achieved an almost virtuoso brilliance, and have since become text-book cases in the Secret Service training schools. Most, by their very nature, must remain firmly on the secret list. The few that can be mentioned give just a small idea of the range and scope of his success.

One of Bond's so-called 'copy-book affairs' occasioned a swift visit to the Far East. 002, who for the previous three months had been inside a gaol in Canton, had broken free, killed several Chinese guards and somehow crossed the border between China and Portuguese Macao. In London it was realized that this was a situation that could all too easily get out of hand. But almost before the Chinese Communists had time to put pressure on the Portuguese for the 'foreign murderer's' return, Bond was in Macao. It was a perfectly planned and executed coup – so perfect that when 002 disappeared from the Portuguese police headquarters where he was being held, there was no shred of evidence of who had taken him. (This was in fact almost the first operational use of Oblivon, a safe but instantly effective sleep-inducing drug which had been recently developed in the laboratories of 'Universal Export'.) The escaped agent travelled to Hong Kong – impeccably disguised as an ancient Hackar woman – on the morning ferry, and was back in London by the following midday.

Another mission Bond undertook this year led to the recovery of several pounds of top-grade Uranium 235, and in doing so he saved the British Government from considerable international embarassment (to put it mildly). For the uranium had been stolen by mistake by a group of London gangsters from a consignment to an atomic power-station on the coast. The lorry had been hi-jacked. The thieves had clearly thought the uranium was gold or some other straight-forward precious metal. But when the lorry was recovered, the uranium was missing. During the weeks that followed, Interpol was alerted. Rumours began to buzz around the underworld about the uranium being 'on offer' for a reputed million pounds. And the Government was suddenly shocked at the prospect of a group of criminals offering the raw material for an atomic bomb to anybody who could pay the price.

Bond spent some time in France, where he was operating in conjunction with his old friend Mathis. He took a lot of trouble building up his cover as an envoy from an Arab power wanting the uranium to be used against Israel. This was dangerous work, involving the penetration of at least one Arab underground network from North Africa. And in fact Bond finally did 'purchase' the uranium – from a villa on Lake Geneva for a million pounds in gold, provided on British government orders by the Bank of England. The gold was recovered by Mathis and his men that same afternoon, whilst Bond and his lethal cargo were flown back from Switzerland to Gatwick by a special aircraft of R.A.F. Transport Command.

That autumn Bond returned to London just in time for the publication of Fleming's second book, *Live and Let Die*. It was obvious to Bond that Fleming was now getting in his stride as an established author. He was very proud of the dust-jacket for the book. Bond liked it too, but something about the author's attitude was troubling him. Fleming had actually suggested he should come to a publication party for the book. When Bond refused, Fleming replied 'but why on earth not? It'll be amusing and no one will realize who you are.'

This, as Bond admits, was just the trouble. Arabs are wary of being photographed in case they lose their face: Bond began to feel that he was losing, not his face, but his whole personality. And Fleming was beginning to act as if James Bond were his creation. Bond told him so. Fleming replied, quite logically, that this was all part of the original deception. Bond had to agree, but still felt uneasy. This time he couldn't bring himself to read the book.

Bond was not the only member of the Secret Service to be

worried at the course the books were taking. After the publication of this second book some very strange reports got back to Moscow. Urquhart was worried that someone in the press would stumble on the truth, and Fleming was summoned to an anxious meeting of the security committee in the 'Universal Export' building. Once again his ingenuity appeared to save the day.

'If we're so afraid that Smersh will smell a rat,' he said, 'perhaps we ought to give them a really big one to sniff at.'

M. asked him what he meant.

'I think the time has come to give them what they think they're getting – a piece of total fiction built around our famous superman. Something so obviously far-fetched that our old friend, Guy Burgess will have all the arguments he needs to convince his critics that Bond is pure and unadulterated fiction.'

This was the origin of his next book which he called *Moonraker*.

The plot was a favourite one of Fleming's – a mammoth British rocket project built by a rich industrialist who plans to use it for his Russian masters. But he and Bond spent a weekend together to discuss it. By an odd coincidence, Fleming owned a house not far from James Bond's boyhood haunt at Pett Bottom – the Old Palace, Bekesbourne. They went to Fleming's club, the Royal St George's, Sandwich where they played a lot of golf and then sketched out the plot. Fleming's idea, like all the finest thriller plots, was just conceivable. His villain was an immensely rich industrialist who offered to use all his vast resources to build a British rocket – he called it 'The Moonraker'. The project would go ahead, the villain would get praised for his vision and patriotism. And then, at the last minute, James Bond would discover that he wasn't what he seemed. In fact he was working for the enemy, and the Moonraker would be part of a plot to hold London to ransom – either the British Government would give in, or the Moonraker, complete with atomic warhead, would be fired directly at the heart of London. Bond was again impressed by Fleming's ingenuity,

and also by his knack of welding fact to fiction. It was
Bond's idea to place the rocket-launching base on the cliffs
at Kingsdown. This was a stretch of coast that he knew well.
He took Fleming there to get the atmosphere, and afterwards
they stopped at the pub, The World Without Want on the
Dover Road, which was to feature in the book. Here they
discussed Bond's office routine, and M.'s latest fads. They
even talked about the villain. He was based on a mutual
acquaintance but, to avoid the libel laws, they had to find a
different name for him. For some reason Bond remembered
the dog he had owned as a boy in France – Drax.

'Good name for a villain,' Fleming said. 'Villain's names
must all be short and sharp and memorable.'

12

Bond Cocu

'Love?' said James Bond. 'The best definition of it I ever heard came from a friend of Ian's, a man called Harling. Used to work with N.I.D. during the war and was supposed to have been a great expert on the subject in his day. He defined love as "a mixture of tenderness and lust". I think I agree with him.'

'And that's all?' said Honeychile.

'That's quite enough,' said Bond. 'For me at any rate.'

It had taken him several days to explain how the Bond books had started. During this time he had appeared distinctly tense and it had clearly been an effort to recount the facts of this strange story. I knew him well enough by now to recognize when he was ill at ease. The voice grew sharper and he became impatient at any interruption. Plainly the loss of his identity into the Fleming books still rankled. He seemed relieved when he could talk of other things; much to my surprise he even accepted an invitation from the indefatigable Mrs Schultz for a day's cruise aboard her yacht, the *Honeychile*, and suggested I should come along.

We set out early. The Schultz 'Corniche' picked us up from the hotel at eight. By eight-thirty the long white boat was gliding from the harbour to the open sea.

We spent that morning cruising between the islands and

enjoying the immensity of sky and ocean. I had never seen Bond quite so happy. All his anxieties of the last few days seemed to have been left ashore; it was revealing to see how he took command. He looked every inch a sailor (or was it once again an actor playing the part of the distinguished naval officer?) He spent the morning at the helm, ordered the crew around, and even took over navigation from old Cullum, the *Honeychile's* professional skipper. (Cullum, a philosophical man, didn't seem to mind. He must have been well trained by Honeychile). Bond seemed most competent with charts and sextants and nobody resented his authority. True, Cullum smiled occasionally, but he addressed him as 'Commander' which Bond seemed to like. Honeychile played the part of Bond's devoted slave.

She had insisted on preparing lunch herself – a P.J. Clark salad, cold pheasant, strawberries and cream. Bond was allowed to manage the champagne. Honeychile looked suntanned, desirable and rich, and by now was wearing nothing but the bottom half of her bikini. Bond had told her that he could not bear tanned women with what he called 'undercooked' white breasts. She was obediently doing what she could to improve them.

It was after lunch that the combination of alcohol and sun and Honeychile's near naked presence, had brought the conversation round to sex and love. And it was then that he had given his definition of love.

'Tenderness and lust,' Honeychile repeated. 'Those sound like the words of a true male chauvinist bastard.'

Bond grinned cheerfully. The land was out of sight, Cullum at the helm, the yacht was ploughing a furrow of white wake to the horizon. Honeychile got up to fetch a second bottle of champagne. Her breasts were browning nicely. When Bond refilled her glass she sipped and then said very softly, 'One day, J. Bond Esquire, you're going to get your sexual comeuppance. It'll be very funny and I hope that I'm around to see it.'

Bond didn't seem at all put out by this.

'Oh, but it's happened,' he replied. 'Not that it's

231

something I've ever looked for in a woman, but I have been treated very badly in my time.'

'Like when?'

'Like during the time I was with Tiffany. I'd been in America in 1955 working on the diamond case that Fleming wrote about in *Diamonds are Forever*. There was a gang that called itself "the Spangled Mob". It virtually controlled the illicit international diamond traffic. We had to deal with it – and in the process I acquired this girl. Her name was Tiffany Case. Fleming mentioned that I brought her back to London, but never described what happened afterwards.'

From Bond's account that afternoon it was quite clear that the beautiful Miss Tiffany Case, ex gangster's moll and sometime blackjack dealer from Las Vegas, possessed that extra something that a woman needed to get through his habitual sexual defences. In her case this something was her vulnerability. He had sensed it beneath her 'brazen sexiness and the rough tang of her manner' that first evening that he met her in her London hotel room at the start of the assignment. As Fleming noticed Bond had an instinct for female lame ducks. He probably detected some reflection of his mother in them, and his protectiveness was roused from the beginning.

He is essentially a sentimentalist; the story Felix Leiter told him of the girl's childhood touched his heart. Most men would have steered clear of a girl with such a past, however beautiful. But for Bond the wounds that life had given her added to her interest. He was intrigued to learn that this brash, knowing girl had never had a man since she was communally raped at sixteen by a bunch of California gangsters. There was a challenge in a girl like this. The fact that her mother had once kept 'the snazziest cat-house in San Francisco' added, if anything, to her allure. So did the desperation with which she tried to drink herself to death after the disaster. As Bond admits now, she was the ideal romantic victim-heroine to appeal to him.

Fleming has told how Bond finally made love to her that night aboard the *Queen Mary* – 'I want it all, James.

Everything you've ever done to a girl. Now. Quickly.' Once this had happened and her phobias were safely overcome, Bond's fate was almost sealed. He had always said that he would only marry someone who could make love and *sauce béarnaise*. Tiffany did both. On top of this she satisfied his hidden vanity. It was as if he had created sex in her when they had finally made love. She was his Pygmalion. She needed him, as no one else had ever done. It was inevitable that they should talk of marriage.

From the way that Fleming writes it might appear as if James Bond were dangling marriage at the girl simply to get her to come and live with him. But Bond insists that he was totally sincere. He never spoke of 'love' unless he meant it. With Tiffany, he was all for marrying her at once. She was the one sufficiently hard-headed to suggest the trial period together in Wellington Square.

They made a point of being very honest with each other. Even during the exciting days aboard the *Queen Mary,* Bond had told her all his drawbacks as a potential husband – the hazards of his job, the fact that he was in a sense 'already married to a man called M.'. He also told her that, much as he liked the idea of children, it would be unfair to think of having them until he was retired from the 00 section. But it was not until they were safely settled into Wellington Square that they discovered there were other problems.

Fleming described how James Bond sent May a telegram in advance saying that he was coming and ordering flowers and Floris bath essence for the arrival home. It is revealing that there was no mention in the telegram of Tiffany. For the truth was that Bond was just a little scared of May, and how she would react to another woman in the flat. As it happened he need not have worried. He had forgotten that May was away in Scotland, visiting her mother in a village near Glencoe. He and Tiffany had the first ten days in London quite alone.

It was an idyllic time. One of those rare occasions when Bond felt entitled to relax. M. had been satisfied at the way the diamond racket had been dealt with, and Bond felt justified in self-indulgently enjoying life – and Tiffany.

She was the perfect mistress for him now. This was the first time he had lived with anyone since Marthe de Brandt, but he was never bored. One of the reasons why he had avoided living with his women previously was that he had dreaded being bored. With Tiffany he was kept busy teaching her a whole world she had never seen. She was an apt pupil, Bond a dedicated teacher.

He showed her London, not the London of the guide-books, but his private London – London of the river and docks, the City empty on a Saturday evening when there was just one pub by Cannon Street still open, Covent Garden in the early morning. They ate in the last Chinese restaurant in Limehouse (Bond had first met the owner in different circumstances in Hong Kong), and dined at the Ritz ('the finest dining-room in Europe') at Scott's (the inevitable grilled plaice and black velvet at Fleming's 'Honeymooners' table') and at a taxi-driver's shelter in Victoria ('the best sausages and mash in London').

Bond also showed her the crown jewels, the Soane Museum, Savile Row, the reptile house at London Zoo and took her on a late-night tour of the London sewers. They bought smoked salmon in a shop off Cable Street, caviare in Clerkenwell, steak in Smithfield, and had champagne and strawberries sent from Fortnums.

The only time they clashed was when Tiffany wanted to go to a theatre. Bond refused. In the event they spent the time in bed.

For both of them, the greatest source of pleasure lay in novelty. Neither had lived like this before. In her disorganized wild way, Tiffany kept house – cooking when they were hungry, stacking the dark blue Minton unwashed in the kitchen, pulling the covers over the bed when they had finished making love. The flat looked as if a boys' club had adopted it.

At the time Bond didn't mind – rather the reverse. Like most meticulous and over-organized people, he had a secret longing for disorder. It seemed a breath of life, a much-needed shake-up. Order brought James Bond boredom – anarchy rejuvenated him. Then things began to change.

They had gone off to spend their second weekend together at Le Touquet, putting the Bentley on a Bristol Freighter flight at Lydd and staying in some style at the Hotel Westminster. As Bond told her, this was a treat – to celebrate their time together, and to mark the end of their brief 'honeymoon'. On Monday morning he returned to work. They had to make the most of these last hours of holiday. They gambled wildly, ate compulsively, made love extravagantly. They arrived back in London late on Sunday night. May was waiting.

May had a certain way of sniffing when she disapproved. It was a private signal Bond had always recognized. She sniffed when she surveyed the flat, her 'handsome closed face', (as Fleming once described it) eloquent with mute distaste.

'If ye'll be excusin' me,' she said, 'I'm just a wee bit tired. I'll get started on the place tomorrow.' And in the morning Bond and Tiffany were woken by the angry sound of washing-up as May got going in the kitchen. It was the clarion-call to battle.

Bond was very male in the way he had closed his mind to May – also in the cowardice and his assumption that 'things would work out'. They didn't. Almost from the start these two women in his life reminded him of two determined cats – one of them old and wily, the other young and in its prime, circling the same disputed patch of territory. Both were fighters.

May brought 'the Commander' his customary boiled egg and copy of *The Times*. Tiffany insisted that he preferred kippers and Cooper's marmalade and the *Express*. May began tidying compulsively – Tiffany produced more mess than ever. May sniffed. Tiffany slammed doors. Bond shaved, dressed, dodged both breakfasts and was late arriving at the office.

For the remainder of that week the battle rumbled on with May and Tiffany embattled in the flat and Bond a somewhat wary referee longing for one thing only – peace. This was a situation he was not prepared for, the sort of warfare where this 'man of war' became a coward. He could take on a Smersh, a Chiffre, a Mr Big, but he would suffer agonies at the thought of having to lay down the law to May – or Tiffany.

The sad thing was that suddenly he seemed to have lost the best of both worlds he had known. Tiffany's insouciance had left her. So had May's order and discretion. During the weeks that followed Wellington Square became a sort of no-man's-land.

Bond became edgy in the office and bad in bed. He felt tired. The unshakeable Miss Goodnight became difficult. Bond's work suffered. He felt M.'s hidden disapproval in the background – and at the same time his 'available male rating' with the secretaries plummetted.

He still loved Tiffany, in some ways more than ever, but she had started to annoy him. The female débris that surrounded her no longer seemed appealing. Nor did her ignorance. She drove the Bentley and dented the offside wing. Once he would have ignored it. Now he was annoyed, and there were tears.

Finally Bond asked Bill Tanner, M.'s Chief of Staff for his advice. This was something Bond had never done before. He wasn't one for revealing his personal affairs to anyone, but Bill Tanner was an old friend, a married man, and eminently sane. His advice was quite uncompromising. 'It looks as if you've got to choose. Either you marry, get a house and kick out May – or you risk losing Tiffany. You can't have both.'

In fact, Bill Tanner's words were truer than Bond suspected. Early that June, May was on the edge of handing in her notice, whilst Tiffany was growing more and more depressed. She was having to find out the hard way James Bond's defects as a potential husband.

She still loved him, and thought him glamorous and kind as ever. When they were together life could still be wonderful. But, as she sometimes asked herself, what was in all of it for her? She had no friends in London. Bond was away all day. May was a bitch.

Nor had she any money. Bond could be generous, in certain strictly limited ways. He loved to give her presents, often expensive presents – a diamond clip from Cartier, a jumbo-sized bottle of scent, silk underwear, the luxuries of life. But when it came to bread-and-butter he was downright mean. She found the housekeeping he gave her quite inadequate; this too became a source of friction.

The truth was that Bond had really no idea about money, nor the cost of running a *ménage*. May was an economical old Scot who had always managed everything, cut the expenses to the bone and worked wonders with the salary of a civil servant. Tiffany was not. The life that she had led had made her quite indifferent to money. It had always been around her in large quantities and she had spent as she wanted. Now she was short for food and short on clothes. She couldn't buy a lipstick for herself. Inevitably they argued over money – something they both hated but could not avoid. It was almost a relief to Bond when, in the second week in June, he was sent off abroad on a brief assignment, even if it was the sort of faintly servile and routine affair that he would normally have loathed.

M. was predictably embarrassed by the whole business, and cut the briefing to a minimum. From his few clipped phrases Bond gathered that his task was simply 'to keep an eye on' a British cabinet minister holidaying at Eze-sur-Mer. The man, not entirely to Bond's surprise, was homosexual – M.'s phrase was 'one of them' – and Bond had simply to make sure that no enterprising agent of a foreign power attempted to involve him in a scandal or to blackmail him. Recently there had been several cases which involved businessmen and politicians with such tendencies. The minister had been showing an extraordinary compulsion to get into trouble – there had been discreet warnings from the C.I.A. after the man's recent visit to the States, and, as M. said, 'prevention is better than a messy scandal.'

When Bond told Tiffany that he was off to France for a brief assignment, she begged to be allowed to come along.

'All I want is a bikini and a suite in the Negresco. I'm just a simple country girl at heart.' Bond was tempted. On a job like this it was a always relief to be assured of some straight heterosexual company. But then he reflected that it would be a dangerous precedent to set; she would soon be demanding to go everywhere with him. Nevertheless he felt uneasy when he left.

Bond had five days of what the section used to call 'Nanny duty' watching the private and at times preposterous behaviour of this leader of the nation. It was a difficult assignment, not least because Bond had to act unofficially. The Minister had his own detective, a Scotland Yard man Bond had known for years. Luckily, Bond and the detective understood each other.

The Minister was staying at a villa near the sea, a long white house belonging to a Paris businessman of dubious repute. From the detective Bond obtained a copy of the guest-list – which he immediately checked over with Mathis at the Deuxième Bureau in Paris. That evening Mathis rang back to say that one of the names was known to the police. He was a man called Henri, part-time male model, mother Hungarian, father French. There was a record of petty convictions for theft and minor drug offences; the year before he had been on the fringe of a scandal which involved the death of an American Embassy official and a suspected leak of NATO information. Nothing conclusive had been proved against him, but Mathis said, 'he's hardly the man I'd choose to be my brother's best friend.'

Bond alerted the detective who replied that there wasn't much that he could do, but Bond was worried – especially when he learned that Henri and the Minister had been seen together at a restaurant in Cannes. It was a tricky situation. All of Bond's instincts were against this sort of squalid prying into private lives and he was inclined to agree with the detective.

But on the other hand he had a job to do: after Mathis's warning he could hardly leave things as they were. If anything went wrong, M. would be holding him responsible.

He thought of having a discreet word with the Minister, but dismissed the idea at once. He could just picture the man's fury, and the letter of complaint to M. that would follow. He also thought of trying to see Henri and warning him off; that would be even clumsier and riskier. In the end he telephoned his old friend, Reynard, at his house near Grasse. Reynard knew everyone and was very shrewd. Bond suddenly had an idea.

Next morning the telephone rang early in the villa by the sea. The manservant who answered it replied that he was sorry but Monsieur Henri was asleep and could not be disturbed. The voice on the telephone then gave a name that made the manservant suddenly respectful. Seconds later he was knocking urgently on Henri's bedroom door. When Henri mumbled that he wanted to be left in peace, the manservant whispered the name. Five minutes later Henri was on the telephone to Paris.

It was Reynard who arranged the chauffeur-driven Rolls that called at the villa twenty minutes later, and Bond, from a car parked opposite, was relieved to see the slim young man in the immaculate brown suit hurry from the villa and get in. The car purred off. No one else within the villa stirred.

But the name of the film producer which had so impressed the manservant had been genuine – Reynard had seen to that. So was the screen test which the young man took in Paris late that afternoon – so was the part they offered him. In years to come, Bond was to watch the young man's burgeoning career in films with interest and was always proud of what he called his 'skill as talent-scout'. 'The only pity', as he says, 'is that I never asked for my percentage.'

The rest of the assignment passed off without incident. The detective told Bond that the Minister was put out at the way the young man left without so much as a goodbye. Bond said he sympathized. The detective said that he was most impressed.

'How did you do it? Fear, I s'pose?' he said.

'No,' said Bond as he sipped his first martini of the day.

'Vanity. It's stronger.'

During these days when Bond was in the South of France, Tiffany remained dutifully in the flat. By now she and May had reached a state of stabilized hostility, but life was tedious and she was lonely. There was not much to do with Bond away. She remembered one of Bond's earliest remarks about getting married, 'Most marriages don't add two people together. They subtract one from the other.' At the same time she hadn't understood him. Now she did.

Thanks to Bond she had been admitted to England without a passport. Immigration had told her to obtain one later from her embassy. With Bond away it seemed an opportunity to do so; she took a taxi off to Grosvenor Square.

It was the first time she had been inside an embassy but from the moment she entered she felt at home. Perhaps it was the smell, that curious American smell of mouthwash, air-conditioning and percolated coffee; perhaps it was the transatlantic tone of voice; perhaps it was the stars and stripes outside and the copies of the New York *Herald Tribune*. Whatever the cause, Tiffany was suddenly affected in a way she had not thought possible: she was homesick for New York.

There was a query on her passport; a good-looking young American major attached to the Embassy showed her to the office she required. He was from California and they chatted briefly about San Francisco. Suddenly she longed to talk about the places that she knew. And so it started. Five minutes later he was asking her to dinner. She refused, but was delighted to be asked. As she walked back across the square she was happier than she had been for weeks.

Good-looking majors working in embassies have ways of finding out the names of pretty girls who ask for passports. It is not legal but they do. This major also found her telephone number. This was not legal either: nor should he have rung Miss Case and told her that the passport office needed her next day at twelve. Just the same, she came, and when he asked her out to lunch, accepted.

This was the position, more or less, when Bond returned from France. He was at a strange disadvantage. Had it been anyone but Bond, he would have recognized the situation straight away. Tiffany had changed: she was alternately distant and over-loving, gentle yet rejecting, critical and then subservient. In short she was showing all the classic symptoms of a woman having an affair. But Bond, who had not been cuckolded since the age of twelve, was merely puzzled.

What was wrong with her? Was it her period? The condition seemed to last too long for that. Had he neglected her? He tried spoiling her – more scent, more underwear, another trip to France: but all too late. Never before had any woman treated him like this and all his wide experience of doting and adoring women had left him quite ignorant of the female heart. He made mistakes that no suburban husband would have made. Then, final degradation, he became jealous.

This unfamiliar emotion floored him completely, and he suffered like an adolescent youth. He tried to reason with himself. There were other women; no one was worth this sort of anguish – not even Tiffany. He suffered just the same.

It was a complete reversal of his character. Once away from her he tried to be sensible. It was no use. He was emotional by nature and had had no training with women he could not control. He tried to question her. Worse still, he threatened her. One night he hit her. He was very drunk. Next morning, sober, he was most repentant. She was icy. That evening, when he returned, the flat was empty.

At first he could not believe it, even when May announced, 'She's gone. The body's gone. She's left you.' But there was a letter on his desk.

Darling James,

We have enjoyed ourselves, and I shall be always grateful. But the truth is that you don't need a wife but I need a husband. When we first met you told me that you were married to a man called M. I think I know now what you meant.

Do understand, my darling, I'm not blaming you. But

I have met this major at the Embassy. His name is Nick. You'd like him, and he wants to marry me. I've said I will.

Do understand, dear James, that this is best for all of us. I know you love me, and that you will be hurt. But in time when the hurt is less you'll know that I am right.

Tiffany

Bond took it very hard. He had left many women in his time, but he had not been left before; he felt lonely, and betrayed. His pride was hurt. He realized that he had truly loved her.

Soft, sentimental as he was, he thought that he might still succeed in settling down and marrying her. Somehow he found the hotel where she was staying. He sent her a letter. It was returned unopened.

Presumably his vanity was hurt. At first he couldn't quite believe that she was serious. No woman had done this to him before. But when he finally did reach her on the telephone she calmly told him she was leaving for the States next morning. She did agree to see him – briefly.

Bond drove round to see her. He was still certain he could persuade her to come back to him and he was convinced that he loved her. Then he saw her; and he knew at once that everything was over.

She was waiting with her new fiancé, and introduced him straightaway as 'Nick'. He seemed a pleasant fellow, 'nothing extraordinary to look at and not over-bright, but clearly top-grade American husband material.' And Tiffany had a certain look he'd never seen before, 'the look of a woman who has got her man – and is all set to eat him.'

It was that look, says Bond, that cured him. Just a few hours before he had seriously thought of shooting the American. Now he was grateful for the chance to buy the man a drink.

It was all most civilized. They talked about New York and San Francisco. Bond promised to look them up next time he was in the States. He wished them both good luck, and then kissed Tiffany good-bye. As he drove back to Chelsea he thought of sending Tiffany some roses, but couldn't find a flower-shop.

'Perhaps,' as he says now, 'it was as well.'

13

The Soft Life

Honeychile Schultz was winning, there was no doubt about it. Now Bond was in danger of becoming Mr Schultz the second. The story he had told of his affair with Tiffany merely underlined the fact. Until then I hadn't realized how weak he really was with women once they had got through his defences. I should have recognized the pattern earlier. Those one night stands of his, the hit-and-run affairs, the rigidly controlled relationships with firmly married women were quite simply the manoeuvres of a man determined to keep womankind at bay.

Fleming had understood this perfectly when he said that Bond, like most hard men, was soft inside. Bond was essentially sentimental and at heart a vulnerable lover. And Honeychile, who was quite the opposite, must have appreciated this, especially after yesterday. The moral of the Tiffany affair was certainly not lost on her.

Bond though, appeared oblivious of what was going on: he had other worries on his mind. After our day aboard the *Honeychile* I had been hoping to continue with the story of his life from 1955 – the year made memorable by the assignment Fleming has described in that most colourful of all his books, *From Russia With Love*. Bond had other ideas. I was sitting on the terrace after breakfast and wading through a day-old copy of the *New York Times* when he appeared. He was smartly dressed in regulation James Bond dark blue shirt and freshly laundered white duck trousers. He had, he said, to spend the day with Mrs Schultz, but was expecting a telephone call from London. Would I please be sure to take it for him when it came.

'From whom?' He paused.

'From Universal Export. From M. to be precise. I've been attempting to get through to him all week. I can't imagine what he's up to. Moneypenny promised to make sure he rang.'

'And if he does, what do I say?'

'Just tell him that we've nearly finished and that I hope to see him soon. Tell him . . . ' At that moment there was a sharp blare from a car at the front of the hotel. Mrs Schultz was waving from her Rolls. Bond shrugged his shoulders.

'Tell him I'd like to know what's going on.'

But M. didn't ring, and it was late that evening when Bond reappeared at the hotel. Honeychile was with him looking, as the gossip columnists say, 'quite radiant'. There was a hint of power in her beauty now, a subtle gleam of triumph in those wide blue eyes. She did the talking, Bond, by and large, the drinking. They had been deep-sea fishing. Bond had apparently caught an eight-foot swordfish. The idea seemed out of character, but she made much of how he had played and handled it, 'just like a real professional'.

'I never knew you were a fisherman,' I said.

'I'm not. Fishing's for old men.'

'Not our sort of fishing, darling,' Honeychile insisted. 'Ours is for rich men.'

Bond said nothing, but when she left asked, 'Well, did he call?'

When I said no he shook his head and said, 'Well, I suppose that settles it. This would have amused Ian. Didn't they try to make him take up fishing when he retired?'

'Who's talking of retirement?'

'I am. I've had enough of hanging on here, waiting while they decide whether to have me back or not. Thank God for the lamented Mr Schultz – and for his fortune, and his wife.'

'Won't you be bored?' I said.

'Bored? Not as bored as I would be in London, waiting while they decide if I'm still fit for just one more assignment. I've had enough of it. It's always been the same.'

'What has?'

'The uncertainty and boredom – waiting and wondering whether you're still up to scratch, and all the time hanging on until M. is ready to employ you. Fleming knew how it felt – he described it when he wrote about the summer after Tiffany had gone. That was the first time in my life when I actually woke up in the morning feeling bored.'

This had been an ominous development for Bond, the first but not the last time in his life when he had found himself without his customary zest for living. Normally Bond lived at such a pitch of sheer activity that this stagnation was unbearable, and what Fleming called 'the blubbery arms of the soft life' soon had him round the neck. He started feeling suffocated.

At first Bond put this whole mood down to Tiffany's departure. When it refused to go he realized the truth. The life that he had led was catching up with him, nature was taking its revenge. Perhaps he had asked too much even of his iron nerves and shatter-proof physique, and that summer's boredom was no passing phase but a cumulative affliction of the spirit which was to cause him trouble in the years ahead.

It also set a pattern to his life. From now on he would increasingly rely on his assignments to keep the boredom of his normal life at bay; and not for nothing was he to describe boredom as 'the only vice I utterly condemn'. The strange inertia I was seeing in him now, clearly began way back in that summer of 1955, when he was thirty-four.

The Turkish mission, which Fleming wrote about in *From Russia With Love* was an important one for Bond in many ways – not least because it stopped him wallowing in depression. But there were other factors too which made this whole assignment something of a turning point in Bond's career.

Fleming's outline of the mission is surprisingly accurate (indeed at one stage M. was threatening to stop the book under the Official Secrets Act. He still maintains it gave too much away). Certainly Smersh did plan to involve Bond in a carefully planned scandal in Istanbul, as Fleming said they did. The bait was a beautiful young woman carefully trained and selected from their own organization. Her name, as Fleming says, was Tatiana Romanova and she was pretending to defect with the latest Russian cypher machine, the Spektor. Bond was sent out by M. to meet her. He slept with her, became convinced she was in love with him, and it was during their return to London on the Orient Express that Bond met and, against all the odds, defeated the trained Russian killer Granitsky, alias Donovan Grant.

This was a very real setback to the cold hard men in Smersh. Indeed, this incident was more of a victory for Bond than Fleming could reveal. For, naturally, the Turkish mission has to be assessed against the peculiar background of Bond's whole Secret Service life. The truth was that this attempt by Smersh was simply one more episode in their vendetta against Bond. Granitsky was intended to avenge the one-time top assassin in Smersh, Chiffre's killer, Oborin. But there was more to it than that. By now the directorate of Smersh had found out the truth about the James Bond books and realized the scale of the deception. There was some pressure to have the facts made public, but this was powerfully resisted by the redoubtable General Grubozaboyschikov, the head of Smersh. He had his enemies within the party and as a wily *apparatchik* who had survived both Stalin and Beria, he knew how dangerous such revelations of his gullibility could be. Lesser mistakes had cost much greater men their heads.

Instead the general reacted like the determined man he was. All the proof, so carefully prepared for months, of James Bond's existence was quietly consigned to the incinerators behind the Smersh headquarters on the Sretenka Ulitsa. And at the same time a foolproof plan was hatched to destroy the real-life Bond as well. This (and not the slightly flimsy argument that Fleming gives) was the real reason why a killer like Granitsky was brought in to murder him. This was why such elaborate plans were laid to tempt him out to Istanbul, and this was also why Bond's victory aboard the Orient Express was such a triumph.

But the events of these few autumn days in 1955 played their part not only in Bond's subsequent career but also in his legend. Fleming has described the frantic way that Smersh still tried to murder him. Even in Paris he had to face the arch-spy Rosa Klebb – disguised as a sweet old lady knitting in the Ritz – and as we know, the lethal dose of Japanese blow-fish poison from her knife-edged heel all but finished him. Thanks to Bond's stamina, (and possibly the low quality of Soviet *fugu* that year) he survived.

It was at this point that General Grubozaboyschikov chose to act like the realist he was. The vendetta against this agent Bond was clearly getting out of hand. Smersh had lost Oborin, Granitsky and now Rosa Klebb. Even by Russian standards, this was excessive.

Surely the best plan was quite simply to allow Bond to continue as the hero of the Fleming books. Why unmask him? Why even try to kill him – especially now that it appeared that he was in a dreadful state from *fugu* poisoning? The Russian evidence of his existence was destroyed and it was inconceivable that he would operate against the Soviet again. Quoting the words of an ancient Cossack proverb, Comrade General Grubozaboyschikov decided he would 'let sleeping moujiks snore'.

This decision of the general's produced the ironic situation which has continued ever since – for until today the Soviet and British Secret Services have had a shared interest in concealing Bond's existence. Certainly after the fiasco of the Smersh conspiracy outlined in Fleming's book, *From Russia With Love*, James Bond was safe from inadvertent exposure by the Russians.

Not that this really worried him that autumn. He had more serious problems on his plate, and even Fleming was soon talking as if this book would be the last that he would write about his hero. His summer boredom was essentially a symptom of a more profound disorder and the strain of his Turkish mission (the quite extraordinary physical demands of the oversexed Miss Romanova and the struggle with his appalling enemy, Granitsky) had virtually exhausted him. The real trouble was fatigue. This was why he bungled the end of the assignment. As he says, had he been on form, la Klebb could not have hoped to trick him in the way she did, only his blurred reactions let her get in that all but winning kick.

But others slipped up too – even that normally astute young Frenchman, René Mathis. A man of his experience should certainly have known better than to have consigned Rosa Klebb to headquarters in a laundry basket without searching her. (At the subsequent inquiry he shouldered all responsibility for the woman's death. She had swallowed a concealed cyanide capsule and was quite dead on arrival at the headquarters of the Deuxième Bureau.)

Bond had a bad few weeks that autumn, and he spent several days, heavily guarded and sedated, in a small private nursing home in Paris. He says that the first effect of the drug was enormous pain and a feeling of asphyxia. He never quite lost consciousness, and owed his life entirely to Mathis who gave him artificial respiration till the doctor came. At first it was seriously feared that the drug would cause permanent paralysis or damage to the nervous system. Thanks to Bond's stamina it didn't. A fortnight later Bond was flown home aboard a specially dispatched R.A.F Transport Command Comet. He spent another week in the London Clinic, where he was tested and examined by several of the country's top medical scientists. They pronounced him virtually recovered. M. (who incidentally hadn't visited him in hospital) awaited his return to duty.

It wasn't quite that simple. Bond was in no state to work. The symptoms of the 'soft life' which had afflicted him that summer seemed to have returned and, loner that he was, Bond found that there was nobody to turn to. The Russian girl, Tatiana, had disappeared completely from his life (after a long interrogation she changed her name and went as a sponsored immigrant to Australia. Bond isn't certain where). Aunt Charmian had moved to Sussex.

Luckily for Bond there was one man who could help him – the remarkable neurologist and consultant to the Secret Service, Sir James Molony. Bond is devoted to him, and still insists that he all but saved his reason. Certainly the two men have remained great friends, with Molony as the nearest thing to a psychiatrist and father confessor in Bond's scheme of things. He has also proved to be a useful ally – particularly against M. when the need arose – and has played a vital part in maintaining Bond's efficiency ever since. It is an intriguing story.

Bond still remembers the first evening when Molony visited him in Wellington Square. Bond at the time was incommunicado, finding it hard to sleep or to face anyone. Sir James had quite a job persuading May (who was very worried) to let him in. He had, he said, brought Bond a present – a bottle of Wild Turkey – and was to stay up half the night to help him drink it. At first Bond was suspicious, he'd had his fill of doctors in the last few days, but as he told himself, this was the first who had brought him anything to drink. Sir James seemed unconcerned at Bond's moroseness. A Dubliner, he had what the Irish call 'a way with him' and gradually Bond did what he'd never done before – he started talking of his childhood and parents and his early life. Sir James was a skilled listener – and drinker. Before the night was over he knew more about James Bond than anyone.

From long experience with the Secret Service he recognized Bond's type. He was what he called a 'puritan romantic' whose divided nature was in constant conflict with itself.

'You mean,' said Bond, 'I've never grown up?'

'No, not at all. It's simply that you've never managed to resolve the two sides of your nature. Rather the reverse – the way of life you've plumped for naturally exaggerates them, hence the conflict.'

'How do you mean?' said Bond.

'One side of you, the Scottish puritan, longs to have everything in order. It's basically your father's influence – it's obvious from your flat and from the way you dress. It's in your face as well. But then the other side of you, your mother's side, gets sick of all this order and restraint. That's when you break out and start longing to escape. The trouble is that the puritan lets you do this only in the line of duty, on some legitimate assignment. Small wonder that there's so much tension.'

Molony said all this so calmly that Bond suddenly felt scared.

'You mean that there's no cure?' he said.

'Not really. None at all. This is quite simply what you are. It's probably as well to know it and to face it. Then we can do something about it.'

'But does it mean I'm finished with the Service?'

'Not if you're sensible. This character of yours is what makes you perfect for your job, you have the ideal psychology. Why else d'you think that you've survived so long?'

'What's wrong with me then?'

'At times like this the tension between the two sides of your nature simply gets too much. That's when the boredom and the lethargy begin. And that's what we must fight.'

'Can we?' said Bond.

'Oh, certainly. I've worked out a therapy for men like you.'

The 'therapy' began next day at Sir James Molony's big country house near Sevenoaks. It turned out to be an intensive crash course in what he called 'enhanced living'. (This had been evolved in principle for jaded senior executives and men from the professions. Sir James adapted it to Bond's requirements. He was intrigued to see how Bond responded.) There was a lot of so-called 'basic exercise' – running and swimming and gymnasium work. There was fast driving and an afternoon spent on a carefully devised assault course. There were a succession of complex intellectual and mathematical conundra 'simply to stretch the brain', plus massage, dietary control and medical tests. Sir James drove him hard – and was not surprised when Bond responded.

Even so, he was concerned for Bond – and Bond is still grateful for the way that he stuck up for him with M. M. of course made no allowances for anyone (although he asked for none himself) and many readers of the Fleming books have found the famous conversation between M. and Sir James early in *Dr No* 'heartless and distasteful' as one reviewer put it. Certainly M. did appear unpleasantly cold-blooded in his attitude towards a loyal subordinate. There is something chilling in the way he talked of Bond as if he were totally expendable – 'won't be the first one that's cracked' – and then went on to list that scarifying catalogue of all the bits and pieces which the average human being can dispense with – 'gall bladder, spleen, tonsils, appendix, one of his two kidneys, one of his two lungs, two of his four or five quarts of blood, two-fifths of his liver, most of his stomach and half of his brain'.

But Bond loyally insisted that this was really an example of M.'s rough-and-ready sense of humour, and he pointed out that at this time the head of the Secret Service was under growing strain, and criticism. There had been more losses recently – and leakages. There was fresh talk of traitors and betrayal and within Whitehall itself the ancient feud between the Secret Service and the Security Service was coming to a head. M.'s reaction to this sort of strain was always to be tougher – with others just as with himself. And Bond insists that M. was right. He had to be a hard man to hold down his job.

'Too much sensitivity would have been quite out of place – no one in M.'s position could afford to be too understanding.'

I was surprised to find Bond even defending M. over the way he had to vent his disapproval by the enforced replacement of his favourite gun, the faithful old Beretta.

'He could have been more tactful, but events proved him right – as usual.' The new Walther PPK, so strongly recommended by the Armourer, has justified itself time and again. Bond says he owed his life to it, and that within a matter of weeks the Walther was as much a part of him as the Beretta had ever been: which was just as well once he was battling with Dr No.

The mission against Dr No (for all its hazards or perhaps because of them) brought James Bond back on form. It was the sort of mission in which he excelled. It seemed like a return to home ground to be back in Jamaica. Unlike the Turkish business with its atmosphere of constant double-dealing and betrayal, this offered Bond a chance to fight a clearcut enemy. Fleming has been permitted to describe the way that Bond tracked down the diabolical doctor to his guano-coated hideaway of Crab Key in the Caribbean. Thanks to James Bond he was destroyed, and with him the threat to American space programme from Cape Kennedy. But there was more to Bond's victory than that. Dr No was evil and Bond felt no remorse for the appalling death that finally befell him.

On his return, however, Bond didn't get the welcome he deserved, for suddenly the attention of that powerhouse of the secret war beside the Park was focused on one spot – Eastern Europe. During Bond's absence, Hungary had risen in revolt against its Russian masters. Its borders with the West were open. With all her eastern satellites in disarray, Russia herself was threatened – and the Western Secret Services suddenly seemed offered their greatest pickings since the war ended.

For several days Bond was confined to routine duty inside the department. Headquarters were on twenty-four-hour standby and Bond joined the overworked band of men and women keeping in contact with events in Eastern Europe. There was a sense of history in the making as the reports came humming down from the communications section up on the thirteenth floor. There would be hurried conferences, queries to follow through, and as the fighting raged in Budapest, Bond found himself snatching a few hours sleep on a camp bed in the duty room then slogging on throughout the day without much chance of rest. It was a tiring frustrating time. He disliked the sense of waiting impotently, whilst others did the fighting. He knew that M. was holed up in his office, but hardly saw him now. Just occasionally he had a chance to talk to the Chief of Staff, who looked, if possible, more overworked than ever.

Hungary had overnight become an open field for all sorts of covert operations from the West. The American C.I.A. had played a big part in the rising, and now was seeking to exploit it. So were the British. They had their agents inside Budapest. Bond knew that they were hard at work recruiting others and trying to enlarge their network for the future. When the Red tanks moved in and it was clear that the revolt would soon be over the real pressure started. But even then it seemed that Bond would be no more than a spectator from the duty room at Regents Park. He knew that several members of the 00 section had been in Hungary. He envied them, but knew better than to try to find out more about them. Curiosity could be a dangerous habit in the Secret Service.

Then, without the slightest warning, Bond was summoned for an interview with M. It was the first time he had talked to him for weeks, and M. was showing signs of weariness. His eyes were pouched, the spartan office smelt of late-night conferences and stale tobacco smoke. He leant back in his chair, massaging his neck, then poured himself some coffee from a Thermos jug.

'Well, battle-stations, 007. I hope you're feeling fresher than you look.'

'I was hoping for some action,' Bond replied.

'That's all you ever think of,' M. growled irritably, sipping his coffee. 'Perhaps you're right,' he added, as he heaved himself up in his chair. 'Perhaps you're right. Now, as you've probably deduced, I have been holding you here in reserve during the last few days just in case anything went wrong. Unfortunately it has. I need you out in Budapest as fast as possible. Pull up a chair and I'll explain.'

It seemed that for several days now M. had been concerned about the information coming out of Hungary. There had been unexplained delays and recently the chaos in the country had resulted in a breakdown in communications. Certain facts filtered through, some of them correct, others quite demonstrably false and, as M. said, it was essential now to know 'the total picture'. 009, a former lecturer from the School of Slavonic Studies, had been in Hungary since long before the rising. Forty-eight hours ago, his transmissions ceased. M. said that this was 'most disquieting' (one of M.'s favourite phrases which really mean 'disastrous') for, as Bond gathered from M.'s non-committal briefing, 009 had been acting as liaison man between the different resistance groups inside Budapest. He had had the task of organizing for the future, and he alone had been entrusted with the full list of names, contacts and potential agents.

'Quite contrary to all accepted practice to have one man with so many lives at stake,' said M., 'But there was no alternative. It was a risk we had to take. It looks as if we may have come unstuck.'

M. looked at Bond. There was silence in the room. Both of them knew quite well what would happen if 009's information ever reached the enemy. Both of them knew what needed to be done.

'Chief of Staff has all the information that we have on 009, and he has already made arrangements for your journey through Vienna.' The commanding voice was calm. Only the way he gripped his pipe revealed a little of the tension that he felt.

'I'll do my best to find him,' Bond replied.

'He doesn't matter any more. It's just the list that counts,' said M.

All revolutions seem to smell the same and Budapest that fateful autumn had something in the air Bond recognized at once – the unforgettable scent of violence. It was a sour, acrid smell of burning buildings and unburied bodies. It was the reek of cordite and the fumes from the diesel engines of the Russian tanks that lumbered through the streets. By now it was a hopeless smell. Bond realized that he must hurry. There were still pockets of resistance. The students were holding out in the university and in the southern quarter there were mammoth blocks of flats where the resistance started. In parts of the old city too the flags of the liberation were still fluttering, but it was clear that the uprising was now doomed. The Russian tanks controlled the streets. Government troops were slowly recovering the city. Soon the arrests would start, the trials, the reprisals. Soon it would all be over.

Bond was dressed as a workman – grey shirt and cap, a pair of ancient overalls. During a revolution it is as well to be as inconspicuous as possible. He spoke sufficient Russian to maintain his cover-story as a skilled man from the big Soviet car works on the outskirts of the city. In Vienna he had been provided with his documents and local currency. His only weapon was the Walther PPK in its shoulder holster. He was used to it by now, and was reassured to feel its solid bulk against his armpit.

During the few hours he had spent in Vienna, he had been given certain leads to 009 – an address in the old city where 009 had often stayed, a girl called Nashda who was said to be his mistress, and a man called Heinkel. Head of Station in Vienna had been slightly vague about the Heinkel man. He was supposedly part German, part Hungarian, and had been working with the liberation movement in the city. He seemed to have some sort of private following and claimed backing from the Americans. Certainly he had money, arms and a transmitter, and 009 had evidently trusted him. It was through Heinkel's set-up that he had made radio contact with the British station in Vienna.

In Vienna Bond's task had still seemed quite straightforward. (Most assignments seem straightforward during briefing – it's only later that the complications start.) But now that he was in the city, he realized how difficult it was. He had to find a man whose very nature was to be elusive. The city was in chaos. There were no telephones, no transport, and if the Russians caught him . . . Bond wondered how long his accent and his documents would satisfy those squat, determined figures with their red-starred caps and

256

their machine guns.

There was a lot of firing that afternoon and Bond decided to hide up till nightfall. There was an unfinished block of flats close to the Deli Station; from there he could see a pall of smoke rising from the far side of the Danube. Once darkness fell it was easier to make his way across the city. The Russians had their searchlights out along the river, but the chief hazard lay in their patrols and checkpoints on the streets. He dodged them without too much trouble.

The address he sought turned out to be a small apartment in a big old block above the river. The lift was out of action, and there was nobody about. The electricity was off as well and Bond had to grope his way up the steep stairway, striking matches as he went to find the door he wanted. He rang the bell. There was no answer, but when he pushed the door it opened. He struck another match. The hallway was in chaos, with pictures ripped down from the walls, furniture smashed up, and drawers emptied across the floor. There was blood too along the wall. The match went out: Bond drew his gun then struck another. There was a bedroom off the hall, and in the flickering matchlight he could see a large brass bed. Someone was lying on it. Bond recognized the staring eyes and narrow features over the hideously gashed throat. It was 009. Then the match went out. Bond knew there was no need to strike another.

What should he do? M. had spoken of a list, but it was unlikely to be in the flat – even if 009 had made it. Whoever killed him had been looking hard for something. But once again Bond had no idea who the murderers could be. Nor, with the Russian soldiers on the streets, would he have much chance now of finding out. It looked as if the mission had aborted. Those weeks of work, the risks, and now the death of 009 had been in vain. All he could hope for was to get out fast – and leave the explanations till he was face to face with M. Others had been at fault. He had done everything he could. He put away his gun and turned to go.

The flat was in total darkness and he groped his way towards the door. He thought he could remember where it was, but found himself blundering against the furniture. He put out his hand to save himself and touched something soft. It was a woman's breast.

'Don't move,' said a voice. 'Just raise your hands.' He did, then in the darkness felt himself being frisked for weapons. Somebody found the shoulder holster and removed the gun. Then a flashlight was shone straight into his face.

'Let's go,' the voice behind it said. 'We're late.'

There were two of them – the woman he had blundered into and a man who held the flashlamp. He also had a gun which was pressed uncomfortably against Bond's kidneys. Bond saw that both of them were dressed in white, like medical orderlies, and just along the street there was a small white ambulance.

'Get in,' said the man. The woman held the gun now. Bond complied.

'Where are we going?' he inquired.

'To see a man called Heinkel,' she replied. 'He's expecting you.'

The driver evidently knew the city and although the ambulance was stopped several times by troops, it was immediately waved on. It travelled fast, its siren wailing through the deserted streets. Bond looked towards the woman. She had a round, white, pudding face and spectacles with stainless-steel rims. She wore a nurse's head-dress with a big red cross and held the gun inside her nurse's apron. Something in her expression told Bond that she would like to use it.

As far as he could judge the ambulance was travelling down a long boulevard. Then they slowed down, and swung in through some high gates. They seemed to be inside a park. There were more gates, trees, a long wall and finally the ambulance drew up outside a squat grey building. There was a strange stench in the air, and suddenly the silence of the night was shattered by a high-pitched scream. It continued, like a soul in torment, then just as it died out, the scream turned into laughter, a hideous, hysterical sound. Bond drew back. The woman laughed and pushed him forward with her gun.

'Come on. Get out. You're worrying the inmates.'

'Inmates?' said Bond.

'Sure. The hyaenas. Haven't you seen a zoo before?'

The building was the monkey-house of Budapest's world-famous zoo. Owing to the rising there were no keepers, but there were lights on in the office. Bond was led in. Behind the desk sat a huge man in a shiny leather hunting jacket, smoking a cigar. He had a sub-machine gun on the desk in front of him, and nodded curtly as Bond entered.

'No luck,' the woman said. 'We searched the place again from top to bottom, but there was no trace of it. This character turned up, though, as you said he might. He's English, by the sound of it. Shall I dispose of him?'

The woman's grey, round face was quite impassive, but Bond could detect an eager glint behind the spectacles.

'Good heavens, Rosalie, my dear. What manners! Dispose of Mr Bond? Whatever will he think if you talk like that. Please leave us, Rosalie. We have important matters to discuss.'

The big man's voice was soft, reminding Bond of Peter Lorre in *The Maltese Falcon*.

'Immediately, Rosalie, my dear.'

The woman jumped, then scuttled off. The big man scratched himself and yawned.

'Forgive all this,' he said, 'but these are most unpleasant times. Sit down. A drink? My name is Heinkel. I and my men have been here since the rising started. We found the zoo deserted when the Russians came. It's a good place to hide.' So you came looking for poor 009? Vienna told me to be on the lookout for you when I spoke to them this afternoon. You were extremely lucky to get through.'

A big hand backed with thick black hair pushed a bottle of Dimple Haig across the desk. Bond poured himself a generous measure and drank it neat. After the hunger of the day it tasted good.

'Who murdered 009?' he asked.

The big man shrugged his shoulders. 'Who knows? A lot

of people have been killed here in the last few days. He's in good company. What I would like to know is why *you're* here. Vienna didn't tell me that.'

'They felt that 009 needed assistance. It seems that they felt right.'

'Only assistance, Mr Bond? Are you certain there was nothing else?'

'Like what?'

'Like, shall we say, a list? Just for the sake of argument shall we suppose that the deceased 009 recorded certain names before he died?'

The big hand on the desk moved towards the gun. As Bond looked at Heinkel, he thought how appropriate his hideout was. Those simian features and the bloodshot eyes could have been staring at him through the bars. Even the soft voice and the expensive jacket couldn't disguise the ape-like essence of the man – nor the unspoken threat that he was making.

'Mr Bond,' said Heinkel softly, 'I require that list.'

'What are you up to, Heinkel?' Bond replied. 'Just whose side are you on?'

Heinkel laughed then – not an attractive sound.

'My own, my friend. It's the most profitable I find. I work for anyone who pays me. During these last few days the money has been good. It will be even better if I can somehow find that last will and testament of 009. Who would pay most for it – your British Secret Service, or the Russians?'

'That's a dangerous game you're playing,' Bond replied. 'But even if there were a list, how could I have it? As you know, 009 was dead when I arrived.'

'Ah yes. He was most certainly dead. We know that. But you had your orders where to come, and you knew where to look. That list please, Mr Bond. Immediately.'

The hand was on the trigger and Bond recognized the dull flat tone of Heinkel's voice. Heinkel was a killer. Bond tried to bluff.

'Suppose,' he said, 'Suppose I had this list you speak of. How much would be in it all for me?'

'No deals, Mr Bond. Either you give it freely or we use force. If we use force it won't be pleasant. Remember what happened to your friend 009.'

Bond had been coolly working out the line of fire from the sub-machine gun. This was a situation he had often had to face in training. There was a man called Roscoe who was on the staff at Regents Park. The Service's Armourer had recruited him from a circus. His speciality was dodging bullets and he instructed the 00 section in this invaluable trade. The secret of it lay in speed and creating some diversion. Bond had become quite good at it, but he had never had to use his skill against a man like Heinkel.

Luckily his brain was very clear. Once again he found that danger was a stimulant, and when he moved he moved with the co-ordination of an athlete. His right swung out and sent the whisky bottle shattering against the wall. At the same time he threw his body sideways so that he fell protected by the desk. When Heinkel started firing the bullets were a foot above him.

It was a brave attempt but it was useless. Before Bond reached Heinkel, the woman and two men with automatics had rushed in, and from the floor Bond found himself facing the black muzzles of their guns.

'D'you want him killed, Heinkel?' shrieked the woman.

'Not yet, Rosalie. He deserves something better than a bullet. And he could still be useful. On your feet, Mr Bond. And do be careful. I rarely miss a second time.'

Slowly Bond lifted himself up. Heinkel prodded at his stomach with the sub-machine gun.

'Now Rosalie. Please search this gentleman – thoroughly.'

It was an obscene performance, but there was nothing Bond could do as the clammy fingers started to undress him. The woman's small red tongue was visible. The eyes were glittering through their spectacles.

'Take your time, Rosalie,' said Heinkel, as she started to explore him. Bond closed his mind to what was happening.

Finally Heinkel ordered her to stop.

'That's enough, Rosalie. It isn't there.'

Bond felt more naked than ever in his life before.

'Now Mr Bond', said Heinkel. 'I'm feeling generous, but don't abuse my generosity. I'll give you one more chance. We're leaving in the morning. There's nothing else for us in Budapest and we must be getting back for our hero's welcome from the Americans. You have until then to remember where you have hidden that list we want. If your memory improves, you can have your freedom. If not, you stay here till the Russians find you – and I'll make certain that they know exactly who you are.'

He rose to his feet, and paused to light a fresh cigar. One of the men twisted Bond's arm behind his back as if in warning.

'Oh, and incidentally, Mr Bond. You'll be having company. Be careful how you treat your room-mate. He's bigger than you.'

Bond was dragged out into the main corridor of the monkey house. None of the cages had been cleaned for days – the stench was overpowering – and as Bond passed, small bright nocturnal eyes watched this strange naked ape walking along the wrong side of the bars. Some of them shrieked at him. There were the small grey monkeys, huddled like birds along their perches, gentle orang-utangs, neurotic rhebuses, and iron-faced mandrils with their bold backsides. Bond passed them all, and at the far end of the corridor he saw a small steel door. One of his captors slid it open and pushed Bond inside.

'Sweet dreams, Mr Bond. Your taste in exotic bedfellows is legendary and I am only sorry we are unable to provide you with something more stimulating. But at least we can guarantee you won't be bored. Goodnight Mr Bond, and goodbye.'

A guttural, self-satisfied laugh echoed round the steel cages. Footsteps receded down the corridor. A door clanged shut. Bond strained his ears but could hear nothing.

The straw beneath his feet was moist and spongy and the stench in the cage was overpowering. The stink of accumulated dung fought with the nauseating sweetness of rotting food, but above them both Bond detected the rank and unmistakeable odour that only a terrified animal can exude.

He stood rock still waiting for his eyes to get used to the darkness. Looking up he saw that this part of the cage was open to the sky: low, dense cloud obliterated what light the moon might have shed, but he could make out the bars of the cage and a concrete walk beyond.

Suddenly he heard the straw rustle and a black shape bounded forward and crashed heavily against the bars. The creature shrieked and leapt back into the darkness, and immediately hurled itself again at the bars and shook them violently. Gradually it subsided and after throwing straw in the air and covering its head completely, it returned to its corner.

Bond did not need a zoologist to tell him his cell-mate was a gorilla.

He attempted to assess the situation. So far the animal had ignored his presence, but clearly it was only a matter of time until it turned on him. Something in the back of his mind told him that gorillas were exclusively vegetarian, but in the circumstances it did not seem reassuring. He was naked and unarmed, and his adversary was twice as powerful as any man he had ever encountered.

Shambling across the straw the gorilla crouched again near the bars. For a moment it was still and Bond could see exactly how enormous it was. Beneath its huge, overhanging shelf of a brow two glittering eyes glared balefully into the darkness. Thoughtfully, it clasped a bar in each huge hand and gave them an experimental shake. Nothing moved. It screamed with anger and, moving far faster than Bond had anticipated, raced round the cage scarcely touching the walls or floor but appearing to ricochet off each surface like a huge, shaggy missile.

It settled in its corner and Bond heard it breathing angrily and grumbling to itself. Seconds later it re-emerged into the light. Then Bond saw something white behind it. It was the body of a girl. And as he stared, he saw her hand make a barely perceptible gesture: a thumbs-up signal.

Bond felt a solution was within his grasp. If the girl was alive there was hope for him, for both of them. Probably none of the animals had been fed for days: they were desperately hungry, and bewildered by fear. Just like him, all they craved was freedom.

Bond took a step towards her, but the gorilla saw him and barked with rage and terror. It jumped up and down, leapt from side to side, and beat its chest. In a paroxysm of fury it lashed out at the bars. A small piece of cement fell and rattled on the concrete walk outside. Bond felt he had no choice but to attack, and with both hands clasped rigidly together he chopped down on the ape's neck.

It was a mistake. Hard though the edges of his hands were thanks to his karate training he felt them bruise badly against the solid collar of muscle and hair that protected the ape. Its long arm slashed out and caught him off balance. He fell to the floor, but was instantly on his feet again and ready to ward off the attack which he had foolishly provoked.

To his amazement, the gorilla, instead of savaging him, hurled itself once again at the bars. This time a small avalanche of cement tumbled down and one of the bars visibly buckled.

Bond suddenly knew that his only chance of survival lay in terrifying the animal still further. He filled his lungs and released what he trusted was a blood-curdling imitation of a gorilla's cry. At the same time he pounded the steel door with both his fists.

The animal reacted as he hoped. It screamed back at him but seized the damaged bar and shook it with all the power in its 450-pound body.

Bond screamed, shouted and bellowed until his throat was raw. He thumped and kicked the door until his feet and hands were bruised. He yelled at the girl to join in. She shouted and thumped too. The gorilla seemed in the grip of hysteria. It shook the bars and shrieked with them.

At last, with a crash of concrete, the loose bar fell away, and, as it struck the ground, the gorilla vanished into the darkness.

Bond slumped on to the floor. Seconds passed before either of them would move, and then, without a word, they squeezed out of the cage.

The zoo was deserted except for a single man guarding the ambulances. Bond dealt with him, took his gun, and, more importantly, his clothes. Finally they were away.

It was not until they were racing through the outskirts of the city that Bond had a chance to ask who she was.

'Who are you?' she countered.

'My name is James Bond,' he replied. 'A man called Heinkel put me there. And who on earth are you?'

Even as Bond pronounced his name he heard the woman gasp.

'Bond,' she said, 'James Bond? Why did you come so late? We needed you.'

'Who are you then?' said Bond.

'My name is Nashda. I was with 009 when Heinkel killed him. I've been here ever since.

'Heinkel has no idea I'm alive – he thought the gorilla had killed me. I've been in that stinking cage for two days, just lying there playing dead. I am sure he thought the thing would dispose of you in the same way. In fact, he was as frightened of you and me as we were of him. All he wanted to do was get out of his cage.'

It was a nightmare drive. As they raced through the outskirts of the city, dodging the refugees, the burning tanks and the Russian road blocks, they gradually pieced together what had happened. In the beginning 009 had worked with Heinkel and had trusted him – then, as the rising started to go wrong, he had found out the truth. Heinkel was an adventurer – and a criminal: his followers were members of his gang. For some time now they had pretended to be Hungarian patriots. This got them backing and protection from the C.I.A., but they had merely used the confusion within Budapest as cover for a series of armed robberies. They had been looting unopposed – jewelry, banks. Whilst men were dying in their hundreds Heinkel was enriching himself, and his most ruthless move of all was to use three ambulances he had commandeered. As Bond had seen, he had even dressed up members of his gang as orderlies and nurses, and tomorrow morning they would be driving off to Austria with their loot.

'What about 009?' asked Bond. 'Why did they kill him?'

'Because he threatened to expose them – and because . . .' the woman paused.

'Yes?' said Bond.

'Because they wanted certain information.'

'And did they get it?'

'No,' she replied. 'It's safe – with me.'

By late that afternoon they made the Austrian frontier, and by evening they were in Vienna. Their first stop was the office of the British Head of Station A in an impressive office block in Dresdnerstrasse. Suddenly the horror of the last few days was over. And for the first time, Bond could concentrate upon the girl. She was Hungarian and young and very pretty with short fair hair and a big generous mouth. From long experience Bond knew how pleasurable she would be to kiss. One of her eyes – they were green and thickly lashed – was larger than the other: this too for Bond was an almost automatic source of attraction. He had to tell himself that she was simply not available. She had been 009's woman. He was dead. It would be unthinkable to begin desiring her in such circumstances. Besides, they both had work to do. Rather than write the list of agents where it could be discovered by an enemy, 009 had made the girl learn it by heart before she died. Bond was impressed by her extraordinary memory.

'It's simply concentration, Mr Bond,' she said, smiling demurely. 'There's really nothing like it.'

Bond, who wasn't certain if she was making fun of him frowned and told her that his name was James.

'I know,' she said.

Bond spent some time discussing their arrangements with the Station head. He was a tall, pernickety ex Foreign Office man. He had already been in touch with London and M.'s orders were that the list was far too valuable to risk transmitting to London – even in cypher and employing the theoretically secure wave-band used by the station. The girl must be brought immediately to London, and to ensure that there was no chance of slip-up, Bond was to bring her personally.

'M.'s orders are that you're not to let her from your sight for a moment,' said the Head of Station.'

'That sounds romantic,' said the girl.

Bond was expecting to fly back with her that evening, but it proved impossible to get a flight. The station clerk booked them both 1st class aboard the Arlberg Express for Paris.

'Dear Mr Bond,' the girl said when he told her. 'That means that we'll have to share a sleeper – if you're to follow orders.'

The Arlberg Express left Vienna at 8.45 next morning. Bond was still wary of the girl. She was a little too intelligent and beautiful for comfort. But they got on together. By the time they reached the station he had finally persuaded her to call him 'James'.

'What did you do about that devil, Heinkel?' she asked.

'Not much I could do,' he replied. 'Except to get Head of Station to send round a general warning to the Austrians. They'll stop him at the frontier if he tries to get through.'

The train was crowded, but the excitement of the long train journey affected Bond as usual. They spent the day enjoying one anothers company. After the hell of the last few days, it was wonderful to be alive and to enjoy the scenery of Austria. In the evening they dined – expensively. (Bond decided that the British Government owed a girl like this a good dinner in the first-class eating waggon. It was delicious. So was the champagne.) And after the champagne, the coffee, the Courvoisier, there was the long nostalgic journey through the night. Poor 009 was quietly forgotten, as Bond proved (to his silent satisfaction) that he had been right about her mouth. As they fell asleep to the busy rhythm of the wheels Bond told his conscience that he was following M.'s orders to the letter.

It was still dark outside when he awoke. The train was

inside Germany and in their small compartment there was a faint light from the ceiling. The girl was sleeping quietly beside him. But Bond knew that something definite had woken him. His gun was in its holster. He drew it softly, eased back the safety catch and waited. And then he saw the handle moving on the door. Someone was trying to get in.

For Bond it was almost a matter of routine to make sure his bedroom door was locked when on assignment. Before he went to sleep he had placed wooden wedges under it. The handle turned again, and someone in the corridor outside began to push. The door stayed shut. Then the handle was rattled angrily.

'Passport control – open up please,' said a voice. Bond recognized it – from the zoo in Budapest.

The girl was now awake. Bond signalled to her silently to dress, and at the same time started pulling on his trousers and his shoes.

'We've had our passports checked,' he shouted.

'This is a special check,' the voice shouted back. 'Open up please, right away. Police.'

By now Bond and the girl were fully dressed.

The handle rattled once again, and Bond felt someone pushing at the door. It opened half an inch.

'All right then, Mr Bond,' said Heinkel. 'No tricks now if you please. I want the girl. She's valuable, so open up.'

'And if I don't?' said Bond.

'Mr Bond, you are being very irritating and my patience is exhausted.'

The voice was satin smooth but ugly with menace.

'You and the girl are supposed to be dead. I left the Budapest zoo last night happy with the thought that you were both dead. I dined out on your death, Mr Bond. I ate well, I slept well. I returned to my temporary base at the zoo only to discover that you had been impertinent enough to stay alive, and that furthermore you had allowed a very valuable specimen to escape, to say nothing of the valuable specimen you have in the carriage with you. Fortunately, through my contacts in your Vienna office I had little difficulty in tracing you. But now no more of your tricks, Mr Bond. I am beginning to find them irksome. I have five men out here; all of them are armed. We have gone to considerable trouble to join you on this train. Kindly don't spoil our journey. Now, open the door!'

Bond knew that Heinkel wasn't bluffing, and so he withdrew the wedges and pulled back the door. Heinkel was outside, smoking a cigar. In his right hand he negligently held the small sub-machine gun he had in Budapest. Bond handed him his gun.

'How very touching,' Heinkel said when he saw the girl. 'Comforting a dead comrade's girl-friend, Mr Bond? This way, if you please.'

Heinkel had a compartment further down the train, and Bond and the girl were pushed along the swaying corridor.

'No hurry, Mr Bond,' said Heinkel softly. 'You know your Service's security in Vienna could be so much better. We understand from our contact there that the young lady has the information we require, but we can take our time to get it. It's two more hours to the border. I'm sure that we can make her talk by then.'

From the racket of the wheels, Bond knew the train was going fast. Heinkel was just behind him in the narrow corridor. Nashda was following. As usual at the point of crisis Bond's mind was suddenly quite clear, and, almost effortlessly, he found himself working out the odds. If he obeyed Heinkel, he knew that neither he nor Nashda had a chance. Once Heinkel and his gang had tortured her, they wouldn't want witnesses. Bond and the girl were doomed.

But there was just one chance. The hazards were enormous, but it was better than torture and certain death. As they passed the train door at the end of the compartment Bond seemed to stumble. As he turned, his shoulder cannoned into Heinkel's stomach, and at the same time he reached out and grabbed the handle of the door. It moved. The door swung open, and for one frightful moment Bond and Heinkel were hanging over the abyss. Luckily Bond kept his balance. Heinkel didn't. Bond heaved, and, like an overloaded mail sack, Heinkel's great body was sent thudding out.

Bond grabbed the girl. He was still unarmed, but with Heinkel gone the other gunmen paused. But Bond knew that any moment one of them would fire. He had to take a chance. As far as he could tell the train was on the top of an embankment.

'Now,' he shouted to the girl. And clutching her, he jumped. At that moment he remembered night-time parachute descents over the pitch-black countryside of wartime France. Instinctively he hunched his shoulders, tucked in his head and raised his knees. And luckily the earth was soft. They landed heavily, then rolled, tumbling together to the bottom of the embankment. The first thing Bond remembers is of the girl bending over him and tearfully asking him if he were dead.

The spot where they had landed was ten miles from Innsbruck. Somehow they limped into a village. By the time they reached it, it was nearly morning. Bond's back was hurting badly, and it took most of that day to sort things out. At first the police wanted to arrest them. Heinkel's body had been found a few miles back. It had hit a bridge. Bond identified it from its size and from the leather jacket. And finally, after a call to Head of Station in Vienna, Bond and the girl were driven into Innsbruck, then flown home. Just for once, Bond was grateful for a plane.

14

The Truth about M.

I felt sorry for Bond by now. Headquarters had obviously been treating him abominably. He had been here six weeks and he was patently quite fit for duty. He was also desperately anxious for a word from someone in Headquarters. To my certain knowledge he had tried ringing through to M. five times at least during the last two days, ·and once he had even packed and booked himself aboard a scheduled plane to London. Cynically, I thought at first that he was simply running out on Honeychile, but now I realized it wasn't that. He longed to work. The Secret Service was his life and he felt a compulsive loyalty to all his colleagues in Headquarters. It clearly troubled him to think that they had quietly forgotten him.

He had to break off his account of the Heinkel business to take a cable. It was the answer he was waiting for. He read it, pulled a face, and threw the telegram across to me. It was an uptight little message, making me feel the Secret Service still had a lot to learn on personal relations.

'Imperative you stay and await orders stop desist attempts at telephonic contact.'

It was signed, M.

Bond shrugged his shoulders.

'Typical,' he said. 'M. is impossible these days. He seems

271

to think he can go on for ever – just like old Herbert Hoover in the F.B.I. I was hoping to get through to Bill Tanner. Clearly I'm not permitted to.'

There was a tinge of bitterness now as he spoke and I was surprised to hear him finally talk like this of M. Until now he had always carefully defended him. Now the pretence was over.

'I didn't realize that M. was quite that bad,' I said.

'Few people do,' said Bond and smiled. 'He's a smart old monster – wonderful at public relations and great skill at making himself indispensable to a succession of Prime Ministers, but really the old boy's become a menace. Mark you, as I said, he used to be extremely good. He was a splendid leader and had great flair once, but I noticed him beginning to lose touch around the time of the Hungarian affair. It all began to get too much for him. I even saved him once you know. It's a strange story.'

Bond leaned back, lit a cigarette, and stretched himself luxuriously. He grinned as if the memory still amused him.

'No, it was very rum,' he said. 'If you read carefully between the lines of the Fleming books in places you get a hint of what was happening. That incidentally was why M. and Fleming had their final bust-up, but that's another story.'

'But what about the Fleming books,' I asked. 'Once the Russians had rumbled the deception, what was the point of letting them continue?'

'As I said yesterday, at one stage it was planned to finish them with *From Russia With Love*. Frankly, I think Fleming had had enough of them by then. He was getting bored with being what he called "the faithful Boswell to the Secret Service". He even used to moan to me about the way his friends blamed him for all my vices. No, it was M. entirely who was to blame for the books continuing. You see, the Dr No affair came up and M. saw, quite rightly, that this could provide wonderful publicity for his department.'

'But why should the Secret Service need publicity?'

'That,' replied Bond, 'is a naive question. In 1956

272

everyone was criticizing us. There was the Crabbe affair – you remember, the frogman who was caught in Portsmouth harbour with the latest Russian cruiser during Bulganin's visit. Caused quite a diplomatic incident. Well, we were blamed for that – quite unjustly as it happens. And the Americans were getting difficult. Precious little help was coming from the C.I.A. Against all this, Ian's books seemed to drive home the point that our Secret Service was still the finest in he world. And the Dr No affair of course *did* tell the public of that little favour that we did the American space programme. That was the message M. wanted to get over loud and clear.'

'Then why not let the truth come out completely, and have the fact of your identity made public?'

'No. We couldn't have done that. To start with, Ian just wasn't that sort of writer. I think he could only write about this fictional James Bond he had created in the past. He had to have what he used to call his author's licence to play around with facts and characters a little when he felt inclined. And of course it suited M. to have this enormously successful publicity put out as so-called fiction. In any other form it would have been impossible.'

'And you really didn't mind?'

'Quite honestly I didn't – not by now. My few close friends were in the Service, and it amused me to find myself suddenly becoming a sort of popular hero. Remember it was only now – say 1956 and '57 – that the books started catching on. Ian became suddenly excited at the idea of having a best-seller on his hands and I really couldn't tell him it had got to stop. We used to get on very well together.'

Another factor in the story of the books was that just about this time, Bond suddenly began to have the great successes of his career. Thanks to Sir James Molony he had avoided a recurrence of the trouble of the year before. Jamaica – and the fight with Dr No – had put him back on form. He was supremely confident, and fighting fit, and it was in this mood that he embarked upon the Goldfinger affair.

Again, one must be grateful to Ian Fleming for simply

being there to describe this most extraordinary coup in *Goldfinger*. Perhaps he paid overmuch attention to the more bizarre aspects of that arch villain and capitalist extraordinary, Arno Goldfinger. His cheating habits at cards, the game of golf he played with Bond at Sandwich are of no great importance, when put against the real menace of the man. But they were the sort of personal details no writer can resist and Goldfinger's obsession – his Midas-like craving for gold – was at the heart of his whole criminal achievement. Had it not been for Bond, he would undoubtedly have robbed Fort Knox: and once that happened. once the gold reserves of the world's richest nation had disappeared, the whole financial structure of the west would have been at risk. By beating Goldfinger, Bond became the man who saved the world's economy.

But when he returned to London something distinctly odd occurred. He was expecting if not congratulations at least a certain warmth from M. There was no sign of it – rather the reverse. M.'s reception was distinctly frosty. The Prime Minister was anxious to offer Bond a knighthood, and the Americans had suggested the Congressional Medal of Honour. M. forbade both, and in a way that made it seem as if James Bond had actually been seeking honours.

It was then that Bond got the first inkling of the truth – M. was jealous. This was Bill Tanner's theory too. Bond said he really didn't mind about the knighthood.

'And didn't you?' I asked.

Bond smiled ruefully.

'*Sir* James Bond? It isn't really me – but May would have liked it, and of course Aunt Charmian. If it had been offered I'd probably have accepted. But it wasn't.'

Instead, M. recommended Bond for what he evidently felt his due. Bond was promoted to Grade IV. Practical as ever, Bond told himself that it was better than nothing: at any rate his salary increased by £750. And on the strength of this, James Bond decided to indulge himself.

For some time now his old grey 4½-litre Bentley with the Amhurst Villiers supercharger had been giving trouble. He had owned the car for more than twenty years. Marthe de Brandt had given it him before the war and he had been hanging on to it for sentimental reasons. He told himself that this was stupid – especially now that it was needing a new engine and regularly costing more each year to run. Wakeford, the former Bentley mechanic who looked after it for him had obviously grown tired of it, and it was Wakeford who told him about the Bentley Continental which, in Fleming's graphic phrase, 'some rich idiot had married to a telegraph pole on the Great West Road'. Wakeford convinced him that the car could be restored, and Bond finally paid £1,500 for the whole wreck as it stood.

Bond had always dreamed of building his ideal car. This was his chance. Rolls straightened out the chassis and fitted the new engine Bond had set his heart on – a six cylinder with 8.1 compression. Then came the biggest luxury of all – the body built to Bond's own private specification by Mulliners. It cost £3,000 which, as Fleming has revealed, was exactly half of Bond's remaining capital. It was the sort of body Bond had always wanted on a car – two bucket seats in black English hide (not morocco leather as Fleming said), big convex Triplex windscreen, power operated steering, and the paintwork once more the old 'elephant's breath grey' that Bond had made his private livery. It was both simple and luxurious and Bond loved it.

Despite his normal carefulness with money, he refused to think about the petrol it would use or the sheer cost of keeping such a monster on the road. For Bond the Bentley was an echo of that lost rich Europe he had known before the war, and, as he says, 'everyone should have at least one folly in his life'. The Bentley was quite clearly his.

Most of that year Bond was too busy to enjoy it, and the Bentley, lovingly maintained, languished in its garage as its owner rocketed around the world – France and the Bahamas, Canada and Italy – on the assignments chronicled by Fleming in his book, *For Your Eyes Only*. As Bond put it, 'there wasn't much time that year for desk work or for getting bored. True, there were no major missions – rather too many fiddling affairs – but at least I felt that I was paying for my keep. M. couldn't really grumble.'

It was in fact a crippling work load for a single agent and once again one wonders whether M., in some sadistic way, was out to break him. When I asked Bond this he shook his head.

'I don't think so – not consciously at any rate. The work simply needed to be done, and the 00 section was short-staffed that year.'

In fact there had been more casualties – and resignations, thanks to the crises that were still afflicting the Regents Park Headquarters. Bond was unique in never arguing with M. He was also the only member of the section who could last the pace – although by 1959 even he was showing signs of strain. Fleming has explained what happened at the start of *Thunderball*. On the surface it was just a minor upset over Bond's state of health – but there was more to it than that.

As Bond quite willingly admits, he had been 'slightly overdoing things' (entirely in the line of duty one should add) and this had led to certain symptoms which the Service's M.O. had noticed on his annual check-up. These were nothing serious, simply the usual signs of overwork – the occasional headache, slightly raised blood pressure and difficulty sleeping. His work had also forced on him a certain level of rich living. Sometimes he ate and smoked and drank more than was strictly good for him, but this was something of an occupational hazard for James Bond. As he points out, the drinks and rich food Fleming took such pleasure in describing, belonged strictly to the world of his assignments. When he was on a job he needed alcohol (in what for him was moderation) and also nicotine. Rich food, too, tended to become part of the normal ritual of an assignment, simply because his work took him to good restaurants and excellent hotels. It would have been an affectation – and sometimes positively dangerous – to have tried to live off eggs, salad and fresh orange juice.

But the pessimistic tone of James Bond's medical report gave M. the excuse he needed. As Fleming hinted, M. had become a health food addict. This was just one of his current manias and it was typical of him to have forced Bond off to the sitzbaths and meagre diet of the Shrublands health clinic. Not that Bond really minded. As he admits he was a few pounds overweight and the fortnight that he spent there toned him up, and gave the osteopath a chance to deal with the damage to his back caused by his jump from the Arlberg Express. Shrublands also gave him a fortnight's welcome rest at the expense of the department, and offered a vital lead to the operations of the notorious Spectre organization.

Fleming has described the sequence of events – the meeting with the sinister, bronzed lady-killer, Count Lippe, in the treatment room at Shrublands. Bond's recognition of the tattoed 'Red Lightning Tong' sign on his arm, and then the hideous attempt Lippe made to have Bond literally torn apart on the traction machine. This, in turn, led to Bond's first encounter with that extraordinary criminal genius, Ernst Stavro Blofeld – killer, capitalist and founder-chairman of Spectre, 'the Special Executive for Counterintelligence, Terrorism, Revenge and Extortion'.

It was Herr Blofeld who had masterminded the hi-jacking of the NATO bomber and using its atomic bomb to extort £100 million from the Western European governments. Bond had the task of tracking Blofeld's minions to the Bahamas and recovering the bomb. This involved the famous underwater battle with Blofeld's man, Emilio Largo, and his accomplices. It was this battle which undoubtedly did save both Nassau and Miami from the atomic holocaust Blofeld had threatened. Blofeld, of course, survived, but Spectre almost fell apart, and Bond had the satisfaction of knowing he had saved the British taxpayer £100 million, and even worse extortions from the power-mad Blofeld.

But once again for Bond success had to be its own reward. There were no medals, no citations for his bravery. He was used to this, but he admits that he did find M.'s behaviour strange. There was no word of congratulation when he returned. Even the personal note of thanks from the Prime Minister to Bond aroused no comment from the steely martinet, and Bill Tanner told Bond later that M. had vetoed the P.M.'s suggestion of a private lunch at Downing Street. M. had apparently ruled that it would be 'quite improper' and that it would set what he called 'dangerous precedents' for members of the Secret Service to have any contact with politicians. (Bond says that he was secretly relieved.)

Late in the autumn of 1960, things started going strangely wrong for Bond. His carefree years were over.

Most of the trouble lay not in him but in the Secret Service. During this period it was under fire from the politicians and there was fresh talk of purges from security. This had produced the customary irritated reaction from M. He was on his guard and there was talk now of disbanding the 00 section. It had come under frequent criticism as a source of provocation to the enemy, and M. was tired of defending it. These rumours naturally worried Bond: without his 00 rating, it was doubtful whether he would wish to stay within the Secret Service. Then on top of this came the big re-shuffle at Headquarters just before Christmas. For Bond, a true conservative at heart, the shake-up was more disturbing than he cared to admit.

M.'s office was moved up from the sixth to the seventh floor, and Bond, to his horror, found himself relegated to 'a small, cream-painted, hencoop of a place' up on the eighth. In the circumstances, the move seemed ominous. Then, just a few days later, the devoted Ponsonby announced that she was leaving to get married to her mysterious broker boyfriend from the Baltic Exchange. For Bond, who had always liked to think that she was secretly in love with him, this was 'the last bloody straw'.

That Christmas he was champing for a long, involved assignment, preferably somewhere warm, which would keep him out of range of M. and Regents Park as long as possible. Instead he found himself dispatched to Canada.

It was the sort of dirty, brief assignment Bond had come to loathe – a trip to Toronto to protect a man called Boris from a hired assassin. Boris had defected from the Soviet

Union, and, after giving his secrets to the British, had been settled in Toronto. The Russian K.G.B. had recently discovered his address and made a deal with the still functioning Spectre network to destroy him.

Bond worked efficiently, but without much relish, finding the would-be murderer (an ex-Gestapo man called Uhlmann), taking the Russian's place on the night of the killing, and then quite calmly shooting Uhlmann in a gun-fight. Bond played his part like the professional he was, but it left him mildly disgusted with his calling. He liked to think that he was something more than a salaried trigger man for the British Secret Service. But it was obviously too much to hope for another of those missions like the Thunderball affair which gave him the luxury of feeling that his work had real value to society.

M. seemed obsessed with Spectre and with Blofeld, and on Bond's return to London insisted firmly that from now on they were to be his sole concern. Bond tried to argue. M. was unsympathetic.

Throughout that spring and early summer Bond persevered – still without success. He was convinced by now that Blofeld must have died and that M., for some perverse reason of his own, was keeping him at this pointless drudgery. Perhaps he wanted to deflate him after the success of the Thunderball affair. Perhaps . . . As he said to the sympathetic Bill Tanner during one of his periodic moans, 'the trouble with the old man is that he's become so odd and difficult that one just never knows what he's up to.'

Tanner nodded wearily. 'And to make it worse,' he replied, 'he still has an infuriating habit of sometimes being right.'

Another source of irritation to James Bond cropped up then. Urquhart reminded him that it was time that Fleming wrote another book. This had become an annual event. The publishers expected it. The public would think something had gone wrong if a new book failed to appear. Bond replied curtly that his life had now become so dull that there was nothing that would make a book.

This time the argument was carried up to M. He still seemed anxious for the Bond books to continue. Urquhart had told him that what he called 'the James Bond cult' was catching on, and that there was talk of making a film now of the famous British agent. Bond hadn't heard and was horrified. Not so M.

'One must be forward-looking in such matters, 007,' he insisted. 'Forward-looking' was a phrase that he had recently taken to using. Bond mistrusted it. But M. appeared pleased that it was a British agent – and not an American or a French one – who was involved. Something else had pleased him too. 'Look at this,' he said to Bond, and pushed a magazine across the desk. It was the current issue of the American *Life* Magazine, and somebody in the press department had underlined the article. It was by the White House correspondent, High Sidey, and it listed the ten favourite books of President John F. Kennedy. Number six in the list, after the *Charterhouse of Parma*, was a James Bond book – *From Russia With Love*. M. was delighted.

But even M.'s enthusiasm was unable to produce a subject for a further book. 'It had been', said Bond somewhat bitterly, 'a fallow year.' And then another complication cropped up which seemed to end all chance of a fresh Bond adventure for that year. That April Fleming had had a heart attack, and even as M. spoke, he was in the London Clinic. When James Bond heard this he went to visit him.

Fleming appeared quite cheerful. He and Bond laughed about the Kennedy enthusiasm for *From Russia With Love* and Fleming seemed relieved not to have to write another James Bond book that year. Despite all this, Urquhart was not so easily diverted from his purpose. The same April he flew specially to Canada and it was while he was there that he found out about the girl called Vivienne Michel. Bond hadn't mentioned her in his departmental report on the Toronto job, although he did briefly mention his involvement with two gangsters in the motel she ran outside Toronto. This had no bearing on Bond's mission. The gangsters were two thugs attempting to extort money from the girl. Bond dealt with them, and handed the case over to the local police.

But Urquhart had found out about her. She was attractive. Bond had slept with her. And Urquhart discovered something that Bond didn't know. The demure Miss Michel had literary ambitions; and she was more than willing to tell all. The result was that oddity among the James Bond books – *The Spy Who Loved Me*. Bond says it is the one book he regards with real distaste. Indeed, he feels that he was treated badly over it, and blames Urquhart for getting Fleming involved in the book at a time when he was obviously far from well. (Ian Fleming finally appeared as 'co-author' with Vivienne Michel.) Bond says that he was 'hideously embarrassed by the whole enterprise'.

Certainly one has to sympathize with Bond. Miss Michel's womens'-magazine style revelations would have worried any self-respecting male. For somebody as reticent as Bond these 'true confession' type descriptions of the night he spent with the ardent Miss Michel in the Shady Pines Motel must have made quite horrifying reading. Bond says he 'hit the roof' when he was finally allowed to see the proofs of the book, but there was nothing he could do except complain to M., and M. dismissed the whole affair as 'just not worth discussing'. Urquhart had cleverly kept the text away from Bond as long as possible, and as Bond says resignedly, 'What can one do about that sort of woman?'

In July M. went on holiday. He was no better when he got back – in fact he was quite intolerable, snappy, bad-tempered, getting on everybody's nerves. Even the glacial Miss Moneypenny seemed to be finding him impossible. Bond found her in a state of near prostration after one afternoon non-stop with M. and took her out to dinner. She came gratefully and Bond took her to Alvaro's in the Kings Road, where he thought the *pasta* was the best in London. Over the *spaghetti alle vongole* Moneypenny told him all her troubles.

'I'm really worried for him, James,' she said. 'I know he's difficult, but he's never been like this before.'

'Like what?' said Bond.

'Actually losing all control. He's been nagging on at me, and then this afternoon he flew into a rage.'

That cool naval presence in a rage? Bond hadn't thought it possible.

'What was he like?' he asked.

'Terrifying. He started shouting and shoved all the papers off his desk. I simply fled.'

Bond tried hard not to smile at the thought of the stately Moneypenny in precipitate retreat.

'Perhaps it's the male menopause,' he said.

'He should have got over that by now. No, James, the odd thing is that this should have happened *after* his holiday. He was all right before he went, a little tense and snappy but nothing at all like this.'

'Any idea what happened on this holiday of his. I don't remember hearing where he went.'

She shook her head. 'That's the strange thing about it. He was most anxious nobody should know where he was going, and told me to keep it to myself. In fact the forwarding address he left was for a Greek island called Spirellos.'

'A bit different from his usual fishing trip to the Test,' said Bond.

'Perhaps he's in love?' said Moneypenny, looking suddenly quite gentle.

'Perhaps he is,' said Bond. 'For all our sakes I hope so and the lady soon says yes.'

The idea of M. in love gained credence in the section. It explained everything, and everybody started to make allowances for M.

But as Bond said to Mary Goodnight, "She really must be putting the old boy through the hoops. He's getting worse and worse.'

Indeed he was. Bond heard that he was drinking heavily at Blades. And then, the next day, there was a worried telephone call from a friend in the Ministry of Defence.

'What's the matter with your boss?'

'What do you mean?' asked Bond.

'Yesterday he blew his top at the Joint Chiefs of Staff

conference. Nobody knew why. It was most embarrassing. They were discussing possible subversion in the Secret Service, and he suddenly seemed to go berserk. Quite between the two of us, the Chief of G.S. asked me to have a word with you to see if there is anything on the old boy's mind. And could you just keep an eye on him?'

'You've been pushing him too hard too long,' Bond replied loyally.

'Point taken. But that makes it all the more important that there shouldn't be anything unfortunate. We couldn't have the man crack up.'

* * *

M. cracking up! The idea was unthinkable. And yet the more Bond thought about it, the more possible it seemed. But what to do? M. was not the sort of man one could invite out for a drink and ask to share his troubles. He was a guarded unforthcoming man and Bond had no idea what went on behind that lined, distinguished-looking face. Nor had he any more idea about his private life. M. kept it rigidly apart from his work. Indeed, the more Bond started thinking about him, the more he realized just how little he knew about this man who ruled his life.

Bond knew he had a house at Windsor, but at that time hadn't been invited there (nor for that matter had anyone else inside the section – M. made no pretence of being hospitable). Nor did Bond know about his friends. He'd never heard of any. It was almost as if M.'s life stopped entirely once his old black Silver Wraith slid away from the Regents Park Headquarters in the evening. And as Bond realized, he really didn't *want* to know about M.'s private life.

Fortunately Bill Tanner was now back from hospital (but off all alcohol and almost all the food the canteen had to offer). When Bond discussed the situation with him, he was emphatic that something must be done. But they both realized the problem – how can you start investigating the Head of the Secret Service?

Bond tried to make a start next day. M.'s servant, Chief Petty Officer Hammond was in the office, and Bond made a point of talking to him over coffee in the downstairs canteen. Bond knew he was devoted to M. and was not surprised at the suspicion on his ruddy face as soon as he asked about him.

'Sir Miles well? I'd say he has his ups and downs like all of us.'

Bond said of course, but recently he'd felt that he was under some sort of quite unusual strain.

'I couldn't say, Commander Bond. That's not my business.'

Clearly Bond wasn't getting anything from him, but he did his best to tell the Chief Petty Officer that if he did feel anything was wrong with M. he could always get in touch with him or with the Chief of Staff.

'Thank you, Commander Bond', said Hammond loyally.

That same evening, Bond rang Sir James Molony.

'Trouble with M? No, I've heard nothing, but I hope to God you're wrong. M. is the one man in Britain I'd not take on as a patient if you paid ten times my normal fee.'

Bill Tanner also made inquiries – just as fruitlessly. But Moneypenny was thinking of applying for a transfer, and two days later there was another worried query from Bond's contact in the Ministry of Defence. And then, that evening, Hammond rang Bond at home. He and Mrs Hammond wanted to see him urgently. Bond arranged to meet them in a Windsor tea-shop early next afternoon.

Mrs Hammond was the sort of wife who did the talking. She was a forthright little woman who began by telling the waitress exactly what she thought of her scones and strawberry jam.

'Now, Commander Bond,' she said as she condescended to accept a slice of cherry cake, 'me and my husband are agreed that we should talk to you about Sir Miles, but on condition that not a word of this gets back to him.'

Bond solemnly agreed.

'For some time now, Sir Miles just hasn't been himself.

284

He's off his food, and he's so snappy with us both.'

Bond made sympathetic noises.

'Particularly of a morning. Sir Miles has always been an early riser. Merry as a lark, and never any trouble. But lately he's been getting up late and missing breakfast. Hammond here has heard him talking in the night. It's our belief, Commander, that he's being blackmailed.'

'Blackmailed?' said Bond.

'That's what I said, Commander.' She dropped her voice. 'Twice recently we've had this man phone – with a foreign accent.'

'What sort of accent?'

'Just foreign. Not nice at all. And afterwards Sir Miles has been just terrible.'

Neither Bond nor Tanner had considered blackmail, but, as they realized, it *was* a possibility.

'After all,' said Tanner, 'he *is* human.'

'Is he?' said Bond.

'And there he is without a woman. He's just the sort to get himself involved with some cold-faced jezebel and then not know how to handle it.'

'D'you think it's political?' said Bond.

'Let's just hope not, although it's quite a danger. Think what an enemy would pay for a set of compromising photographs of the head of the British Secret Service!'

'I already have,' said Bond.

Bill Tanner and James Bond both realized that they were in a difficult position. Theoretically, their course was clear. They had a duty to inform the head of the security forces of their suspicions. But they knew quite well what this would mean. The Secret Service and Security were at daggers drawn. Think of the rumpus that would follow – and think what would happen if their suspicions were unfounded! Clearly they had to be a lot more certain of their facts before they could do this. Instead they both agreed that they would carry out their own investigation. It was a risky business. If anything went wrong they would inevitably be blamed, but, as Bill Tanner said, 'whatever the old devil has been up to, we owe it to him to do what we can to stop it going any further.'

Bond agreed.

As Chief of Staff, Bill Tanner had no difficulty tapping M.'s home telephone. It was a fairly routine operation in conjunction with the Post Office. The only problem was that officially M. had to see and approve all orders of this sort (and be prepared to justify them to the Home Office). His Chief of Staff for once made sure he didn't.

At the same time, Bond began checking on all M.'s acquaintances. There was a younger brother, once an Oxford don and now retired. There were a few friends from the navy. There were, as far as Bond could see, no women in his life. He tried to find out more about M.'s holiday. He had apparently gone alone. Bond rang a friend in the Greek Embassy to ask about the island of Spirellos.

Next day they had their first success. The phone-tap had worked. The mysterious caller with the foreign accent had rung up again and on the tape there was recorded the brief stormy conversation he had had with M. The man was saying he must see him. M. had told him to go to hell, and the man had said that that was fine and he must take the consequences.

To Bond and Tanner this confirmed what they suspected. M. was clearly being blackmailed and, thanks to the Post Office, they had a lead to go on. Tanner had been able to get the call traced to an address in Kensington. It was a flat and it was owned by an Italian. His name was Del Lungo. He was a photographer.

It was no time for too much subtlety – the stakes were too high for that. Tanner had his car parked underneath the office, and that evening, after dinner, he and Bond drove round to the small turning off the Cromwell Road where Del Lungo lived.

At first they 'cased' the place. It was a typical Victorian block with a big front entrance and a mews behind. Del Lungo had a first floor flat. A light was on. Bond and Bill Tanner waited. Just before midnight it went out.

Bond was a skilful burglar. During his wartime training he had spent several weeks learning 'breaking and entering' from an old lag specially brought up from Dartmoor to instruct the members of the Secret Service. Bond had considerable talent in this direction, and it was not difficult to reach the back of Del Lungo's flat from the garage opposite. He hauled Bill Tanner up after him, then began tackling the window. It was a simple sash affair with a 'burglar-proof' catch. Bond cut a circle from the glass, lifted the catch, and they were in.

Bond worked professionally. He and Bill Tanner both wore rubber gloves and silk stocking masks; as soon as they were in they cut the telephone. From then on the burglary was simple. The photographer was in bed with a woman. Bond switched the light on and Bill Tanner bound and gagged them. Then the real work started.

There were three big filing cabinets in the studio that led off from the bedroom, and they were filled with negatives. Somewhere, presumably, among this mass of celluloid lay the few pictures that could destroy M.'s reputation and career. But there was no guide to where they were. There was no filing system. Every negative had to be examined.

It was an interesting collection. The Italian was a press photographer who worked mainly for society magazines. There were a lot of very famous faces, and not only faces. For Del Lungo obviously ran a sideline in the sort of pictures people would pay a great deal *not* to have published. Bond says there were some real surprises: he rather wishes he had had more time to savour them.

They had been working nearly four hours when they found what they were looking for. There were six negatives; by the look of them they had been taken by some sort of long-range camera. But even so, they were quite recognizably of M. He was on a beach. In some he was quite alone, and in others he was with people of both sexes. All were as naked as the day that they were born.

'Oh my dear Lord,' said Tanner. 'What has the silly old buffoon been up to?'

It was just after four when two figures climbed out of the first floor window of the block of flats, slid down onto a garage roof, then disappeared into the shadows of a wall. Five minutes later, James Bond and William Tanner of the Secret Service were driving safely back to Chelsea. On the way they stopped at a telephone box and rang the police to tell them there had been a burglary at the photographer's address.

'You know, I rather enjoyed our night's work,' Tanner said.

'Perhaps we should do it for a living,' Bond replied.

When they got back to his flat, they had a drink, turned in for three hours' sleep, and woke to eat the biggest breakfast May could cook for them.

Over breakfast they discussed the photographs. They were both embarrassed by them. The idea of M. in such a situation was so undignified that, as Tanner said, 'it's as if you're looking at a picture of your parents.' Bond nodded, and suggested that they ought to place the negatives in an envelope and post them straight to M. Tanner agreed.

'Let's just hope,' he said, 'that once he gets them his temper improves.'

'Amen to that,' said Bond.

But that wasn't quite the end of the story. Presumably M. got his photographs, and certainly he had no more phone calls from the man who took them. Bond's spot of burglary had saved the Secret Service from a squalid piece of blackmail. But two days later Bond discovered more about the pictures. They were not quite what he and Tanner had originally imagined.

Bond was rung up by his friend in the Greek Embassy. He was apologetic for the time he had taken over Bond's inquiry.

'Inquiry?' said Bond.

'Yes,' said the Greek. 'About that island called Spirellos.'

'I'd clean forgotten about it,' said Bond.

'Perhaps you should go there for a summer holiday,' said the Greek. 'It's a nudist island, like the Ile de Levant off

Toulon. It's very smart – lots of young girls, and I'm told it's very popular with old men like you.'

And then Bond realized the truth. He should have guessed earlier. Ever since the *Thunderball* affair he had known of M.'s taste for health foods and nature clinics. What could have been more obvious than for him to have moved on to naturism? Bond only hoped that M. had enjoyed himself. But somehow he doubted whether he would be going back.

15

'The Bastard's Gone'

Honeychile gave a party. The beautiful white yacht, the flawless evening with the full moon rising, candlelight and good champagne, the island glittering against a phosphorescent sea – it should have been romantic. Instead that whole evening seemed unreal and quite extraordinarily sad. The telegram from M. had settled things. Bond was resigning from the Secret Service and marrying Honeychile. The party was to celebrate the fact.

Honey had laid on all the guests, along with the champagne. There was a retired U.S. Army General (who had a speech impediment or was very drunk), a beetle-browed Greek millionaire with bright gold teeth, a recently divorced young actress and several distinctly baffled guests from the hotel invited, presumably, to fill the space. Most of them seemed like wakes attending a burial at sea.

Bond was the only one who seemed entirely at ease. He wore a beautifully cut white dinner suit and had a presence to be proud of. It seemed absurd to think that this tall figure with the lean tanned face was in his early fifties. He was extremely affable, laughing and joking and cheerfully talking golf to the general – this in itself a notable ordeal. Was he really happy – or resigned? Or was this one more role that he was playing? What a strange, enigmatic man he was.

Honey, for all her youth and nervous energy, was looking older now. She also seemed distinctly anxious; vibrant and restless as a yo-yo, chatting to everyone and flashing her extraordinary smile.

'The smile on the face of the tiger,' said a voice beside me. It was Sir William Stephenson who was benignly watching what was going on.

'Well, she's succeeded – like the tiger,' I replied.

'I wouldn't be so sure,' he said, 'She's not the first one to have tried, you know.'

But if James Bond was harbouring doubts about his future, he was keeping them strictly to himself. I saw him smiling frequently at Honey. When I congratulated him he nodded and replied that he thought that he'd enjoy himself. This seemed an odd remark from someone on the eve of marriage.

'You're really giving up the old life then?' I said.

The grey eyes narrowed. 'Oh yes, I think so. All that's over. Time for a change. I'm getting on, you know.'

'What are your plans,' I asked.

'Oh, I've a great deal to catch up on. I really won't object to being out to grass. Between us we've a lot of friends around the world, and Honey's business interests will be taking up my time. I thought I'd even try my hand at writing. There's that book I started on self-defence. Fleming was very keen that I should finish it. He even suggested a title.'

'What was that?'

'*Stay Alive!* From now on that will be my motto.'

But despite Bond's optimism about his future, the air of melancholy lingered. As I left the yacht somebody was playing the Beatles' record, 'Yesterday'. I noticed Bond was on his own and staring out to sea. An era suddenly seemed over.

*   *   *

He had promised to conclude his story whilst he and Honey

stayed on in Bermuda to complete formalities for their marriage – 'that will be my last task for the Secret Service'. (Honey apparently had wanted the invaluable Captain Cullum to give them a shipboard wedding. Bond had vetoed the idea.) He also said he needed to make his official resignation from the Service. This would apparently take a little time.

'I want it all done property,' he said. 'I'm not having anybody say that I left out of pique or that I've acted badly. I simply feel that the time has come . . . '

He raised both hands and made a slight grimace. This morning his confidence seemed to have deserted him and his face looked haggard. He had come down to see me in my room and we were sitting, as we had on that first morning after my arrival, out on the balcony. Bond was in the bamboo chair. When I think of him today, this is how I picture him – the strange mask of a face outlined against the sapphire waters of the harbour. Below us in the hotel pool the everlasting honeymooners giggled and splashed and swam; a fat girl was astride a plastic duck; the pool professional bounded from the spring-board, jack-knifed, then speared his languid way into the water.

Bond took no notice as he sipped his coffee and began describing the conclusion of that frustrating year he spent trailing his vanished enemy, Ernst Stavro Blofeld.

Although Bond had saved M. from the threat of blackmail, the atmosphere within headquarters still seemed distinctly fraught. M. was as difficult as ever – particularly with Bond. (Indeed, Bond wondered if M. knew what he had done for him. Far from feeling grateful, he may have secretly resented him knowing what had happened. It seemed likely.) As summer ended Bond was still stuck behind his desk in London. This seemed ridiculous. Boredom enhanced his discontent, and he suspected that behind all this inaction, he was being quietly forgotten. By September 1961, when Fleming showed him at the start of *On Her Majesty's Secret Service,* Bond was about to kick. As Fleming revealed (Bond was to wish he hadn't) he was actually composing his letter of resignation from the Secret Service when the book began. It was against this background that one of the key episodes in James Bond's life suddenly occurred.

It all started with his visit to the grave of Vesper Lynd at the small French seaside town of Royale-les-Eaux. It was ten years since the Casino-Royale affair, and during this time he'd scarcely given her a thought. But when he found himself suddenly back at Royale, her memory began to haunt him. He had been on one more fruitless European trip to track down Blofeld and the soft September weather, the melancholy nostalgia of the time of year, caught him off guard. He had a private sense of failure – in his life as well as his career – and now he was indulging in remorse. The dead Vesper Lynd reminded him of all the women he had loved and who had died.

As he described her Bond made it clear that these deaths still troubled him, for as he said, 'when it's too late you realize what you've done'. As he said this the sardonic mouth relaxed, the cruel eyes softened and I began to understand something of the tragedy that had occurred that autumn.

Fleming has described the way Bond met the girl he was to marry – the Countess Teresa di Vicenzo. Her father was a man called Marc-Ange Draco, head of the Deadly 'Union Corse' which still controls most of the organized crime in France and her ex-colonies. Her husband had conveniently vanished. She drove a white two-seater Zagato-bodied Lancia Flaminia – very fast. This was a favourite car of Bond's and when he first encountered her along the N.1 between Abbeville and Montreuil she seemed like just another rich, disposable young woman for Bond to pursue, sleep with, and forget. But in the sentimental atmosphere of Royale-les-Eaux that autumn, she became something more. He was soon calling her not, 'Countess di Vicenzo' but plain 'Tracy' and saved her from the 'Coup de Déshonneur' in the casino by paying her gambling debts. He made love to her that night, and as she gave herself to him she cynically remarked that this would be 'the most expensive piece of love of your life.'

But Bond wasn't feeling cynical and after that one night

found himself in love with this vulnerable young blonde. In retrospect this must have been inevitable. For Tracy was the sort of girl Bond could never quite resist, part waif, part wanton and in constant need of his protection. There was a touch of Vesper Lynd about her, and by marrying her Bond felt that he could save her, and redeem himself.

This love affair took place against the events which Fleming has described in *On Her Majesty's Secret Service* – events which ironically proved M.'s hunch about Blofeld to have been correct. Blofeld was alive and still as dangerous and threatening as ever. Under the unusual cover of an official from the London College of Arms, Bond tracked him down to his mountain hideaway above Geneva and found Blofeld, his face re-structured through skilful plastic surgery and his eyes hidden behind dark contact lenses. And it was here too that he met the unappetising Fraulein Irma Bunt of the yellow eyes, fought his great battle with the Spectre killers, and finally destroyed the Blofeld plan to bring Britain to her knees by waging biological warfare on her agriculture.

But Bond clearly felt that Fleming had failed to do justice to his love for Tracy. 'When I decided I would marry her it wasn't quite the spur-of-the-moment thing he makes it seem. We had it all carefully planned out. Both of us realized that we had to settle down and that this was suddenly our chance. I was still debating whether to leave the Secret Service. I hadn't quite decided, but I would certainly have moved out of the 00 section – it wouldn't have been fair to her to have stayed. We also planned to give up the flat and move out of London – probably to Kent. I even found a house for sale that would have suited us – on the cliffs above St Margaret's Bay. You could see France from the bedroom windows.'

'You'd have been happy there?'

Bond shrugged and smiled ruefully.

'How can you ever tell? Certainly we both thought so. I'd learned a lot since my affair with Tiffany and neither of us was exactly innocent. She'd been married already and I'd had enough affairs to last a lifetime.'

'But what about that old enemy of yours, the soft life as

Fleming called it? Wouldn't the boredom of a settled married life have caught you in the end.'

'No,' he said. 'Not with her. I honestly don't think it would. She wasn't in the least possessive and I think I'd – shall we say I'd mellowed since my time with Tiffany?'

He paused to light a cigarette. He was smoking heavily.

'As you know, that madman Blofeld had to destroy it all. Even today I sometimes find myself unable to believe what happened. When the assignment finished I took my two weeks' leave and we were married in Munich. We'd finally succeeded and we were very happy. That of course was the trouble. I still reproach myself for what occurred. Normally I'd have been on my guard and Blofeld wouldn't have been able to get away with it. For that matter, instead of marrying Tracy, I should still have been after him. Instead of which I let him go. Still, one pays for one's mistakes. Or rather, this time Tracy did.'

'Fleming described it all. We were driving to Kitzbühel for our honeymoon – I hadn't been there since before the war, but for me it always had been one of those special places where I had once been very happy. I'd always promised that I'd take the woman that I married there.' He paused. 'You've no idea how many times I've been over those last few minutes in my mind. You see, it really was my fault. I think Fleming explained how we passed the filling station and saw a red Maserati standing there with two people in it. It was an open car, and the people were muffled up and wearing goggles. I didn't recognize them consciously, but you know how it is. There was something familiar about them, something that rang a warning at the back of my mind. Normally I'd have paid attention to that warning – you have to in a job like mine. That's how you stay alive. But I ignored it. I was happy and I ignored it. That was why she died. The man in the Maserati was Blofeld: the woman with him was Irma Bunt. When they overtook us and the Bunt woman fired at us, the shot was meant for me. Instead it caught Tracy. It went through the heart. She died immediately.'

Bond described this unemotionally, almost casually, as if it had all happened years ago to someone else.

'Didn't you want revenge?' I asked.

'No, not particularly. There was no point in it – no point at all. People were very kind – even old M. in his funny way. Bill Tanner came out to help clear up the mess and Marc-Ange came and buried her. Not that it made the slightest difference. She was dead and that was that and of course I thought that I had killed her. You see, so many women I had loved had died, and suddenly it all came home to me. Aunt Charmian had always talked about the curse of the Bonds. It was a sort of joke, but now I honestly believed it. It was partly shock, of course, but I believed that I was damned – that I could never hope to get away from this one life I knew. I felt I was condemned to go on in the Secret Service.' He smiled. 'Stupid, wasn't it?'

He lit another cigarette and then the telephone rang in the room. I got up to answer it. The operator said, 'London on the line.' There was a pause, the line clicked, and another voice said crisply, 'Universal Export for Commander Bond.' I called him in. I heard him say, 'Oh, hullo Bill. You at last. Where have *you* been? Yes certainly – I've quite made up my mind.' Then he said, 'Oh, I see.' And then, annoyingly, he shut the door.

He was on the telephone some time, twenty minutes or maybe more. When he came out on to the balcony he seemed preoccupied and sat smoking, saying nothing. Finally he said, 'Sorry, but something's just cropped up. May I use your telephone again?' I heard him ask the operator for Sir William Stephenson.

'I've just had London on the line. It seems they're serious. Could I come up and see you? Yes, straight away. Fine. Many thanks.'

Then he apologized to me, and said he would continue his story later that afternoon.

But he didn't. I lunched alone, then went to sleep beside the pool and woke just before five with a headache. The hotel suddenly seemed empty. When I rang Bond's room he wasn't there, nor was Sir William. I dined alone and was in bed by ten.

Next morning Bond was back again soon after breakfast. He seemed quite jaunty but he made no reference to his telephone call from London nor to what was going on. Instead he took out the gun-metal cigarette case, stretched himself out in the bamboo chair, and continued his story. That mask-like face was adept at concealing what he was thinking. He described the aftermath of Tracy's death. When he got back to London, May was waiting for him in the flat. Winter had started. Nothing had really changed. Even Bond's old arch-enemy Blofeld was still at large and still as menacing as ever. Fortunately M. did have sufficient tact not to give Bond the thankless task of trailing him again.

It took some time for the real shock of Tracy's death to hit him. He had such self-control that his grief remained inside him. Few people realized what he was suffering. Probably the only one who did was Sir James Molony, and his advice was simple. 'Work!' Bond did his best to follow it. But something indefinable had gone.

Everything he did was a disaster – he says that he's not certain why. 'I can't believe that I was any less efficient or aggressive than in the old days but my luck had gone. Gamblers run out of luck. So do agents in the Secret Service. With Tracy's death all my luck turned. None of my 1962 assignments seemed to go right.'

The worst was the Prenderghast Affair and once again Bond's luck let him down, this time, however, with results that shook the whole structure of the Secret Service. Prenderghast was Station Head in Rome. Bond had known him for years and liked him. He had a distinguished record as a Fleet Air Arm pilot during the war and later served with Bond for some years in the 00 section. For the past five years he had been in Rome, and Bond never failed to see him when he was in the city. For Prenderghast was fun. He knew all the gossip and his apartment just behind the Via dei Coronari was a splendid place for lunch. Bond also found him a good friend and a sympathetic listener. He was intelligent, efficient and he knew his job.

It was Bill Tanner who gave Bond the first hint of trouble about Prenderghast, when he mentioned that a man called Croxson had been sending in unfavourable reports about him. Croxson was one of his subordinates and currently was acting Station Head in Milan. He was young and inexperienced – Italy was his first posting after his transfer from the army barely a year before. For this reason Tanner had been treating these reports with what he called 'a fairly generous pinch of salt'. Croxson and Prenderghast had clearly failed to hit it off, and Croxson had taken to complaining of him at every opportunity. Tanner had tried to smooth things over, but recently the complaints had started up again.

'What sort of complaints?' Bond had asked.

'Oh, quite incredible accusations. Corruption and inefficiency; he even says he's homosexual and that he's working as a double agent for the enemy. If one didn't know old Prenderghast one might be really worried.'

'This Croxson fellow must be off his head,' said Bond. 'It's Italy. They're all mad there.'

Tanner had agreed but added that something would have to be done – probably a transfer for young Croxson at the earliest opportunity. In the meantime it might be useful for someone experienced from Headquarters to go out to Italy and have a quiet word with Croxson and with Prenderghast. Quite unofficially of course, but often a tactful word or two could prevent a nasty scandal. Bond agreed. Tanner suggested that a trip to Italy at that time of year could be enjoyable. And a few days later, Bond found himself aboard an early morning flight to Milan.

He didn't take to Croxson. He found him arrogant and earnest and lacking in all sense of humour. More to the point, he soon found out that he had not one shred of proof to back his accusations against Prenderghast. As far as Bond could see he was suffering from an outsize persecution complex and he tried suggesting that it was best not to go making wild accusations against a head of station without fairly solid proof.

From Milan Bond flew to Rome where he called on Prenderghast. He was glad to see him, especially after all the rumours he had heard. For Prenderghast was looking splendid and clearly was in great form. After the wretched Croxson with all his moanings and complaints, it was good to be with someone who enjoyed himself. It was also good to see an old friend who was doing well. They walked through Rome and Bond enjoyed hearing what was going on. After Americanos at the 'Tre Scaline' they strolled up the hill of the Pincio and dined at the Casa Valadier – that is to say, they dined extremely well. They were drinking their sambuccas when Bond brought up the subject of Croxson and his reports: Prenderghast appeared to understand the problem. Croxson was young, his wife was difficult, and possibly he had been a little tactless with him in the past. As for the accusations – Prenderghast grinned at Bond. They had both been within the Secret Service long enough to know how easy it could be to make accusations without proof. There was of course no proof? Of course not, Bond replied. And there the conversation ended. Bond returned to London, and a few days later Tanner told him that Croxson was about to be recalled. He had been in Italy on probation and was obviously unsuited for the Secret Service. Perhaps it was hard on him but in the circumstances . . . Two days later Croxson shot himself.

Then all hell broke loose. The Italian press seized on the case. Prenderghast was accused by Croxson's widow as the man responsible for her husband's death. That same evening he was named as the organizer of a homosexual diplomatic network in Rome. More accusations followed and in the midst of this furore, Prenderghast lost his nerve. Two officers of British security caught him as he was about to board a Czech aircraft at Fiumicino. He was brought back to London, and at the Old Bailey, some months later, Prenderghast was sentenced to a total of thirty years for treason. The trial was held in camera, but Bond read a transcript of the evidence. It proved every word of Croxson's accusations.

Luckily for Bond, not a breath of his meeting with the two men came out in court. (Bond is still grateful to Prenderghast for not mentioning it.) But the whole case received so much publicity that M. offered his resignation to the Prime Minister in person. It was refused – but the whole sordid case had clearly cast little credit on the British Secret Service. As for Bond, he felt that it was the final proof that he had lost his touch and that luck had turned decisively against him. M. evidently thought so too (he lacked the P.M.'s generosity towards erring servants) and by this time had virtually decided to dismiss him, not just from the 00 section, but from the Service as a whole. As he put it to Sir James Molony, he had no room in Headquarters for 'a lame-brain'. Bond was drinking and gambling too much. According to M. this made him 'dangerous to others', and once again it was Sir James who really saved him, by suggesting that M. should send him off on some all but hopeless assignment to redeem himself, forget about Tracy and restore his luck. The result was the Japanese assignment described by Fleming in his book, *You Only Live Twice*.

* * *

Bond was somewhat vague about the Japanese affair, although he did confirm in outline Fleming's version of this most bizarre of all assignments. He went originally to make a deal of sorts with the Japanese Secret Service; they had a cyphering machine which could decode the very top classified Soviet information, and, thanks to Bond, we got it. But in the process he became involved with his old enemy, Ernst Stavro Blofeld, who had moved here from Switzerland and set up a suicide establishment in an old castle near Kyoto. Because of this the mission ultimately turned into a journey of revenge.

'From here,' he said, 'my life became very odd indeed. Japan's a funny country and in many ways it suited Blofeld. That poisoned garden that he built – Fleming called it his 'Disneyland of Death' – was very Japanese.

'But wasn't it satisfying to kill him finally – after all he'd done to you?'

Bond slowly shook his head.

'Not really. I'd dreamed of killing him almost every night since Tracy died, but when it came to it he was so mad that it was like putting down a lunatic; and everything was happening so quickly that I didn't have much time to savour the finer points of killing him. It was all very odd, what happened then, Blofeld's castle going up in flames, my escape in the balloon and then my plunge into the sea off Kuro island. I owe my life, of course, to that girl that Fleming wrote about, Kissy Suzuki. She pulled me out of the sea and fed me and looked after me, and although my memory had gone, we were very happy.'

'Was she your ideal woman then?'

'In some ways I suppose she was. I'd always said that I'd wanted to live with a Japanese – they seemed to restful and obedient – and at a time like that I was lucky to find her. She did everything for me, fed me, bathed me, clothed me – even made love to me, which was very pleasant. But no – I think one would be deceiving oneself if one thought of living with a girl like that forever. Kissy was sweet – but we hadn't really much in common, and once my memory started to return I left. Somehow I felt I had to find my own country and my own people. Instead, of course, I ended up in Russia.'

'And what happened to the girl? According to Fleming she was pregnant when you went.'

'Quite right, she was. To do myself justice, I didn't know – nor could I have done much about it if I had. I really was a mental wreck still. But I went back to Japan, you know – two years later – and I found her, through my old friend, Tiger Tanaka of the Japanese Secret Service. She'd moved to Tokyo where she was working for a U.S. advertising agency. She's a determined girl, and the boy was wonderful – very strong and wonderfully good-looking, although it did feel strange to have a Japanese child as my own.'

There was no mistaking the touch of pride in Bond's voice

as he spoke about the boy. He even produced a photograph from his wallet. It was odd to think of James Bond suddenly as a father – especially when one looked at this snapshot of a solemn, eight-year-old oriental version of Bond himself. He had enormous almond-shaped eyes and a Japanese snub nose, but the jaw-line and the mouth were Bond's all right and it seemed as if he had the beginning of an authentic comma of black hair falling across his forehead.

'What's his name?' I asked.

'James,' he replied. 'His mother named him after me, although of course, he has her surname.'

'And does he know that you're his father?'

'Good heavens, yes. When I returned to Tokyo I suggested to his mother that we ought to marry, but she wasn't very keen. In fact soon after, she married a Japanese in Shell.' Bond pulled a face. 'But to give the man his due he's looked after the boy marvellously, and never stopped me seeing him. I've been out to Japan several times and had him back in England too. I even took him up to Glencoe to meet the family – his family. He's a proper Bond. I've got him down for Eton. He's ten now, so he'll be going in a year or two. Let's hope he does a little better than his father.

'Will he?' I asked.

Bond nodded. 'Oh I think so. He's more serious than I was at that age, and apparently he's rather clever. Perhaps he's more like my brother Henry. That'd be a joke.'

Bond was so obviously keen to talk about his son that it was difficult to get him to complete his story – especially as he clearly didn't care to discuss in detail the episode that followed his time in Japan. This was the period when he was brain-washed by the Russians before being sent back to England with one deadly purpose – to murder M. Beyond a brief remark about 'using certain drugs and playing on my subconscious resentment of old M.' Bond wouldn't talk about how this was done. When I tried asking him if they used Freudian techniques to tap his hostility to all father figures he simply said that it was 'a murky business', and that the reconditioning treatment from Sir James Molony quite obliterated the memory of what had happened. As for M., he said that the old man was remarkably calm about the bungled assassination bid which James Bond attempted with the Russian cyanide pistol.

'He was expecting it of course. He'd had sufficient warning, and I imagine he was secretly delighted to have guessed what I was up to and to have beaten me. He'd won again.' And certainly the missions Bond was given immediately afterwards were something of an anticlimax when compared with his big important operations of the fifties – assignments like the Thunderball affair or the grandiose Goldfinger business. Bond clearly felt the come-down. I felt he blamed M. for it.

There was another trip out to Jamaica to deal with the gangster, Scaramanga. 'That was second division stuff, although old Ian did his best to make a story of it all in *The Man with the Golden Gun.*' There was another minor Jamaican operation too. Fleming called it *Octopussy.*

Bond was obviously moved as he talked about Ian Fleming during the last months of his life.

'For some reason we saw a lot of each other now, you know, and it was really quite a funny situation. Neither of us had foreseen what would happen when he started writing about me back in 1952, and since then his books had changed their character completely. The films had started – *Dr No* was filmed in 1961 – and now what someone called the 'Bond boom' had begun. I've no idea quite how many million copies Ian's books sold. I don't really care. All that I knew was that this James Bond fellow on the screen wasn't really me at all. It was a funny feeling – not very pleasant. But Ian seemed rather proud of what had happened. "You should be grateful to me", he used to say. "There aren't many people who become myths in their lifetime." But I replied that this was something I could do without. He said that in the end he could too. I think that both of us grew just a little bored with all the fuss.'

I asked him if he saw the James Bond films.

'Oh yes. I think that I've seen most of them. At first I was a bit put out to see that Connery fellow supposedly playing *me*, but I suppose that's normal. I remember Ian asked me to a special showing of the first film – wasn't it *Dr No*? – in 1962. He thought it was quite a joke to have me sitting there while all the critics thought he'd simply invented Bond. Instead it was rather – shall we say, disturbing. I felt as if my character, my whole identity had gradually been usurped by someone else. After a while I really wondered whether I existed at all. Ian gave a party after the film. There was more caviare there than I've ever seen in my life but that was Ian for you. I think he'd won several hundred quid a few days earlier at Le Touquet and spent it all on caviare. I remember standing next to some appalling woman who would insist on saying what an oaf this James Bond fellow was and how he simply wasn't credible. Then Ian came up and insisted on introducing me. I remember she was very cross and seemed to think that we were trying to pull her leg.'

'And did you make money from the films?'

'You must be joking. Still, Ian didn't make much either, did he? A few thousand, and he died before the real money started. I was in Germany when he died. I heard it over the car radio. It was a dreadful shock. I'd known him so long. It was almost as if a bit of me had gone.'

'And then?'

'If you'll excuse me now,' he said, 'we'll have another session later and I'll start filling you in about these later years.'

Bond didn't say where he was going but I presumed that he was off to visit his fiancée.

'And so you're really getting married, then?'

He smiled quite cheerfully.

'Yes, certainly. I've finally come round to it. Tomorrow in the city hall. Top hat and tails – the lot.'

I presumed he was joking about the top hat but I wasn't sure.

'And what about the Secret Service? It's really over? All these calls to you from London. They're not trying to make you change your mind?'

He flared at once.

'They always act like that. While you're available no one's interested, but when you say you'll go they need you. It's too childish. And anyhow, they've left it just a bit too late this time. I've quite made up my mind.'

'Really?' I said.

'Yes, really. It may seem odd, but I've grown tired of being treated in this fashion. Also I want a little peace and normal living. Now that the chance is there I'm taking it.'

When Bond had gone I changed, swam, ordered myself a whisky sour, then had a solitary lunch beside the pool. I had notes to write up, but Bond's restlessness was catching. There is a limit to the time that one can spend on islands. Suddenly Bermuda seemed too hot, too soporific. The hotel, the whole island seemed to have nodded off to sleep, and I thought enviously of all the honeymooners taking their siestas there behind the hotel shutters.

One really couldn't blame James Bond for settling for the soft life at last. He'd earned every bit of luxury he got. I thought of Honeychile. She was a dominating woman, but Bond would cope with her. Certainly she loved him and he seemed fond of her, probably the best way round for both of them. She would have the man she loved, and he would have, not passion, but at least a rich and beautiful adoring wife. There were worse foundations for a marriage. There was still time for him to have the children he had always wanted – half brothers and sisters for the almond-eyed young James Suzuki. And possibly he'd even buy his house in Kent, with its view of the English Channel and the coast of France.

These sentimental maunderings of mine were interrupted by the bull-frog presence of Augustus.

'Sah. Would you be knowing where the Commander's gone to?'

I shook my head.

'Who's wanting him?'

'Sir William Stephenson. He's on the phone and asking for him. P'rhaps you'd kindly speak to Sir William personally?'

Sir William sounded impatient. 'Any idea where James has got to?' I replied that I hadn't seen him since before lunch but that I imagined he was now with Honeychile.

He muttered something beneath his breath and there was a pause as if he were speaking to someone else in the room.

'You couldn't come up for a moment? Some friends of his have just arrived from London. I'd be most grateful if you could help them find him. It's slightly urgent.'

I took the private lift up to the big glass penthouse on the roof. It was the first time I'd been back there since the evening I arrived. Sir William greeted me. He had three guests with him. One was a short, elderly man with bushy eyebrows and dark piercing eyes; one had a scarred, amusing looking face; and the third was boyish-looking with wild grey hair.

Sir William introduced me. 'Sir James Molony – head shrinker-in-chief to the Secret Service. I think you've heard of him. And this is Bill, Bill Tanner, M.'s hard-worked, long-suffering Chief of Staff. And finally, Professor Godwin, of the Department of Genetics from the University of Adelaide. They've all come out from London especially to find James Bond. Where is he?' I told them he was probably aboard the yacht and offered to help them find it.

We took Sir William's big gold Cadillac, and drove towards the port where I knew the *Honeychile* was moored.

'Well, how is he?' Tanner asked.

'Marvellous. In great shape.'

'So your idea about the holiday has worked, Sir James. Bermuda suits him.'

We chatted then about the book. Tanner appeared surprised that Bond had talked so freely.

'Simply the last few years to finish now,' I said. 'The period between the Colonel Sun affair and his arrival here. But he's promised to give me that material after the marriage.'

'Marriage?' said Tanner. 'Who's getting married?'

I told him.

'Christ,' he said.

I had wondered if the *Honeychile* had put to sea, but luckily it was still mored beside the quay. There was no sign of life aboard her, but as we trooped up the gang-plank, we were immediately met by the bland, all-purpose sea-dog, Captain Cullum. He was not over-welcoming.

'The Commander? He and madam are resting. They left me strict instructions they were not to be disturbed.'

I told him that three important friends of the Commander had just flown in specially from London and were most anxious to see him – at once. The captain began to argue and suggest that we came back later. In reply, Bill Tanner suddenly began thumping on the deck and bellowing,

'007. On deck at once please. Your Queen and Country need you.'

'Sir. If you please,' said Captain Cullum.

'That's all right, captain,' replied Tanner, grinning. 'We're old friends.'

A window from the saloon opened. Bond's tousled head peered out.

'What the hell . . . ? Good God – Bill – what are you doing here, making such a filthy racket? And you Sir James. Wait while I get some clothes on.'

Five minutes later we were all sitting cheerfully on the stern. Bond appeared delighted. Captain Cullum was pouring us champagne. There was, as yet, no sign of the mistress of the ship.

We were an odd quintet. Professor Godwin remained silent. So did I. But the other three immediately began chatting and exchanging gossip from headquarters.

'M. sends his regards.'

'He does, does he?' said Bond.

'And Moneypenny sends a loving kiss.'

'Pity you couldn't bring her with you. She could have been our matron of honour.'

'She'd have been pleased,' said Tanner. 'You know she always fancied you yourself.'

'And how did you come?' Bond asked.

'By Vulcan bomber – a specially diverted flight. It was

laid on specially by Transport Command.'

'That was a bit excessive wasn't it? Just to be here to see me getting married?'

There was a pause, and Tanner suddenly looked awkwardly towards his feet.

'That isn't why we're here, James. I'm sorry, but we need you, pronto. It's most important.'

There was an uncomfortable silence. Professor Godwin started to light his pipe.

'But that's quite impossible,' said Bond. His voice was like a whiplash. 'Impossible. I've had this out with London and they know quite well that I've resigned. Nothing will make me change my mind. I've had enough.

'Enough of what?' said Tanner softly.

'Enough of this sort of thing. Enough of the whole bloody racket. I want to live.'

The argument would have gone on, but at that moment Honeychile appeared. She wore a blue silk caftan and was looking cool and tall and very beautiful. Love in the afternoon appeared to suit her. I admired her for the way she took this sudden gathering of her fiancé's friends so calmly in her stride. She chatted, smiled and charmed them. It was as if she'd known them all her life. Nothing more was said about the mission, but as we were leaving, Tanner said that Sir William was expecting us that evening. There was a lot still to discuss.

'You bet there is,' said Bond. 'Honey and I will be delighted to attend.'

Tanner's invitation was for nine-thirty and I felt that it had been general enough to include me. Certainly I wasn't missing this part of the battle if I could help it, and turned up in Sir William's penthouse after dinner. The enormous glass rectangle of a room looked magnificent. The lights were low, the shutters were drawn back and we seemed suspended high above the ocean. Far to the right the lights were glittering along the coast. The lighthouse flashed. Lights twinkled from the fishing boats far out at sea.

Everyone was there including the impeccable Augustus

who was handing round the drinks and serving coffee.

'And so,' I heard Bond saying from the far side of the room, 'suppose you tell us just what all this is about.'

'Can't we talk privately?' Tanner replied.

'No. Let's hear it straight away. I want Honey to be in on this. It concerns her as much as me.'

Tanner spoke very calmly then – one could detect the ordered mind, the logical delivery of the well-trained military intelligence. I suspect that there was an echo of one of M.'s briefings. I almost expected him to call Bond 007. In fact he didn't.

'Basically, James, it's a bit of unfinished business we need you to attend to.'

'Unfinished,' said Bond quickly. 'I don't get you. There's nothing open on the files.'

'It's not a file, James. It's an old friend of yours. Irma Bunt.'

'She's dead,' said Bond impatiently.

Tanner shook his head.

'Fraid not. Naturally we all accepted your report after the Japanese assignment when Blofeld's castle went up in flames. She was certainly inside the castle with friend Blofeld. But even then we had our suspicions. Tanaka told us that his people found a male skeleton corresponding to Blofeld's, but there was no sign of the woman's.'

'It might have been completely burned up in the flames.'

'Might have been, but wasn't, I'm afraid. We've been getting odd reports about her during the past year. Recently they've all been from Australia. It seems that she's been carrying on Blofeld's biological studies – but turning from plants to animals. The last definite report we had of her was from a place called Crumper's Dick.'

'Impossible,' said Bond. 'There's no such place.'

'I see that you don't know Australia. Anything's possible out there. This is a bit of it that most Australians would never know about – a trading station on the edge of the Stoney Desert, north of the salt-lake of Lake Eyre.'

'And just supposing, for the sake of argument, that

Fraulein Bunt is still alive, what in God's name is she up to in a place like Crumper's Dick?'

This,' replied Tanner. As he spoke he produced a photograph of an animal. It had small eyes, attenuated rat's face and fangs that hung below the jaw. The body was hairless, and it had powerful back legs.'

'What is it?' asked Sir William.

'Never seen anything like it,' said Bond.

'Not surprising,' replied Tanner. 'Until a year or two ago it had not existed. It's been artificially produced. Originally it was some sort of desert rat. The professor will explain, but apparently it's possible to produce mutant forms of animals by radioactive treatment of the genes. It's also possible to increase power and stature by certain drugs called steroids. This is what Irma Bunt has been concerned with in her laboratory at Crumper's Dick.'

'How big is it?' asked Bond.

'The latest reports say that it is around the size of a Yorkshire terrier. Isn't that right professor?' Professor Godwin nodded.

'But it's ten times as powerful. Biologists have always been surprised by the ferocity of these desert rats. Originally they come from the Sahara, and it seemed as if nature was doing us a good turn by keeping down their size and making sure that they remain in burrows in the desert. It appears that Fraulein Bunt has totally reversed nature. She's obviously a genius, but a diabolical one. The desert rats that she has produced are no longer subterranean – nor are they frightened nor are they confined to deserts. As a zoologist, I would describe them as the most dangerous animal on earth today.'

'What do you mean?' asked Honeychile.

'I mean this,' he said, and opening a briefcase he produced a batch of photographs. Some showed the partially devoured carcasses of sheep. There was the body of a horse, with the hindquarters stripped down to the skeleton. Finally there was a picture of what had been a man. It was not a pleasant sight.

310

There was silence in the room and I was grateful for the way Augustus tactfully refilled my glass.

'How did this happen?' Bond asked finally.

'Nobody knows for sure,' Godwin replied. 'Previous attempts to manufacture mutant forms artificially have all produced sterile animals. These rats of Fraulein Bunt are anything but sterile. For months now she's been breeding them like rabbits – and now they're spreading. And they're hungry.'

'Why don't you stop them?' someone asked.

'Good question, replied the professor. 'We've been trying for some months. But easier said than done. You remember the great rabbit plague that hit Australia last century? This could be every bit as bad – except that the rabbits didn't bite.'

'And what about Irma Bunt,' Bond asked brutally. 'I suppose you're letting her continue her interesting scientific work?'

'No,' replied Tanner. 'I am afraid that that's where you come in. Irma Bunt has disappeared – completely. The breeding station is deserted. She has produced these animals and left. But the Australian Government has recently received an ultimatum from her. Two ultimatums, to be strictly accurate. She threatens that these rats of hers will spread and soon start preying on the sheep. Within a year they will have multiplied so fast that they will really threaten Australia's sheep farming industry. Within two they will have moved into the cities.'

'Is that possible?' said Bond.

The professor nodded. 'But she's also said that she can destroy them almost overnight. Apparently they have some inbuilt instinct which she alone knows how to control. She has promised that in return for one billion dollars she will make these rats turn back like lemmings to the desert where they came from. She wants the money in cash. And she wants it fast.'

'I think you'd better pay,' said Bond.

Tanner tried arguing. It was useless. He said, quite rightly, that Bond was the only man who could recognize Irma Bunt. He was also the only man she feared. He alone could understand that twisted mind of hers sufficiently to hope to catch her. Because of this the Australian Government had asked for him. He was their one remaining hope.

But Bond just shrugged his shoulders.

Someone else could have the honour of catching Irma Bunt. There was nothing very special about her, and Australia must have some good policemen of its own. He was sorry, but he'd quite made up his mind. He had left the Secret Service and was getting married. Finally Bill Tanner realized that it was hopeless. Bond meant what he said.

At this Bill Tanner simply said that he was sorry and hoped that Honeychile and Bond would be happy. He and Sir James and Professor Godwin would be flying on to Adelaide at dawn. The Australian Prime Minister would be there to meet them. If Bond should change his mind . . .

'Thanks very much,' said Bond, 'but somehow I don't think it's likely. And now Honey and I must go. We've a busy day tomorrow.' If Bond was feeling upset at refusing his old friend he didn't show it. The two men shook hands.

I found it hard to sleep. Bill Tanner's story had disturbed me, and I dreamed of desert rats leaping across the English countryside. Then when I woke I couldn't get to sleep again. The idea of the Vulcan bomber leaving for Australia preyed on my mind. I looked at my watch. In less than an hour now it would be off. Finally I dressed and, breakfastless, drove to the airport to see it go.

It was there, like a great black shark, stranded along the margin of the runway. The aircrew were abroad, and just as I arrived, a car drew up, with Tanner and Professor Godwin. We chatted briefly, Tanner said he was still hoping that Bond would change his mind and come.

'D'you think he will?' asked Godwin.

'If it was his decision, certainly,' he said. 'But with that woman—' he shook his head. 'Pretty damned hopeless, I'm afraid. Pity though.'

'You're damned right it is,' said the professor.

By now the Vulcan's engines were awake. The plane was fuelled for the long fast journey round the rim of the earth, and I watched Godwin pull on a flying helmet and stride off, a determined grey figure, to the aircraft.

The dawn was coming up out of the Atlantic – long strips of oleander pink were in the sky – I heard the first bird sing, and felt the sweet freshness of the tropical morning.

Tanner looked at his watch, and shook his head.

'Well, you can't blame him. Really not blame him at all. She was pretty. Let's just hope he's happy.'

'Can't wait much longer sir,' shouted the pilot over the screaming engines. 'Flight Control's expecting us, if we're to make it back to Adelaide in time.'

The sleek cigar-shaped body started to roll forward. Tanner walked out towards it.

At that moment there was a blare from the edge of the field. A big white Rolls Corniche approached the runway. Honey was driving. Bond was beside her, with his old pigskin case, his lightweight blue suit, black knotted tie – his uniform for an assignment.

He seemed quite breezy, quite unruffled, and gave no explanation why he had come.

'Morning, Bill. Good to see you. Are we all ready?'

He saw me and nodded.

'I've enjoyed our little chats,' he said. 'Hope that you didn't find them all too tedious. There's a lot I left out and a great deal more to come, if you're still interested. When I get back we'll meet and I'll do my best to finish off the story.'

Then he turned to Honeychile who was still sitting in the car. She was no longer the tough Mrs Schultz. Her face seemed pale beneath its sun-tan, her eyes unnaturally bright. Bond kissed her and I heard him saying, 'Soon, darling, soon. I'll soon be back.'

How many times, I wondered, had he whispered that before?

Then he turned. I could see the pilot beckoning from the cockpit, and Bond hurried off across the runway, clutching his case. He turned and waved, then hauled himself up

313

through the entrance. The door was slammed behind him and the engines whined impatiently. Then the brakes were off, the engines thundered, and as the bomber turned the dust was whipping up around us, and I could smell the sudden stench of kerosene, the universal scent of modern man's departure.

Honey had left the car, and was standing all alone, watching as the bomber gathered speed. She didn't wave, but when she saw me she said flatly, 'I was the one who made him go. He said he wouldn't but I knew he'd always blame me if he didn't. Just the same, I never thought . . .'

The plane had turned and, as it passed above us, her voice was drowned in the departing roar of its engines. As it sailed off into the dawn it dipped its wings.

Honeychile smiled and watched as it receded to a small dot in the sky.

'Well, that's that,' she said as she turned back to the Rolls, 'the bastard's gone.'